Contemporary Economic Thought

Contemporary Economic Thought

By
Paul T. Homan

Essay Index Reprint Series

BOOKS FOR LIBRARIES PRESS, INC.
Freeport, New York

LIBRARY OF CONGRESS CATALOG CARD NUMBER:
68-20310

TO

C. C. H.

Whose complete indifference to the contents
of this book has been a solace and relief
during the period in which it took form.

Preface

SO M E years ago the writer undertook the task of comparing the doctrines, opinions, and points of view of contemporary writers in the field of general economic theory. This effort was induced by a growing realization of the fertility and incompatibility of the ideas that were being currently expressed. The fluidity of economic thought was strangely in contrast to the dogmatism and finality which found expression in university text-books. Even professional economists, having become engrossed in those specific tasks of investigation in which their efforts have been so fruitful, seemed frequently but little aware of the stirrings of thought in the field of theory, or but little interested in them. Yet it has been to the central body of theory that economists have been wont to point as the accumulated scientific accomplishment of economics.

Out of these studies grew a project for a general survey of contemporary economic thought. The difficulties of properly accomplishing in a creditable fashion so ambitious a project led, however, to its abandonment. Economic doctrines and viewpoints are so numerous and so personal, and relate themselves to so many strains of thought outside the economist's

characteristic discipline, that a survey of economic
thought seemed to involve almost an inquiry into all
the intellectual diversities and controversies of our
times. Added to this was the absence of perspective
which inevitably attaches to general inquiries into contemporary thought, and the failure to find any scheme
of classification by which a large number of economists
could be domesticated to orderly treatment. Consequently, a less ambitious and apparently more fruitful
project was conceived of setting alongside each other
a series of personal studies, setting forth the points of
view, methods, and conclusions of a number of economists picked with the idea of presenting as many as
possible of the diversities of current economic theory.
The present volume is the outcome.

No defense is to be entered of the choice of men for
treatment. It must of necessity be an arbitrary process.
The most that can be said for the choice made is that
the subjects of the following essays seem to the writer
to illustrate a wider diversity of thought than could be
attained by selecting any other group of English and
American names, and to represent as great an influence
upon contemporary economic thought as could be found
in any five men.

A certain objectivity has been attempted in the treatment of the economists selected for analysis. The aim
has been, not to award praise or blame, but mainly to
display the thought of men whose theories are mutually
incompatible, to relate their economic thought to the

wider spheres of thought which color it, to consider the relation of their thought to the external reality which it purports to explain, and to raise questions concerning the validity and adequacy of the types of theory displayed. The real point of the essays lies in the attempt to explain why at a given point in time men engaged in the analysis of approximately the same objective data come to such disparate conclusions. In a sense, then, the implications of these studies are much wider than the field of economic theory, since they demand a consideration of the whole framework of thought which men bring to the analysis of social facts, and a critical examination of the assumptions which underlie the disciplines of all social sciences.

Since the aim of these studies has been the accurate analysis of the thought of others, it has seemed advisable, for the most part, to suppress the personal bias of the writer. That bias will, however, no doubt be sufficiently apparent to most readers to make any personal avowal of faith unnecessary. It is such as might be expected of one who, brought up in the faith of Marshall, then dallies a while in the camp of Veblen, and thereafter seeks for himself an independent position which shall commit him to the dogma of no one. It arises from a type of eclecticism which, were any full statement of it attempted, would doubtless be unsatisfactory to all who entertain strong convictions concerning economic theory. The aloofness of the viewpoint from which these essays proceed is, in consequence, not quite a pose. The writer has, for the moment, no economic faith which he is much interested in propagating. He is more interested in disentangling those strains of thought which lead to the present confusing uncertainty in the field of economics and in asking what fruitful constructive leads appear therein. A beginning is sought for that perspective which only time can complete.

Parts of these studies have previously been published,—the essay on John Bates Clark in briefer form in the *Quarterly Journal of Economics,* the one on Thorstein Veblen, also abridged, in *American Masters of Social Science,* published by Henry Holt & Company. An expression of appreciation must be made to the Robert S. Brooking Graduate School of Economics and Government which made possible the leisure in which the essays took form. It is desired also to acknowledge the debt to many friends for their critical observations, and in particular to thank Miss Helen R. Wright for her patient reading and criticism of practically the whole manuscript.

P. T. H.

Ithaca, New York.

Contents

Introductory

Introductory

MEN'S minds have always, it seems, furnished them with some sort of explanation of the phenomena which surround them. Such explanations have in the past prevailingly run in terms of supernatural forces. It is only during the last three centuries that the physical universe has been searchingly subjected to minute inspection and made to give up the secrets of its being. Out of the knowledge so distilled by scientific investigation has been derived that vast technical and mechanical development which has given shape and form to our contemporary civilization. The growing belief that the universe was controlled by natural laws acting in a uniform fashion, rather than by the immanent hand of the Deity and of his arch-enemy, extended its influence to the sphere of human activities. Thus, though speculation concerning the nature of human institutions was already an ancient and honorable occupation, it received a new impetus and took a new turn which has led with the passage of time to the development of the so-called "social sciences."

The new impetus was the scientific spirit, the new turn a search for the natural laws which govern the activities of mankind. This search was first pursued with any assiduity in the fields of political and legal thought, and the end in view was a valid and satisfactory explanation of the nature of the state, or the sovereign, and of the relationship between it and the individual. It was out of speculation along these lines that there emerged that characteristic and persistent body of eighteenth-century doctrine which is summed up in the phrases "natural rights" and "natural liberty." Mediæval thought passed out of the picture with the rise of the new view that social relations are the outcome of contractual relations between individuals.

Such a view had become commonplace when, about the middle of the eighteenth century, attention was directed more specifically to the examination and explanation of economic relations between men. Economic science in its infancy thus was furnished with an intellectual background of a very definite sort. From physical science it was furnished with a scientific analogy and a controlling scientific principle, the heart of which was the tendency of forces toward a state of equilibrium or rest. From political philosophy it was endowed with an individualistic view of the relation of man to man, as the "natural state." The natural, and therefore, by a refinement of thought, the right relations between men were such as arose out of their private, individual contracts with one another.

In economic activity, the acquisitive desires were seen to be the primary motivating force, but since the pursuit of such desires led to the performance of services for others, their effects could be interpreted as socially desirable. The organization of economic activity was viewed as a competitive struggle between individuals for wealth in its manifold forms. And such restrictions as limited this competition between individuals was viewed as "unnatural" and undesirable, and prejudicial to the wealth (and therefore to the welfare) of all.

Economic science in the hands of Adam Smith, and even more in the hands of economists of the succeeding generation, became primarily a technique for explaining the relative values for which economic goods exchange, and the uses and rewards of the various agents which lend their assistance in the productive process. The analysis ran in terms of a mechanical analogy, and consisted in seeking the logical outcome of the forces of individual self-interest operating through a competitive organization of economic activity based upon private property. Its precept for public policy was the expediency, for promoting public and private wealth, of imposing as little control upon the pursuits of individuals as was consistent with the preservation of property and personal or national safety. Under the sheltering protection of the Utilitarian philosophy, political economy acquired its niche, along with politics, law, and ethics, in a consistent and harmonious scheme of thought, designed not only to explain social phenomena, but as well to lay down the fundamental principles of a desirable social policy. It was in this comprehensive mechanistic scheme of late eighteenth-century thought that the theoretical defences were perfected for the predilection which persists to the present day against governmental interference with the "natural" processes of individual activity.

If in this scheme of thought wherein political economy took its appointed place the element of scientific explanation seems somewhat overborne by that of philosophical speculation, that is only to say that the terms in which mankind shall explain its own activity must of necessity be forged out of ideas and points of view not themselves easily reducible to scientific form.

Such, briefly and inadequately expressed, was the type of thought and method of analysis which early political economy passed on as an intellectual heritage to later generations. Since this early beginning, each generation has seen the rise of new economists who have undertaken to revise, modify, or reshape the body of economic laws or doctrines which have been passed down to them, in order to frame a more adequate explanation of the relations of cause and effect in the operation of economic processes. Such revision has been due partly to the changing external facts to be explained, partly to changing ideas of the nature of human motivation, partly to changing scientific concepts and general habits of thought, partly to the imponderable influence of the economist's own general outlook and point of view. But however much subsequent generations have pared away from or added to their early heritage, one may discern an unbroken line of descent which includes all those who have to some considerable degree remained loyal to the early nineteenth-century idea of the scope and method of economic science. Building up gradually and laboriously a scheme of analysis and explanation of economic phenomena, this group in the outcome must be recognized as having exerted a vast intellectual and practical influence during the past century. Out of their concepts and methods and doctrines has grown much of the current common sense upon economic matters, or, if one wishes to emphasize the reverse aspect, their thought may perhaps be said to have rationalized the common sense of a highly individualistic century.

It is beyond our present purpose to attempt any summary of the varied developments of economic speculation during the nineteenth century. In the main, those who have come to be regarded as representative of the "classical school" were engaged in developing or modifying the views of Ricardo upon the subjects of prices and the distribution of income. Variations of emphasis and treatment are less important than the maintenance of a striking uniformity in general concepts and scientific method. For it was persistently assumed that a science, inexact, indeed, but authentic, could be built by the method of logical deduction mainly upon a premise of the competitive pursuit of individual self-interest. Variations of emphasis have been too numerous to recount in detail. But, in spite of sporadic protests, Ricardian political economy for the half-century before

1870 held its ground as the best available explanation of economic phenomena and as the best available guide to public policy on economic matters.

The latter part of the century was, however, too fertile with new developments in science, industry, social life, and general thought to permit the continuance of such delightful unanimity. The devastating theory of evolution cast doubt upon the validity of natural laws conceived in terms of a tendency of forces to achieve a state of rest. Historical research emphasized the evanescence of human institutions and consequently the ephemerality of economic laws postulated upon the fixity of the existing competitive system. The persistence of poverty and distress in England in the face of the enormously increased productivity of the industrial system belied the beneficence of individualistic enterprise, and placed the ethics of utilitarianism under critical scrutiny. The growing concentration of economic power seemed to be encroaching upon the free contractual relations which were posited by political economy. And finally, a new psychological interest sent economists burrowing into the shadowy places of the human mind as the ultimate hiding-place of economic causes.

Such a combination of circumstances—and the list is by no means complete—injected into economic science so many controversial elements, that two decades of quarrelsome conflict sufficed to transform a well-established and practical body of doctrines and precepts into

a congeries of highly speculative and mutually conflicting theories. Out of this dismal morass the science was
rescued in England by Alfred Marshall, but not to the
satisfaction of all. In the United States and on the
Continent, while his work was highly influential, his
Messianic quality was less widely accepted. Consequently, while controversy has been less prevalent and
less virulent, it has not been stilled. In the nature of
the case, when data of growing complexity must be interpreted and when the canons of scientific knowledge
are so flexible as in the past generation, no complete
meeting of minds upon questions of economic generalizations could be expected.

One must not fail to notice that at no time has the
dogma of economic science failed to elicit dissent from
some quarter. During the period in which it placed its
blessing upon the head of unregulated competition, it
was the target for reformers, whether radical or reac-
tionary, of all sorts who were not impressed by the
beneficence of the existing framework of society. From
Tory defenders of ancient privilege to socialistic
dreamers, the anvil chorus proceeded. The most direct
and most powerful challenge came from Karl Marx's
system of "scientific socialism," and for a generation
economists were concerned with laying the ghost of this
distressing intruder, who disconcerted them with an
equally effective armory of logical dialectic, but with
different premises. Robert Owen, Carlyle, Ruskin,
trade-unionists, all humanitarians who refused to be-

lieve that mankind was doomed to submit to the fell
hand of circumstance, as directed by immutable natural
(or divine) economic laws working through the agency
of an undirected scramble for pecuniary gain, swelled
the chorus.

In more recent times, when economists have more
largely stripped their thought of ethical implications,
resigned from the position of authentic counselors of
statesmen, and recognized the hypothetical character of
their doctrines, the opposing chorus has declined in
power. The measure of the decline is the measure of
the declining practical importance of economic theory
in shaping public policy. Such controversy as remained
thus transferred itself more largely to a strictly intellectual sphere—to the refinement of concepts and
methods, to the discussion of canons of scientific explanation applicable to social phenomena. Largely
removed from the arena of current strife, economists
have been enabled to pursue in more objective spirit
the search for economic truth. Yet still they fail to
agree. Indeed, they seem in our own day to be sep-
arated by more impassable barriers of thought than at
any time in the past. After a century and a half of
persistent research and thought by men of outstanding
intellect with no other purpose than a scientific explanation of economic activity—a disentangling of the complex skein of cause and effect in the economic process—
the utmost difference of opinion prevails, reaching down
to the very terms in which the process shall be described.

Such a situation seems to offer abundant food for reflection. One may well ask whence arises this strange stubbornness of economic phenomena against orderly domestication. Are the facts too complex for simple generalization? Are the methods of analysis inadequate? Has science no tool for coping with the life of man in society? Does some strange obliquity affect men's minds when they essay an examination of affairs human? It would not be true to say that economists are more ignorant of their environment than in the past. Too much patient investigation has been done to permit an absolute lapse, even in the face of increasingly complicated economic arrangements. The curious disparity of thought arises apparently out of the varying complement of ideas which economists bring to their tasks. If this be true, it must be supposed that the present disordered state of economic thought is in some large degree the reflection of divergent habits of thought in contemporary society which are wider in their sweep than the mere field of economics.

Under the circumstances, it appears not to be a waste of time to inquire, not only *what* men think, but *how* they think, about the contemporary organization of economic activity. At no previous period have more harassing economic problems had to be faced by organized societies. Never have men been more mystified and more perplexed either in explaining or in controlling their economic environment. What service the economist may be expected to perform in the one or the other seems properly a matter of interest. For if not to him, then to whom, may those burdened with political or economic responsibility turn for light or guidance?

In the pages that follow, an attempt has been made to penetrate somewhere near to the heart of the thought of five recent or contemporary economists. They have been chosen for treatment because of the varied viewpoints they represent and in view of their extreme importance in influencing the direction of economic thought in recent years. No five men can comprehend within themselves the infinite variety of contemporary economic theory, yet within the thought of these men may be found at least the germs of almost every idea that has been pressed into the service of economic analysis during the twentieth century. From a study of individual approaches to the province of economics, one may hope to acquire a clearer view of the range of ideas which are fertilizing that field of knowledge than from any other angle of attack. Indeed, there seems no other point at which to enter, since individual differences between economists are too numerous, too fundamental, and too detailed to lend themselves to any reasonable scheme of classification.

Alfred Marshall, in spite of the generation that has elapsed since the first appearance of his great work, still dominates the field of economic theory in a remarkable fashion in England, and to a lesser degree in America. Against his perpetuation of the classical tradition, John A. Hobson is the most effective dissenting English voice.

John Bates Clark achieved the most imposing recognition that has been attained by any American theorist, and his thought is imbedded to some degree in almost all American texts of economic theory. In opposition, Thorstein Veblen has set in motion a more impressive and influential current of dissident opinion than is elsewhere to be found. In Wesley Clair Mitchell's work may be found imbedded a view of economic science too representative of much contemporary thought to be overlooked. To these outstanding personalities we shall confine our attention in a limited exploration into the economic thought of our times.

John Bates Clark

John Bates Clark

I

PROFESSOR JOHN BATES CLARK
is perhaps the most distinguished of the American
economists who may be regarded as the legitimate offspring of the classical line. He is certainly the American theorist who during the past generation has made
the most original and impressive contribution to abstract
economic theory. Of international reputation, he has
been classed by Professor Alfred Marshall as among
the three or four great theoretical writers of the early
twentieth century. And many economists have concurred in Professor E. R. A. Seligman's judgment that
his writings have "earned for him the reputation of
being one of the five or six great Anglo-Saxon theorists
of the nineteenth century, putting him on a level with
Ricardo, Senior, John Stuart Mill, Jevons, and
Marshall." [1]

A brief account of Clark's early training may assist
us in appreciating the turn which his later thinking took.
His undergraduate days were spent at Brown University and Amherst College. They were twice inter-

[1] In *Essays in Economics*, p. 151.

rupted by the illness of his father, and in these intervals he was engaged in selling plows to farmers in
Minnesota, which was then decidedly pioneer ground.
His later college days thus found him a much more
mature and experienced person than the ordinary student, and it is recorded that he was a student of exceptional brilliance. His particular intellectual interest at
this period lay in philosophical studies. He was first
inducted into economic studies in his senior year under
the tutelage of President Julius Seelye of Amherst,
who included a course in political economy in his department of mental and moral philosophy.

Both Amasa Walker's textbook, which was used, and
President Seelye's instruction left Clark with a feeling
of the incompleteness with which the subject was
treated. It was, he thought, a subject of supreme importance to the welfare of mankind, and his mind
turned to an attempt to fill the gaps that neither teacher
nor textbook had been able to close for him. During
his last year at Amherst he worked out for himself certain ideas concerning the nature of wealth and the relation of labor to wealth, which were the starting point of
his later book, *The Philosophy of Wealth*. Approaching economics through the channel of philosophy, Clark
seems from the first to have been engaged in the attempt
to relate it to social ethics. He was trying to give to the
theory of economic life a form which would permit it
to be dovetailed into a larger theory of the organization of the social life of mankind, placing it upon a

defensible moral basis. The philosophical and ethical approach is displayed throughout all his later writings, and one at times thinks of his mind as more like that of a Greek of the age of Aristotle than that of a modern scientist.

Encouraged by his professors to think well of his ideas and his abilities, Clark, upon his graduation from Amherst in 1872 at the age of twenty-five, proceeded to Germany, where he continued his studies for nearly three years under the direction of Professor Karl Knies at the University of Heidelberg. He was thus the first of that group of American students who repaired to Germany during the 'seventies and who later lent such distinction to the field of economic studies in the United States. It is perhaps evidence of the peculiar independence of Clark's mind that this period of study under so distinguished a representative of the historical school as Knies has left little or no lasting stamp upon his later writing.

Upon returning to the United States he engaged in university teaching and held positions successively at Carleton College, Smith College, and Amherst College. Until his recent retirement he was a professor at Columbia University since 1895. During the last quarter of the nineteenth century he wrote frequently for the periodical press upon problems of economic theory, and one may trace with some clarity the genesis of the ideas which are embodied in his three important books, *The Philosophy of Wealth* (1885), *The Distribution of*

Wealth (1899), and *Essentials of Economic Theory* (1907). During these years he was caught in the current of renewed interest in the more abstract aspects of economic theorizing, and gradually moved into greater prominence until he came toward the close of the century to be generally acclaimed as the greatest of American economic theorists.

Current economic problems did not fail to occupy much of Clark's attention, and the trust problem interested him particularly. Since, however, our purpose is to fix attention upon his theoretical work, it will be necessary very largely to neglect his writing upon current problems except in so far as they appear relevant to the present inquiry. In the field of economic theory it is not too much to say that he achieved the preëminent place among American economists in point of subtlety, originality, and completeness, and in point of influence upon the generally expounded body of economic doctrines.

Clark's reputation chiefly rests upon the views embodied in *The Distribution of Wealth*. One cannot, however, secure an adequate view of the man's mind and its development without some attention to his earlier work. In the fourteen years which elapsed between the publication of *The Philosophy of Wealth* and of *The Distribution of Wealth* his method of approach to the problems of economic theory underwent at least a change of emphasis, if not a very radical shifting of fundamental views. It should therefore prove illumi-

nating to glance briefly at his views as held during his
earlier years, that we may comprehend the point of
departure from which he set out, to arrive at last at the
rounded and balanced system of theory which represented his mature thought.

The Philosophy of Wealth is in no sense a systematic
treatise upon economic theory. It consists of a series
of more or less isolated essays, most of which had been
previously published, upon the problems of economic
theory and of economic organization. A careful examination reveals the presence of three main trends of
thought. In the first place, the premises of classical
political economy are subjected to criticism. In the
second place, constructive corrections of older theories
of value and distribution are attempted. And finally
the major problems and defects of the existing economic
organization, as Clark sees them, are realistically set
forth, with suggested lines of improvement in terms
both of the immediately practicable and of the more
remotely and ideally desirable.

(1) Three major assumptions of classical economics
Clark finds contrary to truth. The first and most misleading of these is that man, in his economic activity,
is guided only by motives of material self-interest.
It is fundamental, in his view, that economic reasoning
should start from a correct view of human nature,
since the voluntary action of men is the basis of economic law. The mechanical and selfish "economic
man" whose consistent self-seeking has served the pur-

poses of economists is so much a fiction that any conclusion based on his actions is too irreparably inaccurate to
be rectified by allowances for "disturbing forces." So
great is the need and so difficult the problem of establishing a proper psychological basis for economic reasoning that "to trace the elusive laws of human nature
. . . will afford work enough for one generation." [1]
In the absence of a scientific body of knowledge on the
subject, certain tentative additions to the theory of
human nature are put forth. Moral principles and
unselfish motives are advanced as important factors in
the actions of "the man whom God made." The sense
of right in men is "the supreme motive in the market
place as elsewhere" and "the centripetal force in economic society." Another neglected factor in human
nature is the universal and insatiable desire for personal
esteem, a desire which is beneficent, since the ignoble
imitate the noble, thus raising the standards of taste
and of mercantile honor.

The second misleading assumption is that competition is the channel through which economic forces of
necessity discharge themselves, and that economic laws
are laws of competitive business enterprise. True competition, a rivalry for public favor, Clark sees to be
degenerating in modern life into a quasi-combat. The
natural action of self-interest and unrestricted competition are bringing us to the point of annihilating competition. In other words, under modern conditions

[1] *The Philosophy of Wealth*, p. 36.

competition tends to be self-destructive, and in its place we find great groups, labor and capital, achieving an elimination of internal competition and a solidarity of mutual antagonism, a situation which constitutes an essential peril to society. This is where self-interest has led us. Competition at its best is subject to serious criticism. It resolves itself into an "ignoble struggle for personal profit" in which one may look in vain for a providential design and from which a harmony of interests cannot conceivably emerge. The immorality of the market place, its sharp bargaining of the nature of plunder, the inequality of the bargainers, and the absence of an adequate code of justice or morality are evils that must be overcome by the progress of moral law. "Individual competition, the great regulator of the former era, has in important fields practically disappeared. It ought to disappear; it was, in latter days, incapable of working justice. The alternative regulator is moral force, and this is already in action."[1] As to the ways in which moral force shall exert itself, nothing very explicit is offered, but it may be gathered from the context that the conflicts of newly developed groups have shown the necessity and paved the way for a very widespread governmental regulation of economic life.

A further objection is made to the prevalent neglect by economists of the fact that society is an organism, not a mere aggregation of individuals. No attempt is made to prove that society is an organic whole in any

[1] *The Philosophy of Wealth*, p. 148.

true biological sense. The statement is made purely as an *obiter dictum* and a brief analogy is made between ascending types of social organism and the ascending biological classification of radiates, mollusks, articulates, vertebrates. The distinguishing marks of differentiation and cephalization are seen in society as the division of labor with its consequence of social solidarity, and conscious control of economic life in the interest of the social whole. The latter fact is reinforced in advanced societies by a "growing subordination . . . to the dictates of moral law" which "is the great and neglected fact of modern times." The view of the social organism is not presented as a convenient figure of speech, but apparently as a biological fact, and no account is taken of the rather distressing difficulty of having to view man for certain purposes as a mere cell and for other purposes as an intelligent, moral, self-directing individual. No further discussion of Clark's use of the organic analogy is necessary here, since it will have to engage our attention at a later point in our inquiry.

A consideration of the nature of these criticisms of the premises of economic reasoning reveals the curious fact that they present a remarkable resemblance to some of those advanced by Veblen at a later period. There is the same insistence that economic theory must be built upon a correct view of human nature, and the same contention that competition is not *per se* desirable and that in contemporary society its force is too attenuated to make it available as the basis for broad economic generalizations.

(2) Clark's early treatment of the problem of value is curiously inconsistent with his criticism of the postulates of economics. The fixing of values is analyzed as a competitive process in which the cost of production, including average profits, determines "normal" prices, and this in spite of the fact that we are elsewhere led to believe that competition is an obsolescent and undesirable institution. The analysis of value is original in two respects—in the place attributed to the social organism in the valuation process, and in the treatment of utility in relation to value.

Values, as expressed in prices, are pictured as the result of a market process of equalizing supply and demand. But market prices are deemed to express the utility of a thing to society as a whole. The idea that society is the purchaser and user of all goods produced led Clark to obliterate the distinction between "value in exchange" and "value in use," and to adopt the view that values are positive quantities, not mere ratios expressed through a monetary medium.

The argument runs somewhat as follows: Goods have a common quality, utility or want-satisfying power. Utility is capable of quantitative measurement, and value is that measurement. Price is a mode of expressing utility in monetary terms. Utility is measured not by its absolute useful service, but by the effective, or additional, service of the marginal unit. The market

value of a commodity is a measure of its utility to society as a whole; that is, it is in effect bought by
society, whence it is distributed under certain laws to
the various cells, or persons, as nutriment passes to the
parts of the human body. This value is the measurement of a positive amount of utility. Value to society
is determined by the play of the forces of supply and
demand. The price of utilities over long periods is a
"normal" price, based upon costs of production and
affording to the workman "ordinary" wages, to the
capitalist "current" interest, to the employer "average"
profits. Normal costs change with the progress of
society. An optimistic conclusion is arrived at by seeing
the higher wants as those which are indefinitely ex-
pansive and therefore to be more largely satisfied in
the future; by anticipating no such increase in population as to neutralize the gains of improved technical
production; and by a belief in the increasing control of
moral forces over human affairs. The distinction between higher and lower wants might be expected to
raise some question as to the possibility of reducing
these qualitative differences in utilities to a common
quantitative measure, but this difficulty is not faced.

As we shall have occasion to consider these ideas at
greater length elsewhere, they need only be mentioned
here. Their particular importance in the history of
economic theory lies in the fact that they presented
an analysis of the effect of marginal units of utilities
upon the fixing of prices. At the time when they were

first formulated, about 1880, Clark was not acquainted with the work of either Walras, Menger, or Jevons, so that he is to be regarded as one of the original contributors to the marginal utility theory of value. Linked up as his theory was to an organic view of society, it had distinctive features of its own. But its effect was not different from that of Jevons, in emphasizing the fundamental importance of utility as a factor in the price-fixing process.

In the discussion of distribution, as of value, there is a certain mixture of ideas as to competitive laws and ideals of justice which stands very much in the way of brief analysis. Under competitive conditions, supply and demand are conceived to divide the stream of income between general groups representing those engaged in producing a commodity from the raw material to the finished stage, between the subgroups that add to its sum of utilities as it passes toward completion, and between landlords, wage-earners, capitalists, and employers within each subgroup. "There are fixed laws of distribution," it is said, "which society is not at liberty to violate." [1] Then, in view of current injustices, an amendment is broached that "better systems of social circulation may be before us, if we can wait for their development." [2] The argument wavers indecisively between the notion of fixed laws of distribution on the one hand, and, on the other hand, the need

[1] *The Philosophy of Wealth*, p. 87.
[2] *Ibid.*, p. 88.

for amendments in our system of distribution in view
of many patent injustices in the distribution of income
and in view of the social dangers involved in the new
solidarism of groups of employers and workers.

Leaving interest and rent out of mind, the division
of the product of social industry within the subgroups
has, in the view of Clark, been determined in the past by
the relative bargaining strength of employers and laborers.   Since strength has lain predominantly on the
side of the employer, there is a suggestion that labor has
been to some extent exploited.   But a new complica-
tion is encountered in the solidification of labor and
capital into groups and the internal abeyance of competition within the groups.   The automatic scheme of distribution, such as it was, is in the way of supersession.
The primary problem of distribution is to insure equity
in the division of the product, and in the new situation
a new and true theory of wages is called for, in the
interests of justice and of public order.   The development of bargaining relations into a quasi-combat leaves
no alternative, in the pursuit of justice, to the effective
intervention of the government to regulate by arbitration the incomes of wage-earners and employers.

As the purpose at present is only to indicate Clark's
approach to the problems of economic theory, no extended critique of his early value and distribution theory
need be attempted.   The point which it is important
to bear in mind for purposes which will emerge in our
later study is the double approach, the attempt to for-

mulate scientific laws of value and distribution, modified, or one might almost say nullified, by the desire to regulate values and distributive shares on lines of justice and in the light of moral precepts.

(3) In setting forth, as has been done in the preceding pages, Clark's criticism of the premises of economic reasoning and his constructive approach to the problems of value and distribution, some indication indirectly emerges as to his approach to problems of the day. The really important problems of economic organization, in his view, are those represented by the combination movement, the growth of group solidarity in extensive fields of industry and among both employers and workers. In the menace of that movement lies the challenge to our social inventiveness. Seeking to understand where we are and where we are going, he traces in some detail the historical background. In the earlier days of small-scale industry, competition had been relied upon as an automatic regulator, kept within bounds, after the sweeping away of mediæval and Mercantilist regulations, principally by the laws of private property, the police force, and customary morality. But the advent of the machine, leading to the large, concentrated industries of the present, has greatly limited the always imperfect power of competition to regulate economic activity. Monopolistic combinations have arisen, unions have sprung up to combat the overweening power of industrialists and to protect labor from the exploitation of the unscrupulous among the

employers. And that is where we are: the public un-
protected from the greed of monopolies; the wage-
earner unassured of a just and adequate wage or steady
employment; a body politic rent by gigantic conflicts
over the division of the fruits of industry; trade openly
predatory and marked by a refined untruthfulness.

The solution of these serious problems is seen to
involve a number of agencies of which the most important two are government intervention and a spiritual
awakening. The powers of government have been invoked to some extent and they may very well be invoked
to regulate all monopolistic enterprises. The more
immediately practicable alleviative of group strife is
found in a system of arbitration. It is deficient, however, in spite of securing greater justice and intelligence in distribution, in that it leaves attention centered
upon points of conflict, not upon community of interest.
An extension of profit-sharing plans is looked to, to
secure a partial elimination of the area of conflict and
to concentrate attention upon enlarging the product
from which both parties alike draw their reward. The
ideal solution is to be looked for in a widespread system
of coöperative production, wherein the workers are self-
employed, the area of conflict entirely disappears, and
community of interest and justice in distribution are
established. It is not too much to hope for the eventual
appearance of such a system, ideal and remote though
it may appear. The really significant form of competition of the future will be the struggle for primacy be-

tween these alternate forms of economic organization. "The new political economy must recognize, as one of its principles, this special and higher competition by which systems are tested. Individual competition, the basis of the traditional science, is, in extensive fields, a thing of the past."[1]

The moral forces of the community will be tested by the adequacy of their response to the situation. Legislation in the interests of justice and social order is dependent upon them. The shady ethical standards of the market place are in need of a cleansing breath. An adequate teleology is to be sought for, an ultimate goal toward which to guide social tendencies. A rational control will not depend blindly upon the competition of self-seeking interests, but will adapt the means to the end held in view. The Ricardian system of free competition, the apotheosis of selfishness, contains the promise of a social revolution. Almost the fate of society is dependent upon the intelligence with which the higher moral ideas of the community are brought to bear upon the situation. Moral law must control economic processes. "As thus apprehended, there is no apotheosis of selfishness in the theory of political economy."[2]

This is the Clark of *The Philosophy of Wealth*. It is a Clark little known to those who know only his later work, and this analysis may therefore serve as an

[1] *The Philosophy of Wealth*, p. 190.
[2] *Ibid.*, p. 219.

introduction and point of contrast to what is to follow. What is interesting is to see what he was trying to do. At this youthful period of his life, a number of very interesting ideas, a little vague, perhaps not mutually reconciled, but nevertheless fertile, were obviously germinating in his mind. In the first place, he was not content with finding the world chaotic. In the spirit of the natural sciences and of his predecessors in political economy, he was bent upon a search for "laws" governing the economic activities of mankind. And, if what formal theory he gives is of much the conventional sort of his predecessors, it is interesting to note that he was looking for its rectification in a very pertinent quarter—that is, in our view of human nature. As anyone who wishes to consult the periodical indexes may discover, the notion that psychology has any important relation to economics, outside of furnishing some sort of rule-of-thumb working concept of the valuation process, is a very modern notion. It bespeaks a considerable acumen and originality in this young economist of the 'eighties that he made it the center of his theoretical approach.

Again, we find that he was attempting to present economic life in terms of changing institutions, of biological growth; in short, he is talking for the most part in terms, not of static laws, but of changing processes. Here we may perhaps see the influence retained from a German training during the ascendency of the historical school, but the approach is prophetic of a later approach which, even at the present day, is novel and unconventional.

The third thing that he was trying to do was to assist in the spiritual reformation of the world. Now this may appear no task relevant to the work of an economist, who, in the view of some, is properly a scientist working in the dry and impersonal light of objective knowledge. Nevertheless, one may not penetrate far into the processes of Clark's mind without perceiving the high moral earnestness in which he works. Truth is his goal. But man is a moral being, the highest truth is moral truth, and man's pursuit of material welfare, in the abeyance of moral law, will be retarded and disturbed by conflict. The scientist in human affairs can no more discard the moral element in man than a chemist can discard a chemical element. In the spirit almost of a crusader Clark, in his earlier period, undertakes his task of reconstructing economic science.

It will have been seen that the ideas expressed in *The Philosophy of Wealth* lack unity, if they are not at times flatly self-contradictory. The book must be accepted not as a rounded body of economic theory, but as a body of fertile ideas germinating in the mind of a very original and stimulating thinker. One might have forecast in 1886 that this mind would produce something notable, but it would have required the gift of prophecy to foretell what direction it would take.

As matters turned out, Clark became in a sense the

victim of his generation. It was a controversial generation, and the controversy was waged around the theory
of value and distribution. By a certain fatality, therefore, his attention came to be centered upon the range
of ideas which brought him his initial recognition—his
value theory. His questioning of the postulates of
economic reasoning sank into the background and appeared to be forgotten. He no longer inquired into the
complex processes of developing economic life. With
his own generation, and largely in its terms, he began
the effort to elucidate the general laws which control
the economic activities of mankind.

But Clark's mind could not be a mere private in the
ranks. While attention was being principally given to
the marginal utility theory of value, he was quietly
pondering the problem of extending the concepts used
therein to an adequate theory of distribution. When,
therefore, after years of patient thought and preparation, he published *The Distribution of Wealth*, the
logical beauty and precision of the system of theory
there displayed was like an illumination from Heaven
to many of those whose goal for economic science was
the reduction of economic life to terms of law and
order.

II

In *The Distribution of Wealth*, Clark continued the
attempt, characteristic of the economists of the nine-

teenth century, to discover and state laws governing the
fixing of values and incomes. It is conceived that such
laws may be found, of as truly scientific validity as the
generalizations of the natural sciences. It is conceived,
also, that when found such laws should be practically
applicable to contemporary society, both as explaining
its phenomena and as furnishing a basis for public policy. The difficulty that faced Clark in his search, as it
does all investigators who seek to establish general laws
of social phenomena, was that the method of isolation
and experimentation available to physical scientists is
barred to the economist. He was thrown back, like his
predecessors, upon the method of logical deduction.
The measure of the scientific validity of a system such as
Clark's is obviously, then, dependent very directly upon
the preconceptions and postulates on which the system
rests.

Before going into the process by which his characteristic doctrines are arrived at, it will be well to examine
the point from which he starts. A convenient method
will be to list briefly the essential postulates of his system of theory, and then to look at their implications in
a somewhat more leisurely fashion. (1) Private property is accepted as the basic social institution, without
examination of its historical or ethical foundations.
(2) Individual freedom of activity is assumed to be
unhampered and to operate through active competition
in all gainful pursuits. (3) Government is thought of
as intervening in the economic sphere only for the phys-

ical protection of property, for the enforcement of contracts, and for the maintenance of competition. (4) Labor and capital are conceived to constitute mobile funds, the units of which are capable of rapid transfer from point to point in the economic system upon adequate stimulus. (5) Economic activity is deemed to be motivated by the attempt of men to satisfy their subjective wants. Pecuniary gain is pursued intelligently merely as a means of acquiring the goods which will afford satisfaction.

The essential postulates, as thus stated, obviously do not differ materially from those common to most economic theory in the nineteenth century, as amended by the marginal utility school of analysis. They ally Clark directly to the philosophy of utilitarianism. They bind him at the same time to a more rigid set of assumptions, both as to human nature and as to social institutions, than Alfred Marshall had been willing to adopt. These assumptions must be modified by the addition of three others which are essential to the particular turn which Clark's analysis takes. (1) Society is assumed to be an organism, comparable to a biological organism. The laws of economics are organic social laws and not mere generalizations concerning the economic relations of individuals as such. (2) It is assumed that a division may be made between the "static" economic forces which are permanent and the "dynamic" forces which introduce changes in economic life. A proper understanding of static laws is presumed to be essential to the analysis of dynamic forces. (3) A general preconception is held that the natural laws of economics are only to be considered valid when they approve themselves to the moral sense of mankind. With this brief introduction of the bases upon which Clark builds, we may proceed to examine them at some length, postponing the development of the doctrinal system to a later point.

The static condition of economic society with which Clark primarily interests himself would ensue "if labor and capital were to remain fixed in quantity, if improvements in the mode of production were to stop, if the consolidating of capital were to cease, and if the wants of consumers were never to vary."[1] Actual society is always dynamic, but underlying the complexities of a changing world there are static standards with which actual values, wages, and interest tend to coincide. This static shape to which society would conform in the absence of change is its "natural" or "normal" shape. It is not suggested that the phenomena of change are less important to the scientist. They are in fact the more important and difficult part of the field. But an adequate formulation of the laws which govern dynamic change will be a long and difficult task, involving arduous historical and inductive research. Verification and measurement of the results of such research by comparative statistics will present the most laborious task that economists will ever have to undertake. Meantime it is of essential importance that a true

[1] *The Distribution of Wealth*, preface, pp. vi-vii.

conception of static laws be secured, since an understanding of their basic and fundamental character is
necessary to the construction of a body of true dynamic
theory. Such an isolation of static forces, it is admitted,
gives to the study an unlifelike appearance and makes
it "heroically theoretical." The fact remains, however, that the forces analyzed are real forces, constantly
operative in the real world. Their action is merely
made less apparent, but is not at all mitigated, by dynamic movements.

Having made clear the static character of his inquiry,
Clark at once defines its scope. It is to discover those
"natural laws" which apportion the income of society
among the different claimants. The main thesis is immediately introduced in these words, "the distribution
of the income of society is controlled by a natural law,
and . . . this law, if it worked without friction, would
give to every agent of production the amount of wealth
which that agent creates." [1] Or again, "where natural
laws have their way, the share of income that attaches
to any productive function is gauged by the actual product of it." [2] This statement discloses the character of
the study as an analysis of functional distribution; that
is to say, it attributes income to the agents of production
in accordance with their performance of certain productive functions in the economic order. It does not go
afield into personal distribution, or the examination

[1] *The Distribution of Wealth,* preface, p. v.
[2] *Ibid.,* p. 3.

of the claims of individuals, as such, upon the social income.

This inquiry into the source and allocation of incomes, it is conceived, is a matter of very great practical importance. And particularly, the truth of the thesis presented is crucial. "More hinges on the truth of it than any introductory words can state. The right of society to exist in its present form, and the probability that it will continue so to exist, are at stake." [1] It is of importance, also, to examine the dynamic trend. "Having first tested the honesty of the social state, by determining whether it gives to every man his own, we have next to test its beneficence, by ascertaining whether that which is his own is becoming greater or smaller. The right of the present social system to exist at all depends on its honesty; but the expediency of letting it develop in its own way depends entirely on its beneficence." [2]

The problem is thus thrown at the very start into the realm of ethics. If every man receives all that he creates, then "the different classes of men who combine their forces in industry have no grievances against each other." On the other hand, if they do not receive their product in full, there is "institutional robbery," and "there would be at the foundation of the social structure an explosive element which sooner or later would destroy it." [3] If the thesis is correct, private

[1] *The Distribution of Wealth*, p. 3.
[2] *Ibid.*, pp. 4-5.   [3] *Ibid.*, p. 9.

property is ethically justified because "property is protected at the point of its origin, if actual wages are the whole product of labor, if interest is the product of capital, and if profit is the product of the coördinating act." [1]

It is interesting to note that Clark refuses to be drawn into the controversy over the justice of private property as now instituted. The socialists are summarily dismissed with the statement that their plan "would violate what is ordinarily regarded as a property right. The entire question whether this is just or not lies outside of our inquiry, for it is a matter of pure ethics." [2] He is thus involved in this dilemma, that he is engaged in an inquiry with ethical implications, but that another approach to the same problem is irrelevant because it has ethical implications. He resolves the dilemma to his own satisfaction by contending that the truth or falsity of his own thesis is a matter of "pure fact." As we shall see, other institutions of society are later subjected to criticism on grounds of morals and public policy. But the laws of private property are merely sweepingly approved. This fact, of course, will throw no suspicion on the argument as to the allocation of income. It will of necessity, however, create in the mind of the candid reader some question as to the validity of the ethical implications of the argument. The point is of interest as

[1] *The Distribution of Wealth*, p. 9   [2] *Ibid.*, p. 8

illustrating a characteristic of Clark to which attention has already been called. Social arrangements must be morally defensible. A set of social laws that did not commend themselves to his higher moral insight would, in his eyes, be only vile counterfeits. It is, perhaps, not too much to say that this predilection for morality is of the essence of Clark's inner self. It is not so much a part of his scientific inquiry, nor so much a necessary consequence of it, as it is a personal preconception which he brings to it. It is necessary to give vital meaning to his work.

The mobility of labor and capital has, of course, been a time-honored assumption of deductive economists, together with the "economic man" who "remorselessly and intelligently" pursues his own interest. These, the Ricardian premises, are approved by Clark, and it is his opinion that Ricardo's analysis of value on the basis of them is substantially correct, though incomplete. His one criticism of Ricardo is the failure to see that he is engaged in static analysis. "What the Ricardian theory unconsciously and imperfectly accomplished was the separation of static from dynamic forces." [1] "If these early students . . . had completed their system by separately examining the dynamic forces, they would have attained a complete and realistic science." [2] Clark is thus, in his own view of the situation, following out and completing in the field of

[1] *The Distribution of Wealth*, p. 69.
[2] *Ibid.*, p. 70. Contrast the denunciation of Ricardianism, *The Philosophy of Wealth*, p. 150.

distribution a body of doctrine which is approximately correct in the field of value.

Labor is regarded as a fund of working energy, the separate units of which are prepared to gravitate at once to any point where their earnings would be increased. It is a permanent fund, self-replenishing by procreation, so that while the units change, the fund abides. The difficulties of ignorance, family ties, and the like which hinder the intelligent migration of workers in the "real world" are recognized, but the readiness of labor units to move in answer to a financial stimulus is regarded as a sufficiently universal phenomenon to serve as the basis for an economic generalization. It is to be remembered, also, that under the static assumptions of a complete existing adjustment of labor and capital to industrial technique, no further movement is called for. There is "mobility without motion." But the notion of movement is necessary to show the applicability of static forces to a dynamic world in which there are always maladjustments to be smoothed out.

Capital, like labor, is treated as a mobile fund and is distinguished from capital-goods, which are the concrete appliances of industry. The fund originates through "abstinence," but once formed may be regarded as permanent and self-sustaining, through the creation of a product with which to replace the wear and tear of the concrete instruments in which the fund is embodied. Thus while capital-goods are transient, the fund of capital is abiding. Land is included as one of the forms of capital-goods in which capital is embodied. In this case, of course, the practice of attributing the origin of capital to abstinence will not apply. The objection which most theoretical economists have felt to throwing land and other productive goods into the same category is avoided by the static assumptions. Under those assumptions "artificial" capital is as fixed in amount as land itself, so that they may, without confusion, be treated together.

Certain logical difficulties, of almost metaphysical subtlety, arise in connection with the "funding" process. These difficulties Clark never resolves. Whether this fund has a real entity of its own apart from concrete appliances which embody it, or whether it is merely a fund of values, a sum made up of the values of capital-goods is never made clear. Clark seems to be not quite clear on the point in his own mind, as the meanings are alternately used wherever the one or the other will best promote the argument. We should be detained too long were we to go into the difficulties which have been encountered by economists in their search for a proper concept of capital. It is sufficient at present to note the theoretical use which is made of Clark's concept.

Capital-goods are relatively fixed and immobile during their lifetime. A machine shop cannot be converted into a steamship. But capital, as such, is mobile. Its owners are forever on the watch for profitable investment. Its mobility is established by the fact that the appliances which embody it are forever wearing out. It can thus from one generation of appliances to another effect a sort of transmigration. The whole difficulty arising out of the immobility of capital-goods contrasted with the mobility of capital is resolved by the conception that "Competition for capital is an all-round struggle to get *concrete things that are about to be.*"[1] The tenuous character of the reasoning on this point can hardly be grasped without resorting to the text itself. This elusive quality will need to detain us somewhat at a later point. For the present, progress will be hastened by merely accepting the fiat that capital is mobile; that it is productive; that it seeks the point of maximum gain; that in the static situation, gain (productivity) is equalized; and that therefore there is "mobility without motion."

The basic assumption of competition in pursuit of gain is thoroughly diffused throughout the argument. The efficacy of competition is the keystone that maintains the arch, or, to resort to one of Clark's own favorite hydraulic illustrations, the water that turns the mill. By hypothesis, all such modern developments as monopolistic enterprises or price-fixing associations are excluded from consideration. As Clark is concerned that economic theory should constitute a "realistic science," it will be necessary to see how he deals with such abeyances of competition as are very realistic features in

[1] *The Distribution of Wealth*, p. 259.

contemporary life. That can best be done in connection with our later examination of his dynamic theory.

The efficacy of competition is, of course, dependent upon the assiduity and intelligence with which men pursue their financial interest. In a science dealing with human relations no progress could be made in the absence of a theory of human nature. A number of excerpts [1] will make clear the position taken on this point: "In all stages of social development the economic motives that actuate men remain essentially the same. All men seek to get as much net service from material wealth as they can." "The generic motive which can properly be called economic is the desire to make their surplus large." "Altruism has its place in any social system of economics, and so have the sense of justice and the positive compulsion of the law. Altruism does its largest work in causing men to give away wealth after they have acquired it, but conscience and the law powerfully affect their actions in acquiring it. These are forces of which social economics has to take account; but the more egoistic motive, desire to secure the largest net benefit from the wealth-creating process, is one of the premises of any economic science. This involves a general pursuit of wealth." Such is the general tenor of numerous passages. It is no misrepresentation to say that the human being presented in the static theory is that personage of honorable antecedents, the "economic man." Verbal conces-

---

[1] Taken from *Essentials of Economic Theory*, p. 39.

sions to other human attributes are indeed made, but no relevant use is made of them in developing the argument. The logic used is the logic of men in intelligent pursuit of the wealth that will satisfy their own wants.

The wants of men are, of course, the final term in the economic process. It is toward their satisfaction that labor and effort are directed. In Clark's view, the notion of "productive consumption" is an example of mistaken teleology. Men do not primarily consume that they may produce. They produce that they may consume. "Men seek the wealth for a certain personal effect which comes from the use of it, and they measure it, when attained, by means of this subjective effect." [1] It is essential, then, to the task of discovering the values of goods that the subjective process by which goods are valued be explained.

In attacking this problem, Clark retains the conception which we have already seen as being expounded in *The Philosophy of Wealth*. Commodities have one common quality "utility," or want-satisfying power. The utility of anything is, in the first instance, a measurement by the individual of the amount of satisfaction which the particular thing will give him. The utility of each unit of goods of the same kind decreases as the number of units increases (the familiar "law of diminishing utility"), and the "effective" utility of any unit is measured by the amount of satisfaction to be gained

[1] *Essentials of Economic Theory*, p. 39.

i

from the last unit. The rational attempt to secure maximum satisfaction from one's income will lead to such an expenditure of income as will insure that the "effective" satisfaction gained from the "marginal" or "final" unit of each article of consumption will be an amount equal to that gained from every other final unit. Such an acquaintance with this line of analysis of the psychological background of demand may be assumed as to render no extended treatment necessary here. So much it has seemed advisable to include in order that the psychological premises of Clark's system may be entirely exposed to view.

It will be apparent that the validity of Clark's use of the concept of utility (as, indeed, its use by all marginal economists) is dependent upon the answers to two questions. First, do men habitually balance their purchases against each other in order to secure the maximum satisfaction? Second, are satisfactions to be regarded as quantities of pleasure, or are they marked by qualitative differences which defy their reduction to quantitative terms, except in mere objective terms of price? It is simply to be noted here that Clark assumes uncritically the view of the utilitarian school of philosophers that utilities are quantities of pleasure, rationally measured. This involves the view, of course, not merely that the price of admission to a prize fight and a symphony concert are equal, but that the *amount* of subjective satisfaction is equal in the two cases to those for whom the expenditure has been marginal.

A further development of this line of subjective analysis leads to the position that the acquisition of any means of satisfaction is laid over against the pain, sacrifice, or subjective cost of acquisition. The primary painful or unpleasant thing in life is work, or effort. So that the final touchstone in estimating the worth of anything to a man is whether or not he is willing to undergo the sacrifice or effort necessary to its attainment. This conception will need to be developed a little later in connection with Clark's theory of value. It is introduced here merely to make plain the psychological assumptions upon which he proceeds. Enough has been said to show that his analysis is based upon a definitely hedonistic view of human nature. For purposes of theoretical static analysis at least, men are regarded as proceeding through life constantly balancing satisfaction against satisfaction, and balancing satisfactions against sacrifices.

No special mention need be made of Clark's concept of the social organism. The same range of ideas that were suggested in *The Philosophy of Wealth* are carried over into the later work. He was, it seems, the first person to apply to economic theory this item of Herbert Spencer's social philosophy. The concept is not basic to most of the reasoning, which proceeds for the most part upon thoroughly individualistic lines. At a certain point it is aroused from its dormancy and injected into the argument by way of constituting economic principles as laws of organic society, thereby giving the final element of roundness, completeness, and ethical plausibility. The transformation is made without proof, with simplicity, even naïvely. One is apparently asked to believe at the start that Spencer has said the final word upon the nature of the organic life of society.

Clark objects to the customary division of the field of economics into the four departments, Production, Distribution, Exchange, Consumption. The trouble with this classification is twofold. In the first place, production, distribution, and exchange are really merely aspects of a larger process which cannot be logically so subdivided. In the second place, it blocks the way to a proper classification, on which a correct analysis of economic laws may be constructed. It is necessary, therefore, to find a proper division of the field. This is done by dividing economic forces into three groups, in each of which are to be found distinct, though related, sets of economic laws. The three sets of laws are the Universal Laws of Economics, which may be discovered by studying the principles which govern the life of an isolated man; Static Social Economics, disclosing the laws operative in a changeless society; and Dynamic Social Economics, in which the laws governing the processes of social change are unfolded.

As has already been said, Clark, in delimiting the scope of his inquiry, is confining himself in *The Distribution of Wealth* to the study of static social phenomena. He is compelled, however, to give some preliminary attention to the universal laws discoverable in an isolated economy, since they carry over into a social economy. Briefly, these universal principles are, (1) the law of diminishing returns, (2) the distribution of effort between providing for present wants and providing the means for future production (capital accumulation), (3) the law of diminishing utility in consumption, (4) the direction of production by the principle of final, or marginal, utility. Excepting the first, the universal laws may be said to have inherently within them the psychological postulates of the system. Stripped of technical jargon, the man presented to view is one forever taking counsel with himself how he may attain a maximum of pleasure; forever debating whether he will be best served by another bushel of potatoes or another rabbit, whether he shall go fishing or start a new canoe, whether a lean-to to his hut or ten hours' additional leisure will constitute the greater benefit. It is not permitted that these matters resolve themselves into any habitual routine. Every choice of one thing against another, of the present against the future, of work against leisure, must be rationally made in pursuit of the maximum of personal satisfaction. This is in no sense a parody,[1] but expresses the implicit or explicit assumption of the system we are examining.

The remaining universal principle, that of diminishing returns, is of a different stripe. In its time-honored form it refers, of course, to the fact that beyond a cer-

[1] See *The Distribution of Wealth*, p. 48.

tain point a tract of land gives a progressively less generous response to the efforts of cultivators; or, from another viewpoint, that the progress of population calls into cultivation new land which is less fruitful than that previously cultivated.   As thus conceived, it was a principle of dire import to society, but its distressing implications were in the field of dynamics, or social change.   In the hands of Clark, engaged in a static analysis, it has no such power to harrow the feelings or destroy the hopes of mankind.   In a static society, you will not have recourse to poorer lands, nor will you be impelled to more intense cultivation.   You have, instead, fixed amounts of land, of productive appliances, and of available labor.   There is, then, in a true static situation merely a certain productive combination of labor and capital (including land).   By the forces of competition, a combination takes shape based upon what may be called the law of the proportion of factors.

But, while the law of diminishing returns is quiescent, you have it always in the background, or just around the corner, ready to intervene.   And in this case the threat of the law is not confined to the product of land alone.   For if a little more labor be injected into a situation otherwise stable, its product per unit will be reduced because of the necessity of working with a smaller pro rata share of capital and a less effective form of capital.   This adjustment of capital to a new labor situation rests upon the ability of capital, abstractly considered as a mobile fund, to adjust itself

quickly to any amount of labor. [1] Similarly, an increase
of capital, other things being equal, will cause a lesser
return per unit, since the earlier forms will have embodied the more essentially productive qualities. Thus,
an increase of any one factor of production involves a
loss of productivity to each unit of that factor, productivity in this sense referring to physical product,
not value of product. The principle of diminishing returns is thus translated into a general principle of
diminishing productivity, applicable to all the factors
of production, to labor and artificial capital as much
as to natural capital (land).

The idea is implicit in the principle, as thus stated,
that a specific product is attributable to each unit of
each factor. Now concrete products are commonly the
outcome of a coöperation of factors. For example, the
wheat yield of a farm involves the land, plows, reap-
ers, horses, men, and so forth, not to mention the sun,
rain, and air. The latter may be ruled out as irrelevant, since their inappropriable character eliminates
them from the meaning of economic goods, as defined.
As to the others, the central argument is designed to
demonstrate that a separate part of the joint product
is to be attributed to each one, and to elucidate the principle upon which the division is made. It will not be
necessary to pursue the point here, since it will take its
proper place a little later. It has seemed advisable to

---

[1] The same characteristic of capital rules out anything in the nature
of unemployment. See *The Distribution of Wealth*, p. 115: "An industrial society can, in some way, absorb any amount of labor."

dwell at some length on the main aspects of the universal laws, discoverable in an isolated economy and carried over into the social sphere. For they include the psychological laws which determine the personal appraisal of goods and the direction of effort, together with the physical law of diminishing returns, or productivity, which are the most essential underpinnings of the completed logical structure.

III

After so extended an examination of postulates and preliminaries, it should now be possible to get very quickly to the heart of the system. The search is directly for the laws that control the distribution of income in an unchanging society. Since, however, distribution is part of a larger process including production and exchange, we are compelled to approach our objective by a slightly roundabout route. By the mechanism of exchange, through the medium of markets, values are placed upon commodities. These values, or prices, for reasons to be examined later, may be considered as appraisals by society, or social values. These appraisals will determine the extent to which the productive power of society will be apportioned between one group of industries and another. Thus, values of finished woolen goods determine the total amount available for distribution among everyone engaged in the production of woolens from ranch to retail store. Under the stress of competition, productive factors will migrate from group to group until there is no further advantage in migration. You have then a "normal" or static adjustment, based on socially determined values.

Within these larger groups are the smaller subgroups, representing the different stages through which a material passes on its way to becoming a finished product. Competition will act to the same effect, that a normal adjustment is created offering no incentive to movements of labor, capital, or organizing ability between subgroups. Going a step farther, within each subgroup—for example, the woolen manufacturing industry—the total amount which the social appraisal and the action of competition has allotted is yet to be subdivided between the management, the owners of the capital, and the laborers. This is the central and crucial problem of distribution, the point at which any injustice will create class feeling and social disorder. Division is conceived to proceed on the basis of function performed. For example, the land upon which a factory stands is to receive a share as a factor in production, without regard to the matter of ownership. So long as private property is a basic social institution, the progress of the income into a personal pocket is not a matter for comment.

The first fact that emerges is that, when the normal, or static, adjustment has been achieved, profit will have disappeared. By hypothesis, business men are endowed with an uncanny knowledge of every source of profit;

that is to say, every market in which goods may be
sold at more than their cost. Rivalry in exploiting such
markets will force down prices until the source of profit
is dried up. The business men who specialize in the
organization of production must, of course, receive
some compensation. Their reward, however, is merely
of the nature of wages, a payment for organizing ability,
and contains nothing in the nature of a surplus which
they are in a position to claim merely by reason of
their strategic position in the producing organization.
Moreover, by the hypothetical mobility of capital and
the omniscience of organizers, the best available methods of production will have been adopted by all competing firms. There will then be no incentive for
business men to transfer their efforts from one field
of endeavor to another, because advantage has been
equalized over the entire field of production. The
beneficent effects of the competitive system are thus
seen in its apotheosis, the static adjustment, where
profits are nonexistent and buyers procure their goods
at cost.[1]

There are, in consequence, but two sharers in the
totality of social income, labor and capital, and the
problem to be solved resolves itself to what forces control that distribution. As has been said, the thesis to
be proved is that every laborer is paid the exact equivalent of what he produces, and that every unit of capi-

---

[1] See *The Distribution of Wealth*, p. 77: Competition "insures to
the public the utmost that the existing power of man can give in the
way of efficient service."

tal receives the exact equivalent of what it produces. The argument runs in terms of "units" of labor and "units" of capital, terms which should be made clear. By a unit of labor is meant the amount of labor-force which a worker of "average" ability is capable of expending. Distinct workers may embody more or less than a unit of labor. Wage differentials are accounted for by differences in "efficiency"—that is, by differences in the number of units of abstract "labor" embodied in a particular worker. A unit of capital, it will be shown later, must ultimately be measured in terms of labor undergone. For an adequate working concept, however, it is to be regarded as merely a certain number of dollars' worth of capital, or a certain small fraction of the total fund of capital. Then, if one hundred dollars be taken as the unit, a machine costing a thousand dollars or a building lot selling for a thousand dollars equally embodies ten units of capital.

How, then, are wages adjusted? We must hark back to the principle of diminishing productivity. Each worker added to a working force increases the total product by an amount less than the last man of the smaller previous force did. So long, however, as the labor of additional men will yield to the employer a return larger than he has to pay them, an incentive remains to him to enlarge his force. Competition among employers will, therefore, lead each severally to add men up to the point where the last man, or group of men, adds to his gross income only a product equivalent to the amount which he has to pay in wages. Up to that point he is compelled to go by competition. Beyond that point he cannot go without incurring loss. Marginal workers receive their "virtual" product as their wages.

There is thus established by competitive conditions a "zone of indifference" over the whole field of employment, comprising those final, or marginal, men in every establishment whose work brings no net gain to their employers. Such zones are found where men are employed upon land too poor to yield rent, at the intensive margin of cultivation of better land, where men are using rentless industrial equipment just worth operating, and at the intensive margin of use of industrial equipment of all kinds. In all such situations marginal men are paid by what they produce. Competition has brought it about. So long as marginal men are paid more in one industry or establishment, there is an incentive to some men to change their occupations and to some employers to increase their forces. The normal, or static, adjustment then is achieved only when the pay for all marginal units of labor has become the same and all incentive to movement been removed.

The next proposition to be established is that all units of labor will be paid at the same rates as the marginal, or least important, ones. This involves the hypothesis that all units are interchangeable. The tasks that two men of equal ability perform are not of necessity of the same absolute importance. It is of more importance to stoke the furnaces than to clear the yard litter. If, however, a laborer engaged in an essential task were removed, the remaining workers would be shifted in such a way that the essential task would be done while the least essential task would be left undone. So it follows that the *effective* importance of any unit of labor is no greater than that of any other. In consequence one unit of labor will not be paid more than another and the pay of all will be gauged by the product of that large group which, throughout the whole field of industry, is engaged in performing the least important tasks.

Having got so far, we encounter the question as to whether this does not involve an exploitation of labor. Does there not arise from the labor of those earlier in the series a surplus product which, since all are paid at the rate of the marginal ones, escapes into the pocket of the employer? In short, does the wage system not involve systematized robbery? The answer involves an appeal to the hypothetical characteristic of capital, its magical ability to adjust itself to any amount of labor. The argument proceeds somewhat along these lines. If the number of laborers working with a given amount of capital be doubled, the amount added to the total product by the new contingent will be less than that credited to the earlier group in the earlier situation. This is due to the fact that, to be adjusted to a larger number of workers, the capital has had to take new forms. In the new situation, the earlier group is working with only one-half as much capital as previously, and consequently is less productive. Working, in fact, with only as much capital as the second group, its product is no larger. Though wages have been adjusted downward, the specific product of the old group and the new group is the same under the new conditions.

Jumping the intermediate stages of the reasoning, we may say that the addition of any laborers necessitates a readjustment of capital. Whatever amount of labor is working (and in the static condition it is a fixed amount), capital has so shaped itself that each unit of labor is working in conjunction with the same amount of capital as every other. The product of every unit is thus the equivalent of every other. When, then, every unit of labor is paid the same amount as the marginal unit, it is not being deprived of any surplus which it has created. There is, in fact, no such surplus in existence, and every unit of labor actually receives as its reward its "virtual" product—that is, the value equivalent of its product. "Natural law, so far as it has its way, excludes all spoliation." [1] And so is born that famous doctrine, the specific productivity theory of wages. In such bare outline the theory may appear a little unintelligible. It can be grasped only by keep-

---

[1] *The Distribution of Wealth*, p. 324. See the note on von Thünen's use of marginal productivity, note, pp. 321-324: "As von Thünen did not suspect, the natural law of wages gives a result that would satisfy his own requirements, as being desirable and morally justifiable."

ing constantly in mind the three premises on which it
is principally grounded, the principle of diminishing
productivity, the interchangeability of units of labor,
and the fluidity of the fund of capital. Even then a
question arises concerning the internal validity of the
argument.

There are, in fact, two distinct theories of wages
implicit in the argument. One is dependent on the use
of a given amount of labor in connection with a given
amount of capital goods, or concrete instruments of
production. In this situation, "additional men create less
than did the original ones, because their opportunities
are poorer." [1] This gives the result that "wages tend
to equal the product of marginal labor, and that part
of the working force which occupies a zone of indifference is thus marginal." [2] Though really creating a
larger physical product, the earlier men in a series can
get no more than the later, by the principle of interchangeability or substitution. "What a man on the
zone of indifference is getting, another man must accept, if the employer can substitute the one for the
other." [3] Even then, however, no net benefit emerges
for the employer, since rivalry in disposing of the product eliminates profit. The marginal man increases the
total product which can therefore be sold only at a
reduced price, the benefit thus being diffused throughout society as a whole. This view of the case gives

[1] *The Distribution of Wealth*, p. 110.
[2] *Ibid.*, p. 106.   [3] *Ibid.*, p. 112.

what may be properly called a "marginal productivity" theory of wages. It means that no one of a group of interchangeable workers can secure a reward greater than the addition to the total product made by the man performing the least essential task. Merely that and no more. The product on which all wages are based can be detected only where the use of instruments has been pushed so far that the product of the final unit of labor has in it no intermixture of other income and is attributable to labor alone. It is, in effect, a mere "demand and supply" theory of wages, in which the final unit of labor, like that of any other commodity, is strategic in the fixing of price.

The other theory is dependent upon the use of a given amount of labor in connection with a given amount of that fluid essence, true capital. In this view, capital adjusts itself to any amount of labor to the effect that each unit of labor works with an amount of capital equal to that with which every other unit works. Consequently, the "specific" product of every unit is the true equivalent of that of every other unit. Under these conditions, it is obvious that a "zone of indifference" is an impossibility. For no labor is working with rentless instruments, but each unit is working with instruments embodying an equal amount of capital.

The "marginal productivity" analysis permits a testing of wages by merely withdrawing one worker and discovering the loss in product. The "specific productivity" analysis, however, can be tested only by taking the total product of one force, subtracting one worker, reshaping the capital to fit the lesser number of workers, and then comparing the total product under the new conditions with the former total. This measures the worth of the final, and consequently of every other, unit of labor. Some considerable strain would seem to be put upon the employer's omniscience in discovering just what a final worker is worth to him. In the complete static adjustment, however, all defects of knowledge have been by hypothesis removed and all capital has taken its appropriate shape. But it would appear that the "zones of indifference" have also disappeared, since no rentless instruments remain.

Clark is apparently unaware of the difficulty raised by his double approach through "marginal" and "specific" analysis. The latter principle is simply superimposed upon the former to make it "doubly clear that labor on all parts of the industrial field has the same degree of productivity that it has on the marginal zone." [1] Presumably, the difficulty could be resolved by resorting to the late Professor Alfred Marshall's device in distinguishing between the results of the "short-time" and the "long-time" play of forces. In that case, the fixation of wages by "marginal" product could be conceived of as a temporary phase pending a complete static adjustment of capital. The fixation of wages by "specific" product would represent the natural law of wages under the completed adjustment. Some

[1] *The Distribution of Wealth*, p. 332.

such conception was probably dimly present in Clark's mind, without sufficient clearness to lead to explicit statement.

This extended examination has been carried so far only in order to get, as well as one may, into the true inwardness of Clark's meaning. It is to be noted that in the more summary view of his theory presented later in *The Essentials of Economic Theory*, Clark omits the "zones of indifference," whether because he has discarded them or for brevity's sake it can only be surmised. His ultimate resting-point is thus the "specific productivity" theory of wages, which appears to be the correct outcome of his static assumptions. On this position, too, rests his whole defense of competition and the wage system as engines of social justice.[1]

The income of capital remains to be explained. Clark does not attack this question with the same brilliance of argument and fertility of illustration that he lavishes upon wages. The reason is obvious, that to a considerable degree the problems are the same, so that the logic of the one case is applicable to the other. For the same reason, the case of interest may here be abbreviated to less wearisome length.

[1] Those later texts of economic theory which show Clark's influence in the greatest measure have, in general, an exposition based clearly on the marginal analysis. They thus present a theory of wages avowedly divorced from any ethical implications, and applicable to a society in which "flux and change" have not been completely eliminated. It may be said, then, that these later economists are more "realistic" in the sense of keeping closer to the actual state of economic life; but that they fall short in the perspicuity with which they press their logic through to the conclusions made available by their premises.

The first essential fact is that capital does produce something specifically attributable to it. Presumptive evidence of this fact lies in the mere existence of the form of income known as interest. Were there no product there could be no income. As one of the partners in the industrial process, some distinguishable share of the total product must be assigned to it. So far the argument may be said to represent an economic fiat. It is, at any rate, Clark's angle of attack. Other economists have, certainly, been willing to attribute the whole product of industry to labor working in conjunction with certain inanimate aids. Interest can then be explained as a portion of the total product which must be paid to the owners of the stock of inanimate appliances for keeping the stock intact. A continuing incentive of income is necessary to capitalists to reward them for the continuing abstinence upon which the existence of the stock of capital demands. Under this hypothesis, how large the portion shall be is determined by the play of the "money market" in which the capitalists, actual or potential, represent the side of "supply."

Now to Clark, taking his stand at the point of static equilibrium, analysis along the lines just hurriedly sketched appears superficial, if not actually misleading. Abstinence, in his eyes, is over and done with when the initial act of saving is accomplished. The initial act was, indeed, done in the light of enjoying a future income, but, once done, a present satisfaction has been permanently and irretrievably traded for a continuing series of smaller future satisfactions. To put the case more concretely, in one view the setting up of sinking-funds to replace capital-goods as they perish through wear and tear is a form of abstinence as truly as the initial act of saving. In Clark's view capital is automatically self-sustaining and creates a product in addition, the whole amount of which goes, merely by right of title, to those fortunate enough to own it. The ability of capital to perpetuate itself automatically is not conceived to involve quite the eventuality feared by the inhabitants of Erewhon, where, it will be remembered, the possibility that machines might develop the power of procreation and escape from human control was the leading theoretical reason for their banishment from the realm. But the conception runs in not greatly dissimilar terms. It would, perhaps, be better merely to say that Clark takes sinking-funds for granted. He is, then, looking only for an explanation of interest in mechanistic terms of net product, rather than in human terms of incentives.

Assuming the identity of a product directly attributable to capital, the play of the principle of diminishing returns (productivity) comes into view. The action of this principle is to be tested by the device of adding or subtracting an increment of capital in an otherwise stable situation. The point of testing in "zones of indifference," where was discovered the marginal product of labor, is not available in this case.

For there is no extended field of wageless labor in connection with which a product due to capital alone can be isolated. But the method of testing for "specific" product is the same. The addition of a unit of capital to the amount already used by a fixed number of workers will mean that each worker has a larger *pro rata* share of capital. That is, he works with more or better equipment, produces more, and gets higher wages. The last unit of capital, on the contrary, produces less than the final unit in the earlier adjustment. The exact amount that it does produce can only be found by subtracting the total product of the earlier combination from the total product of the later.[1] The result will show the actual product of the final, or marginal, unit. This will be the measure of the product of every other unit of capital.

The "specific" product of the marginal unit is arrived at by assuming the elastic ability of capital to adjust its form, whatever its amount, to a given amount of labor. The "effective" importance, and therefore reward, of every other unit may be arrived at merely by assuming the infinite interchangeability of all units of capital. The fundamental fact is a little deeper. Each unit of capital, if it is to receive its "specific" product as its reward, must have been so adjusted in relation to labor that the actual product of each unit of

---

[1] See *The Distribution of Wealth*, p. 264: "The whole field (of industry) is possessed by men who have made the tests successfully and have so developed the power to use the agents of production with the maximum of efficiency."

capital is the exact equivalent of that of other units. If this were not so, we should have found wages and interest arrived at by differing principles.

In a perfect static adjustment competition will have so searched out the possibilities that the final unit of capital in one field of industry will produce an amount equal to that in every other field. Every unit of capital will, therefore, be equally productive over the whole field of social industry. The rate of interest is merely the amount of this product, in terms of value, expressed as a ratio to the value of the capital which has produced it. Competition is relied upon to search out every opportunity for profitable investment and to bring the ship of industry into the haven of perfect rest. Every unit of labor and every unit of capital is eager to move at the slightest sign of higher pay. But no movement ensues because everywhere remuneration is equalized.

The whole income of a static society has now been reduced to wages and interest. What has become of the income known as "rent"? The term, in Clark's use, has no particular relationship to land. Rent is to be considered as the product of concrete instruments of production. Contractually, it is the amount paid to the owner of such instruments, or, when he himself uses them, the imputed amount for which he might have leased them. This contractual rent, or its imputed equivalent, is, by the force of competition, made to equal the full product of the instrument under static conditions. It appears, then, that rent and interest are identically the same incomes. In the one case, the income is expressed as an absolute amount traceable to various concrete capital-goods; in the other case it is expressed as a ratio of the value of the true capital which the concrete instruments embody. "Rent is the aggregate of the lump sums earned by capital-goods, while interest is the fraction of itself that is earned by the permanent fund of capital." [1] Where, indeed, the static adjustment is incomplete, the two forms of income need not exactly coincide, because in that case capital has not everywhere become equally productive. But their coincidence is implicit in the complete working out of competitive forces.

This deviation from the customary use of the term "rent" involves Clark in a somewhat extended analysis of the income from land which would detain us too long, were we to examine it at all thoroughly. The calculation of land-rent as a differential amount measured from the marginal uses where land produces no net income is considered not so much incorrect as valueless. The rent of land is really its net product. This product is made to conform to the law of interest by the dictum that a specific area of land is to be considered as embodying a certain number of units of capital on which the product will represent a rate of interest the same as the rate elsewhere. This is really no more than a back-handed way of saying that the value of

[1] *The Distribution of Wealth*, p. 124.

land is the capitalized value of its rent, but "capitalization" is a word that Clark nowhere uses. In his competitive paradise, the idea is, of course, not needed except in the case of land, for there are elsewhere no surplus earnings to be capitalized. In the effort to make land amenable to his more general laws, he shuns the idea, so thoroughly, indeed, that he gives the impression of glossing over.

He also rather sidesteps three uncomfortable facts —that land does not arise from abstinence; that it cannot, like other embodiments of capital, shift its form; and that the personal appropriation of the product of land has an ethical significance which differentiates it from other types of income, from the social viewpoint His difficulties are diminished by the fact of his static hypothesis, since the questions related to the product of land are largely of a dynamic character and have to do particularly with personal, as contrasted with functional, distribution. He insists upon the mobility of land, in the sense that it will be put to the most productive uses. Under his own hypothesis, the serious gap in his treatment lies in his somewhat uncandid avoidance of capitalization. While other capital changes its form to bring product to an equalized percentage of cost elsewhere, with land the situation is somewhat reversed and product is the forerunner of a capital value not depending on cost. Otherwise his treatment of land as only a special form of capital fits very well into his static analysis, where the special questions relating to the fixed amount of land do not arise, since total capital is a fixed amount.

When the principle of diminishing returns is applied to land, considered merely as a part of capital, its use must obviously be different from that made of it by earlier economists. Their analysis leads to margins of cultivation, above which rent is measured as a differential gain. In Clark's hands it is used merely to explain the adjustment of land to its various uses. Like other capital, it will be so distributed between one crop and another, between building and tillage, that a maximum total product is obtained. The margins of cultivation for every crop are, like other margins, fixed by value of the product, and competition will nose out the points of relative advantage and eventually equalize all uses, in relation to a given amount of labor and other capital.

The testing method of adding or withdrawing a unit of capital and observing the result is hardly applicable to the case of land, because "units" of land are not areas, but values, while the same piece of land in oats will embody a different number of units than when in peas. About all that can be said to this elusive analysis is that competition will have established the proper utilization of various lands, guided by the value of the product. It will be learned only after the adjustment is completed how many units of capital any piece of land contains, since that depends upon the product. Our analysis undoubtedly becomes very obscure here.

The only defense that can be entered is that Clark is quite as obscure on the points involved. We have merely encountered and faced some of the disconcerting problems involved in reducing income from land and capital to a common formula. Clark can hardly be said to have solved them. Nor has anyone else. His is perhaps the most heroic recorded attempt.[1]

One point of doubt has been carried through the entire discussion of wages and interest to this point. That is whether the principle of diminishing productivity, by which margins are arrived at, has reference to physical product or to value of the product. It may be stated briefly that it is used in both senses. Within a particular subgroup, or industry, the principle is thought of in terms of physical product. In the equalizing of earnings over a wide field of industry, however, it is necessary to appeal to the values of products as the only available common denominator. As the static premises preclude any substantive improvement such as might increase the product while diminishing the amount of capital, there appears to be no objection in logic to this usage. It has to be remembered merely that an argument that proceeds in an apparently simple

---

[1] The existence of rentless land on the extensive margin of cultivation which is still worth cultivating raises the question as to whether it can be classified as capital at all, since it earns no income. This merely repeats the question raised earlier as to the "zones of indifference," but from another angle. Can the rate of wages be traced to such margins at the same time that capital disposes itself so as to furnish each laborer with an equal complement?

way is, in reality, carrying along a double line of implications.

Our survey of the static laws of distribution may be concluded by calling attention to the larger unifying principle to which they conform. The whole economic process is under the control of "one very general law"; "so all-embracing is it that it dominates economic life." [1] "It may be called a law of variation of economic results; and, if it were stated in its entirety, it would give unexpected unity and completeness to the science of economics." [2]   This universal principle is based upon the law of diminishing returns. In the field of production it operates as we have seen above, making incomes dependent upon the productivity of final units of labor or capital. In the field of consumption it appears as the principle of diminishing utility, making values dependent on the utility of final units of commodities. Postponing this latter idea for a moment, we see in the former the basic explanation of the relative incomes of labor and capital. These depend strictly upon the proportions in which labor and capital are commingled in the productive process, a purely quantitative relationship. "The greater the amount of one agent that coöperates with the other, the smaller is the power of a unit of it to create goods; while the greater the amount of goods produced, the smaller is their value. Agents that are perfectly mobile would quickly

---

[1] *The Distribution of Wealth*, p. 208.
[2] *Ibid.*, p. 209.

reach a state of uniform productivity in all industries," [1] by the action of "the universal law of variation." And there, for the time being, the laws of distribution may be permitted to rest, clustered about a common centripetal principle.

IV

There remains now to examine the "natural" laws of value. To this point they have been only briefly mentioned. They are, however, essential to complete and round out the system. For, of course, the prices at which things sell determine the amount which shall be produced, and control the apportionment of labor and capital as between the various groups and subgroups of the industrial system. Values may thus be said to control group-distribution, while productivity, as has been seen, governs functional distribution.

Clark nowhere develops a complete theory of value. That is to say, he does not analyze the market forces by which, under competitive conditions, prices are fixed at the point of equilibrium between supply and demand. He accepts as correct the Ricardian theory that natural price is cost price, since competition eliminates profit. He also explicitly states that John Stuart Mill's theory of market prices is a correct one.[2] To that ex-

---

[1] *The Distribution of Wealth*, p. 289. See also p. 352: "All depends on the quantities of the several agents that are brought together."
[2] See *The Distribution of Wealth*, p. 230: "Mr. John Stuart Mill has told us that, if the tentative price of an article is too high to

tent he is a true representative of the English "classical school" of economists. He concentrates his attention, however, upon the point tentatively stressed in his earlier *Philosophy of Wealth*, the psychological background of consumer's demand.

Briefly, consumers evaluate goods according to the utility, or want-satisfying power, which they expect to realize from them. Earlier units in a series of like goods satisfy more pressing wants than later units. Likewise earlier services in a single commodity are more highly valued than later qualitative improvements.[1] It is in this latter conception, in which a single commodity is viewed as a "bundle" of utilities serving wants of diminishing importance as the quality improves, that Clark's use of diminishing utility differs from that of the Austrian "psychological" school of economists. The quality of utility is considered capable of quantitative measurement, proximately in pecuniary terms, fundamentally by a touchstone of value to be examined a little later. Each individual is supposed to allocate his purchases in such a way that

---

insure the sale of the whole supply, the price is lowered till new purchasers take some of the goods and old purchasers take more than they formerly did. This statement is, in any view, a correct one; and, unless we want to understand the mental operations that determine the action of consumers and bring their purchases to a stop at a certain definite point, it is enough."

[1] Additions to consumers' wealth are conceived more often to take the form of qualitative improvements rather than new kinds of goods. New utilities are thus most commonly designed to satisfy the less essential wants, not for more but for better goods. See *The Distribution of Wealth*, pp. 217-218.

the final element of utility in every commodity that he possesses is equal. The "effective" utility of all elements earlier in the series is gauged by the actual utility of the final element.

The argument runs on the same grounds as the fixation of wages and interest. The process is guided by a rational weighing of the utility of one thing against that of another. It comes to pass, then, that one's purchases for consumption come finally to rest in a perfect balance of utilities, so distributed that the maximum satisfaction is attained from the expenditure of one's income. "The mental process in the case is . . . a balancing of one pleasure as against another."[1] The mental process involves surveying a commodity, weighing the pleasure to be secured from it, balancing that against alternate pleasures, and finally setting a price which expresses the value of the utility in question.

So far the process represents only the subjective operation of the individual mind. It explains an individual's price bids in the market. When, however, one conceives an indefinitely large number of buyers coming into the market, the effect of this individual valuation on market prices is discovered. Out of these lists of individual price offers emerge the complete demand schedules, indicating what quantity and quality of commodities will be taken off the market at various prices. It is in response to these demand schedules that the forces of production adapt themselves, so distributing

[1] *The Distribution of Wealth*, p. 377.

themselves between one use and another as to equalize their earnings at all points.   And here a wonderful result is discerned.   The competitive process insures the result that not only are goods furnished at cost, not only are labor and capital, respectively, paid their whole product, but also goods to consumers are furnished in such kinds and proportions as to produce a maximum of achievable pleasures.   Here we have the beautiful, healthy functioning of the social body operating under natural law, and unmarred by any diseases of mind, circulatory system, or digestive tract.   We might well pause to shake the "unseen hand" of Adam Smith's providential guide.

The analysis of value proceeds, up to the point of the fixation of price by a market equilibrium, in purely individualistic terms.   Clark is not, however, content to consider prices as the outcome of a mere selfish scramble of countless individuals.   He has foresworn himself to translate the whole process into terms of the functioning of an organic being, society.   This is accomplished by the mere sweeping assertion that prices, as they emerge in the market, must be considered to have been fixed by "society."   To "understand the philosophy of value, we must take all society in view as the purchaser of things." [1]   "The motives in this movement are individualistic, but the resultant is collective. Each man pursues his own interest; but, as the outcome

[1] *The Distribution of Wealth*, p. 227.

of his activity, society acts as a solitary man would act under the influence of the law of diminishing utility." [1]

It has not seemed necessary to Clark to enter any extended argument to prove the organic character of society. No analysis of the biological analogy is anywhere attempted. Nor is attention given to any of the numerous aspects of social life of a noneconomic character. The society exposed to view is entirely an economic society made up of intelligent, self-interested, calculating germ cells, each weighing whether another red corpuscle is worth another unit of heat, and wondering whether the nourishment is not better at the base of the stomach. If definitive proof be demanded, there is only to point to the perfect working of the system. But if further demands be entered as to how the life of an organism can be described in mechanical terms of "statics" and "dynamics," of "weighing" and "balancing," no answer is forthcoming. One discovers merely an uncritical and optimistic adaptation of Herbert Spencer's social philosophy, throughout which the assumption prevails that we are studying, by a kind of microscopy, the detailed physiology of an integral being.

The introduction of the organic concept of society sets the scene for the final rounding off of the value theory. So long as the analysis is confined to individual motivation, the balancing of labor pain against utility is a purely personal and subjective matter. The

[1] *The Distribution of Wealth*, p. 46.

balance is maintained by each individual for himself, and rests upon his judgment of the amount of pain involved in a final increment of labor and the amount of pleasure residing in final increments of consumable goods. When, however, society has entered into the scene through the door of market values, it is conceived that society, like an isolated individual, is engaged in striking a balance between its pleasures and its pains. A new set of terms is introduced—"social value," "social labor," and "social utility." Market prices are supposed to express social values, representing an adjustment by which a maximum social utility is achieved with a minimum outgo of social labor. The adjustment is of the nature of an equilibrium between the pain to society of final hours of social labor and the "effective social utility" of final units of the commodities which society demands. This transmutation of value, pain, and utility into social terms puts a heavy strain upon the imagination, until one realizes that it is effected merely by aggregating all individual subjective feelings and calling them social feelings. We may go on to see to what final outcome this concept of society leads.

Values, as has appeared, arise out of a nice adjustment of production to consumers' demand, determined along lines of diminishing and marginal utility. But, to this point, no unit has appeared by which to measure values. Money, of course, furnishes a mode of expressing them. But money is viewed by the light of a mere convenience for facilitating exchanges. Through money can be expressed the ratios at which goods exchange for one another, but what is necessary is to explain "the power that resides in the coins." Value has now been traced to "effective social utility," so that "the price of a thing gauges its importance, not to one man, but to all men, as organically related to each other."[1] The individual utilities, which in the market place are transmuted into the fine gold of "effective social utility," are conceived to be qualities that can be measured. The unit of measurement must be disclosed, and values, long thought doomed to the fate of being mere ratios, will then become absolute quantities. Some little importance is deemed to attach to this new measure, for "the entire study of wealth is, indeed, meaningless unless there be a unit for measuring it; for the questions to be answered are quantitative."[2] The search for the unit of value leads into "the mysteries of social psychology," whence, indeed, values themselves emerge by the route of utility. But these "mysteries" are made plain to the seeing eye, for "essentially simple in nature is the operation."[3]

Two substantial facts are conceived to be present in the world, pleasure and pain. In the economic field, pleasure is represented by the satisfactions of consumption, pain by the expenditure of labor in production. To a single man, the utility of a thing is measured by the effort necessary to procure it. The pain of labor

[1] *The Distribution of Wealth*, p. 378.
[2] *Ibid.*, p. 375. [3] *Ibid.*, p. 378.

increases as labor is prolonged, and will cease where pain undergone balances pleasure earned. "For the final hours of all days in a year, the man will get a miscellaneous list of pleasures and will decide whether the sum total of them offsets the sacrifice of almost three hundred final hours of labor. This is a difficult decision, but the man will make it, and in doing so he will get a unit of final utility in terms of equivalent pain." [1] For an individual, then, the measure of value is the pain of final hours of labor. Converging lines of utilities lessening in power to satisfy and of labor increasing in burdensomeness meet and stop at the point of balanced gain and loss.

The beneficence of the process is again demonstrated when it is seen that a laborer gets paid for every hour as much as for the most painful, and, as consumer, secures all units of his various pleasures as cheaply as the least important, leaving a substantial net balance of pleasure over pain. Reducing satisfaction, or utility, to measurement in terms of the labor cost, or "disutility," of final hours of labor is presumably a mental exercise indulged in by all men. They may work in isolation and balance consumption against production directly. Or they may work in a social system and effect the balance indirectly through a conversion of the wages of labor by money transactions into acquiring utilities. It is immaterial. Here we have, then, a great "universal law" of economics. And it insures that men everywhere, how-

[1] *The Distribution of Wealth*, p. 384.

ever circumstanced, shall reap from their labors a net
gain of pleasure over pain from their economic activities.

To this point, only individual psychological processes
have been invoked. But values, we have seen, are
social phenomena, expressing the marginal utility of
things to society, or "effective social utility." Obviously, there must be a social unit of measurement for
social values. Clark leaps the gap from individual to
social labor pain in the same way that he translates
individual into social value—that is, by appealing to
the market as the great socializer. The market places
a price upon labor which expresses the disutility of any
hour of social labor. The pain of this final hour of
social labor, as expressed by the price paid for it, becomes the ultimate unit of value for which we have
been searching. Thus, "everything that is produced
by one hour of social labor . . . possesses an effective
utility that equals the absolute utility of the final complement of goods consumed; and this, again, is counter-
poised and measured by the sacrifice which all society
undergoes in the labor of its final hour." [1] "Mere
labor time is an accurate gauge of the values of different complements of goods." [2]

It was said earlier that the measure of social value
involves an appeal to social psychology. One may now
see what is meant by that term. It obviously does not

[1] *The Distribution of Wealth*, p. 388.
[2] *Ibid.*, p. 390.

refer to any sort of effect on men's minds and actions
occasioned by their contact with a group. It does not
include such phenomena as imitation or social emulation, group conventions, or habitual mental attitudes,
nor anything of that sort. Social psychology is taken
to mean merely the aggregated mental processes of
many rational, self-seeking individuals. The results
of these processes, as they eventuate in the market, are
forcibly lifted out of the field of individual motivation
by some feat of prestidigitation too rapid for the eye
to follow. There is then a group-mind, capable of
rationally assessing social marginal utility and social
marginal labor pain, and capable of balancing them at
the point which assures maximum social satisfaction and
maximum net surplus of pleasure to society.

Only one or two small items remain to complete the
balancing process. How may the gap be bridged between one man's labor pain and the pleasure of others
who use his product? This is done by keeping in mind
that society as a whole is the evaluator and purchaser.
This formula then appears: one man's pain is the payment for society's product; society's pain is the payment
for his product; thus, his sacrifices and employments are
equated, and "price is, then, an indication of the *social
cost of acquisition* of different commodities."[1] Another
question arises. Men are differently paid. The burden
of labor imposed on one man may bear a reward only
a fraction of that going to another for the same burden

[1] *The Distribution of Wealth*, p. 391.

as measured by time. The answer is that value corresponds to the amount *and efficiency* of labor. Efficiency is measured by "power to give social gratification." The fact that one worker is paid twice as much as another is *prima facie* evidence of the fact that the product of his labor is twice as useful to society. This is the universal explanation of wage differentials under normal conditions.

One further point demands attention. The unit of labor by which all values are measured is the pain of a worker of "average" efficiency in his final hour of labor. Transferred into monetary terms, the social value of consumers' goods, capital, or labor is shown by the ratio their market prices bear to the hourly wage of an average worker. "Induced social labor gauges the power of them all." If the analysis were on purely individualistic lines, to measure values in terms of average labor while averaging labor on the basis of the value of its product would, as Clark points out, be to argue in a circle. The conception of a social value based on a social sacrifice is necessary to a proper evaluation of the labor of any individual. The circle is broken. But if one were to question the validity of the process by which aggregated individual subjective pleasures and pains are transmuted into social satisfactions and sacrifices, he would have again closed the circle. It is a point that might well occupy the attention of economists of the marginal utility school who have modified the tenets of the faith by discarding the ideas of social utility and social labor cost, or disutility.

Enough has perhaps been said as to Clark's analysis of the normal laws of value and distribution under static conditions. It has seemed the most fruitful plan to throw the premises of the argument and the main tenets of the system into a somewhat prominent perspective. There one may see, with more clarity than is usually possible, the whole range of implications of a system like Clark's. Particularly in the premises of such a logical system must be sought the validity of the argument when applied to the actual life of mankind. Upon them must ultimately depend the value of the conclusions. The internal integrity of the argument may be searched to discover whether the conclusions are implicit in the premises. In Clark's case, it may be said that, with some minor exceptions which have been briefly noted, the argument is well knit. The premises, however, give larger room for argument, and a number of questions will need to be raised at a somewhat later point. The static laws of economics may be rested here, and a brief examination made of Clark's conception of the dynamic laws.

v

During the elucidation of his static theory, Clark has made abstractions of the forces of change, by referring to them as "friction," "perversions of economic law," or "disturbing influences." It now appears, however, that this friction constitutes the largest and most important field of economic inquiry, the *terra incognita* of economic law. "The task of developing this branch of science is so large that the execution of it will occupy generations of workers." [1] "There is, indeed, in mundane affairs little of importance for humanity that does not fall within the scope of this division of the theory of political economy." [2] In the absence of the generations of work yet to be done, Clark essays an outline of the tasks to be performed and the methods to be followed. This we shall briefly examine.

There are, it appears, five types of change which are of importance in the world: (1) Population is increasing. (2) Capital is increasing. (3) Technical processes of industry are changing and improving. (4) Modes of organizing labor and capital are changing in the direction of improved efficiency. (5) The wants of mankind are becoming multiplied and refined. It is out of these types of change that the phenomena arise which constitute the data of dynamic economics. A list of questions will indicate the problems facing the economist. What are the effects of trust, labor unions, and other organizations which reduce competition? To what extent do they disturb "natural" wages, prices, and interest, and how may this disturbance be minimized? What are the effects of tariffs, immigration

[1] *The Distribution of Wealth*, p. 442.
[2] *Ibid.*, p. 442.

laws, and currency laws, and what is the proper public
policy in regard to them?   Is survival of the best in-
sured by economic law?   Does humanity gain from
changes in industry?   To what extent do gains accrue
to laborers?   How will denser population affect the
laborer?   Will capital increase more rapidly than labor,
and with what effects?   Will capitalists become inordinately wealthy, and, if so, how will this affect the
poorer classes?   Will ownership of capital become
widely diffused?   In what direction will human wants
change as they multiply?   What are the conditioning
causes of world-wide prosperity?   How will changes
affect the allocation of labor and capital among the
groups and subgroups?   What are the relative effects
of regular and irregular changes?   What are the effects
of widespread and rapid change as compared with the
slower and more local change?   More important still,
what economic laws govern the growth of population
and of capital, and what economic laws govern the velocity of changes in industrial methods?   In general,
what direction is progress taking, with what velocity
does it proceed, and, of supreme importance, what is
the outlook for the laborer? [1]   It is interesting to note
that, though Clark thinks the formulation of dynamic
laws a task for generations, he thinks himself in a
position to give at least tentative answers to all of his
questions.   This he proceeds to do in rather summary
fashion in the concluding chapters of *The Distribution*

[1] *The Distribution of Wealth*, pp. 74-75, and pp. 441-442.

of Wealth, and at greater length in *Essentials of Economic Theory.*

To give any adequate account of the logical processes by which the outlines of dynamic theory are arrived at would extend this inquiry beyond all reasonable bounds. The merest summary of conclusions will be attempted. To make this part of the analysis less strictly theoretical and more lifelike, Clark divides the world into two parts. One, the "economic center," comprises western Europe, most of North America, and other parts of the world with an advanced technology and extended trade relations with the areas mentioned. In this area, economic laws are conceived to work with a minimum of resistance, due to the relative mobility of capital and labor, and freedom of enterprise. Within this area there are, of course, serious obstructions such as tariffs, immigration laws, and the like. But, in a general way, it sufficiently meets the specifications to serve the purposes of illustration. Over this area the forces of change are directed by underlying static forces into the likeness of a proximate static distribution of population and capital, and proximate static rates of wages and interest. The rest of the world does not respond quickly to the action of economic law. Customary modes of life interfere. Population is relatively immobile, response to improved methods of production is not rapid, and enterprise is hampered by defects of character and the dead hand of custom.

It is not obvious why any such divisions of the world

into civilized center and barbarous provinces should be necessary. Clark's entire theoretical structure has been built upon the original nature of man, and society is represented as doing for itself neither more nor less than an isolated man or community would do. It would be supposed that the more primitive parts of the world would furnish an abundance of illustrations, unmarred by the complexity of life in more advanced countries. The admission that this is not so places Clark's premises in some jeopardy. For it appears to mean that there is no universality to his laws, and that, at best, they apply only to limited areas at a particular stage of development. This was all that Bagehot claimed for economic science; but Clark, until this point, seems to have claimed more.

The general conclusions to which Clark's analysis leads may be stated briefly as a series of propositions: (1) Static forces are forever at work and underlie all dynamic changes. (2) Where dynamic changes are widespread over the five fields of change, they tend to neutralize one another, and society approximates a static adjustment. (3) Changes that are slow and regular are desirable, since they minimize temporary displacements of labor. (4) Economic law precludes widespread displacement of labor. The growth of capital and improvement in industrial methods will enlarge the field of employment for labor. (5) Improvements in technology and organization are assured by the lure of profits for those early in the field. But competition will persistently level profits, and the gains will progressively accrue to society. (6) The continued accumulation of capital is assured, temporary profits affording an added potential reservoir of saving. Accumulation brings a declining interest rate and this stimulates saving, which is primarily done for the sake of an assured regular income. (7) Population will increase less rapidly than capital, as the sex instinct will be curbed by the desire of people to maintain a rising standard of living and to escape the loss of social status. (8) Progress will thus accrue largely to the benefit of the wage-earning classes, who will be able progressively to satisfy the higher wants.

A careful reading of these tentative dynamic laws discloses one thread of thought running through them. They are, without exception, optimistic in tone. Mankind may look to the operation of impersonal economic law to insure a roseate future. A still closer examination of the conclusions discloses the fact that the dynamic laws are all based upon the static premises, omitting only the single assumption that change is in abeyance. The relative reward of labor and capital is a matter strictly of their quantitative proportions, and improved methods may be regarded in this matter as increases in capital. Labor and capital maintain the mobility which takes them to the point of greatest remuneration. The accumulation of capital and the limitation of population are based upon a rational and calculating care for the future. Competition is maintained in full force and mankind continues to establish values by balancing pleasure and pain.

The dynamic laws, then, are but minor emendations of the static laws. The continuance of change produces constantly some slight, but unimportant, variations from normal, or static values, wages, and interest, so that at a given time the adjustment is proximately, but not completely, static. It thus turns out that the "friction" which at one stage of our study seemed to retard the action of natural law becomes, when clearly comprehended, rather a sort of divine fuel which will carry the social machine to higher levels where the air is purer and the outlook more magnificent.

Two disquieting clouds mar the landscape, however. The first of these has to do with the relations between the "economic center" and the outlying territories; the second with interferences to competition. Theoretically, a static adjustment would raise wages by allocating every man to the occupation where he would be most productive. If, however, one takes the whole world into view and imagines a movement toward complete static adjustment, a disconcerting result appears. There would be an enormous flow of population from the backward countries to the more advanced and a flow of capital from the advanced to the backward. The result, while marking an absolute advance for mankind, would be a very definite decline in wages throughout the entire economic center. Clark decides that this view gives a "false" result [1] for the central area where, as a matter of fact, wages are increasing. The theory is, then, applicable in an optimistic sense c.. 'y to the central area. The cloud remains, however, in the possibility that an industrial awakening beyond the pale may permanently undercut the standards of living in the more advanced industrial areas. The point is of interest in Clark's exposition because of the startled sensation which the idea produces in his mind. Looking the world over realistically, he is able to see economic law at work in only a part of it. Why human nature fails to act true to its original type elsewhere is not made clear.

The other and more pressing question relates to the efficacy of competition in regulating economic life. Clark himself, it will be remembered, had sung the doom of competition in *The Philosophy of Wealth*. But now that he has reversed his position and built up a body of economic law based on competition, he finds that others continue to sing his earlier song: "To many persons any theory based on competition may seem to have somewhat of the character of theoretical romance." "Have we, then, completed the theory of competitive distribution, only to find that the fact on which the whole of it is predicated has ceased to be?" [2] The reply to such criticism is concise. "It remains for eco-

[1] See *Essentials of Economic Theory*, note, pp. 227-228.
[2] *The Distribution of Wealth*, p. 440.

nomic dynamics to show that competition is an inextinguishable force." [1]   That is the whole answer.

The thought of the answer is, however, developed more elaborately when Clark comes to the discussion of practical problems of economic organization as he does briefly in the final chapters of *The Essentials of Economic Theory*, and at greater length in his writings elsewhere.   The practical import of these realistic studies has, on the whole, a very minor connection with the general body of theory.   He takes up the subjects of monopoly, railroads, tariffs, and labor organization, and his discussion shows wide information, common sense, and a large interest in the public welfare.   There runs, however, through these discussions of practices that place competition in partial abeyance, the general formula that legislation should enforce competition, and where that is impossible, public regulation should fix values and wages as near the competitive level as the facts permit.   The "inextinguishable force" is unfortunately at many points extinguished, and he calls upon government to do what competition would do, if it could.   It is interesting that a system reminiscent of the earlier advocates of *laissez-faire* should end upon a note of government regulation.   But government is not to work out some new constructive scheme.   It is to *enforce* competition, "keeping alive the force on which the adherents of a *laissez-faire* policy rested their hope of justice and prosperity."

[1] *The Distribution of Wealth*, p. 441.

Clark's treatment of the dynamic aspects of economic theory is brief and avowedly tentative. His own work was mainly confined to static analysis, since he thought it a necessary preliminary to dynamics. It was to this latter field, however, that he looked for the fruitful work of the future. One cannot say why he himself has carried his efforts in this direction no further. He was already an elderly man when his static theory took its final shape, and he may have then felt ready to pass on the torch. His own meager treatment of dynamics indicates some of the difficulties that arise to thwart advance. He expected dynamic theory to formulate laws of progress. And these laws must be built upon the system of static theory which he had already constructed. That system is, however, ballasted with a hedonistic view of human nature and a competitive view of economic organization. If he is to work in Clark's terms, therefore, the dynamic theorist is debarred either from investigating economic motivation or from speculating upon the advantages of noncompetitive forms of organization. The two leads which Clark had himself given in *The Philosophy of Wealth* have thus been closed by the nature of his later doctrines. It is not, then, apparent that Clark's statics are a starting point from which a fruitful study of the phenomena of change can proceed. They appear, indeed, definitely to block the way. Whereupon the query naturally arises whether the division of economic theory into statics and dynamics is one designed to promote the advancement of knowledge.

VI

To what conclusion has this closely wrought body of economic logic brought us? Briefly, it is a system of economic harmonies. Social harmony, it is concluded, results from competitive enterprise. The entire exposition may therefore be regarded as a sweeping and complete defense of the competitive form of business enterprise. Competition, working through the general pursuit of pleasure-gains, automatically eliminates conflicts of interest and injustices, and in a changing world spreads its increasing bounties before all classes, whether they love the Lord or not. "If nothing suppresses competition, progress will continue forever."[1] This is, indeed, a far cry from the Clark who could, twenty years earlier, write: "Individual competition, the great regulator of the former era, has, in important fields, practically disappeared. It ought to disappear; it was, in latter days, incapable of working justice."[2]

The harmonic scheme of automatic action of natural laws must be taken to represent Clark's mature thought. It will not be thought by all an advance over his earlier views. It did, however, put him rather definitely

[1] *Essentials of Economic Theory*, p. 372.
[2] *The Philosophy of Wealth*, p. 148.

in the apostolic succession of orthodox economists. He has become the child of Ricardo and Mill and Jevons, with a cognate line running to Bastiat and a pleasant cousinly relation to Alfred Marshall. This is not to say that his ancestors were all "harmonists," or that he is a mere "chip off the old block." There has been in all Clark's work an originality, independence, and subtlety of thought unique among American economists. With the tools that he chose to adopt he was a master craftsman.

To what extent the laws which he so freely distilled will continue to secure the approbation of fellow economists is not as yet apparent. To the present day, his mark may be seen upon most of the text-books from which the present generation is learning its economic theory. The marginal-utility theory of value, of which he was the foremost American exponent, was for a time almost universally accepted and is perhaps still the most widely received value doctrine. The marginal-productivity theory of wages was quite generally accepted, and is today the center about which most wage-theory debates revolve. The analysis of rent was thought by many a distinct advance in the treatment of that difficult subject. The clear division of economic analysis into statics and dynamics has been quite generally considered an advance in economic thought. A narrower range of approbation has attended the concepts of social utility and social value, while the capital concept has been almost unanimously rejected. Even Clark's adherents have generally felt that the ethical implications were not an essential part of his system of thought.

The finality which Clark was disposed to attribute to the main body of his doctrines does not appear to be assured. They are, in fact, at the center of the theoretical controversy which is today in progress. In the confused drift of contemporary economic thought his conclusions are accepted in greater or less measure by some, respected by others, and disdainfully rejected by a few. But the cogency and brilliance of treatment are nowhere questioned.

It would be interesting, if it were possible, to discover what influences had played upon Clark to turn the ardent reformer of *The Philosophy of Wealth* into a deductive theorist of familiar type. In our day, when economists approach their theorizing from so many angles, when they use such varied disciplines and arrive at such discordant conclusions, it would seem almost as important to study the economists as to study their economics. Since no adequate biography exists, any attempt to explain Clark in terms of objective influences must of necessity be somewhat speculative. A few surmises may be hazarded.

Certain tentative conclusions of Clark's on the nature and determination of value, throwing emphasis on the side of demand and involving a new use of "margins," had curiously coincided with those of Jevons in England and of a group of Austrian eco-

nomists. This coincidence brought him a considerable
repute of international extent. The clarification of
these ideas, and their unification into a generally acceptable view, was the occasion of a very great deal
of discussion in the periodicals of the 'eighties and
'nineties. The vogue of the marginal-utility school was
widely established.

The rapid rise of the marginal-utility type of analysis presents an interesting passage in the history of
economic thought. So great had been the prestige of
John Stuart Mill's version of Ricardian economics in
England and the United States that some decades were
occupied with little more than interpreting it or sim-
plifying it for the popular understanding. Receding
under the attacks of the historical school, socialists, and
social reformers, the authority of classical economics
received its *coup de grâce*, while the deductive method
was restored to favor, at the hands of the new type of
analysis which sprang up independently in England,
Austria, and the United States. Clark, as the American representative of the new movement, was one of
the lions of the occasion. Caught in the current of
renewed interest in the speculative aspects of economics,
Clark may be supposed to have moved naturally into
the development of the ideas that had brought him
early international recognition. An examination of his
contributions to periodical literature in the 'eighties and
'nineties shows the waning influence of his training
under Knies in Germany. We find him increasingly

preoccupied with developing the possibilities of marginal-utility analysis and with bringing his critical talent to bear upon the theories of his contemporaries.

The marginal-utility concept was early applied with great subtlety to the problems of value theory. Clark was the first to attempt to link it up with a full-blown theory of distribution. One may suppose that the pioneering of General Francis A. Walker, who made the first serious inroads upon the classical theory of distribution, heartened him to the task. The actual clue which he later followed out seems to have been found in the suggestion of Henry George that wages are fixed by the product of men working upon the poorest land in use. Starting from this dimly conceived relationship between wages and product, he arrived eventually, as we have seen, at a theory of the complete identity of product and reward.

Once he had conceived the self-conscious isolation of static forces, the way was open for the clear-cut presentation of economic principles. The problem became one primarily of the mechanics of the principle of utility. With his attention thus centered upon a problem of manageable proportions, he slowly and painfully cast his doctrines into the rounded form in which they are found in *The Distribution of Wealth*. It was no less than a stroke of genius which enabled him to see the way in which the principles of utility and of productivity could be grouped about the law of diminishing returns in such a way that the whole economic process presented itself as the working out of a universal law of economic variation. It was the roundness, completeness, and beauty of this view of the automatic functioning of economic life that drew economists everywhere to his feet. He appeared to have succeeded in finding the end of the rainbow for which economists had everywhere sought. He became the peer of Ricardo.

We have noted Clark's indebtedness to Henry George. He appears also to have been, in a negative way, in the debt of Karl Marx. It was Böhm-Bawerk who first pointed out the similarity between the methods of Marx and Clark,[1] despite the exact oppositeness of their conclusions. The revolutionary character of Marx's use of the economist's tools constituted a direct challenge to economists to protect their disciples from such profanation. Disproving Marx's conclusion may be said to have been one of the major economic sports of the later nineteenth century. And more than any other economist Clark met him on his own ground, giving him the choice of weapons. A skillful use of dialectic, used with imagination and a genius for systematic thought and based upon premises of his own choosing, led Marx to his theory of distribution and exploitation. The same weapons in almost equally skillful hands brought Clark to a complete refutation of Marx.

In the final reckoning Clark must be subjected to.

[1] In the *Quarterly Journal of Economics*, vol. xxi.

the same sort of inquisition that Marx has undergone. The question will not be whether his conclusions arise out of his premises, whether he is, in short, a master of dialectic. It will be asked rather whether he has not from the outset worked in the rarefied atmosphere of mystical concepts and whether his "natural laws" are not thereby lifted into the metaphysical company of doctrines of the Holy Ghost. The aim of the present inquiry is too modest to permit any final word on that point. Each for himself may examine the premises of the system and determine for himself whether the deductions from them may be considered applicable to the world about him; to the end that an eternal competitive system provides substantial social justice and promises the progressive amelioration of the lot of mankind.

One final influence giving direction to Clark's inquiries and shape to his theory may be suggested. The combination movement which began in the United States after the Civil War and had resulted in some substantial monopolies by the time of Clark's middle life engaged his earnest attention. It seems to have represented an exactly opposite evil to Marxism in his mind. When Marxian revolution sent him scurrying from his youthful zeal for renovating society, he was confronted by the menacing form of monopoly as the logical outcome of things-as-they-are. In this dilemma, there remained the "faith of our fathers, living still," the competitive system. It could be presented as, by its innate justice, guarded from the threat of revolution, while the heavy hand of the government might be invoked to protect it from the monstrous regiment of monopolists.

Were such things as these in Clark's mind as his theoretical system took form? No one can say. They are speculation, but perhaps not vain and useless. We may see in them something of the background of the economists who were at their tasks in the last quarter of the nineteenth century. And their background of ideas may well be as important to understanding their work as the setting of a stage is to the atmosphere of a play.

In taking leave of Clark's systematic statement of economic theory, we may well keep in mind the nature of the problem with which he was concerned. He was attempting to cut through the mass of complicating external facts to the heart of the problems of value and distribution. He was searching for fundamental and enduring forces in terms of which he might explain the pricing process which coördinates economic activity. And he wished his explanation to cut deep enough to relieve it from ephemerality and transigeance. What he sought to establish were natural laws of enduring scientific validity. To arrive at the inner recesses of truth he was willing to be "heroically theoretical." Quite consciously he dispensed with the outward appearance of reality in order, as he thought, to lay open to the eye in some simple and intellectually manageable form the hidden forces upon which economic life is based.

The assumptions upon which he proceeded, the methods by which he worked, and the conclusions at which he arrived have been passed in review. They were such as to commend themselves in greater or less degree to most American economists of the past generation. They have, however, inevitably given rise to questions. It may be asked whether the processes of social life are amenable to treatment in mechanistic terms of "statics" and "dynamics." Are human institutions sufficiently stable to serve as the basis of "natural laws," and is competition the controlling and necessarily enduring force in economic organization that Clark pictures it? Is the hedonistic calculus of pleasure and pain a scientifically ascertained fact of psychology, and thus available as the central premise of another science? Is an organic concept of society which ignores all but economic data an adequate basis for economic generalization? Can an ethical appraisal be read into economic processes without an examination of the ethical standing of the institutions out of which they arise?

A further kind of questioning is also inescapable— whether an objective examination of economic life lends support to the conclusions which Clark reaches. It may be asked whether profits in modern business are evanescent; whether conflicts of economic interest are negligible factors; whether industrial capital is readily mobile; whether actual methods of wage-determination lend any support to a theory of the virtual identity of product and reward.

Such questions could be multiplied indefinitely. They appear to center themselves about two larger issues—whether, in the first place, Clark states his problem in terms that commend themselves to a contemporary mind imbued with a scientific viewpoint, and whether, in the second place, his conclusions can proceed beyond the phase of hypothesis to that of verification. One may ask whether, having arrived at the correct conclusions from a given set of postulates, Clark is not merely at the threshold, instead of at the end, of a really scientific investigation of the problems presented to economic theorists.

It is hardly necessary to say that the scientific validity of Clark's conclusions must ultimately come to depend upon the answers to the kinds of questions that have been raised. Such questions are now the fat in the fire of economic controversy. Clark may well be supposed to have reached the high peak of the development of economic principles by the subtle elaboration of logical processes. The question now is whether economic truth is to be arrived at in that way.

Thorstein Veblen

Thorstein Veblen

A CURIOUS place in the development of economic theory in the United States is occupied by Mr. Thorstein Veblen. Veblen's extraordinary fate has been to become within his own lifetime an almost apocryphal and legendary character over whose oracular utterances economists disagree with a truly religious warmth. The present study is of a man who has compelled a whole generation of economists to search their hearts lest the truth be not in them.

It is perhaps a defensible generalization that what passed as "orthodox" economic theory during the nineteenth century carried an implicit or explicit defense of the existing economic order. The fact that it carried such a defense may, indeed, account for the fact that it was regarded as orthodox. It rose out of the intellectual and economic life of its time and spoke in terms that commended themselves to the more influential classes of the community. Those who ranked as dissenters to currently acceptable systems of economic theory were, therefore, on the whole, persons who were not impressed by the beneficence of the economic order. In this view Professor Veblen must be classed as a latter-day contributor to the literature of dissent. But dissenting economic theory and discontent with existing economic arrangements have almost universally been accompanied by some scheme of social reform designed to remake the world closer to the heart's desire. It is at this point that Veblen dissents from the dissenters. He is primarily interested in analyzing the industrial system, understanding it, and explaining, to use the vulgar tongue, "how it gets that way." His avowed, if not consistently followed, purpose is to subject the origins and the operation of the economic system to an objective, scientific scrutiny, freed from all such irrelevant preconceptions as should predispose him to become its advocate.

In the case of Veblen, so little of recorded history exists that one is unfortunately estopped from any plan to secure a better understanding of his views by investigating the influences which shaped his thinking in the formative period of his youth. The very fact, however, that so little information is available concerning his life and particularly concerning his intellectual development reflects the personality of the man. Of a peculiarly reticent temperament, he has consistently shrunk from any publicity other than that which his books afford. Even toward his more intimate associates his relations have been marked by a reserve which has left him in their eyes an unexplored and enigmatic personality. It will be necessary, then, to let Veblen

speak principally through his own writings, wherein
the nature, if not the sequence, of the influences that
have shaped his thought will abundantly appear.

Veblen's youth during the 'sixties and 'seventies was
spent in a pioneer rural community in Minnesota. His
parents were Scandinavian immigrants and nothing
more can be said of his early years than that they were
spent under the harsh conditions that went with farm
life during the early period of the settlement of the
Northwest. He was graduated in 1880 from Carleton
College, Minnesota, where he was a student under
Professor J. B. Clark. A few contemporary anecdotes
indicate that at that time he had already a definite
independence of judgment and a habit of looking at
people and things in a curiously objective fashion, free
from moral bias or judgment. It may be supposed
that Veblen's peculiar independence of outlook began
to take definite form at this time, when a curious mind
digging about in the intellectual, scientific, and religious
controversies might be expected to react against the narrowness of the ideas circulated in the pious atmosphere
of a small denominational college in the Northwest.
He studied for a time at Johns Hopkins University,
but, not finding it the scholar's paradise his imagination and current repute had conjured, he repaired to
Yale, where he took his doctor's degree in philosophy
in 1884, with a doctoral dissertation on Kant. His
interest in economic studies at this early date is attested
by the fact that he was awarded a university prize

at Yale for a study of the panic of 1837. For a number of years after leaving Yale he was withdrawn from any active work through ill health.

Turning up from somewhere at Cornell University in 1891, unkempt and penniless, Veblen impressed Professor J. Laurence Laughlin with a sense of intellectual ability hidden under an unpromising exterior, and was granted a teaching fellowship. Even at this early date he exhibited evidence of his appetite for those curiously varied fields of learning on which he later drew in framing his economic views. This trait is illustrated by the fact that he was, at an early age, something of an authority upon Norse literature and Cretan and Icelandic archæology. The following year he went with Professor Laughlin to the University of Chicago, where he remained until 1906.

The early years at Chicago were undoubtedly of great importance in fertilizing Veblen's thinking. Arriving with an esoteric knowledge of philosophy and economic speculation and with scattered information upon a considerable range of scientific and cultural matters, he was thrown into an atmosphere designed to stimulate him to effective intellectual work and to furnish him with new information and ideas. The new university had gathered a distinguished group of men in the natural and social sciences, men not too much bound by traditional methods and most sincerely concerned with advancing the boundaries of knowledge. And with them were associated a group of very able younger men, who were later to establish their competence in their various fields.

Association with a competent faculty of economics strengthened Veblen's grasp upon an understanding of the economic order, and the intellectual freedom existing permitted his native originality to function freely. In his own department his mind rubbed daily against those of such different men as J. L. Laughlin, H. J. Davenport, and R. F. Hoxie, not to mention others, each striving in his distinctive way to perfect a scientific technique for economic analysis. Among his associates in other departments one judges that he owed most to John Dewey and Jacques Loeb, to mention no others. Loeb undoubtedly gave him something general in his apprehension of the meaning of science and something specific through the investigations into the physiology of the mind, which bore upon Veblen's nascent problem of the relation of human psychology to economic theory. But Dewey in particular must be supposed to have influenced him, since one finds their ideas so frequently running parallel. In his efforts to bring a realistic psychology to bear upon the problems of human activity, Dewey was forging instruments for Veblen's hand.

One must not, however, make the mistake of interpreting Veblen in the light of this or that particular influence. He has passed through his mind a curiously varied mass of information and ideas. Sorted and combined in its passage by the reaction of his striking in-

tellectual processes, this raw material has emerged as
the characteristic outlook on economic life and interpretation of it which are describable only as Veblenian.

Veblen passed from Chicago to Leland Stanford
University in 1906 and from there was called to the
University of Missouri at the instance of his former
Chicago associate, Professor Davenport. More recently he has been a lecturer at the New School for
Social Research at New York. He has not during
his lifetime displayed any high regard for the conventional usages and amenities which rule in university
circles, nor for the dignity of those in high places, nor
for "middle-class morality" in general. He has consequently tended to be something of a thorn in the
side of the powers-that-be and his changes of base have
not always been of a voluntary sort. This unfitness
of his temperament for American university environment and the occasional unpleasant episodes to which
it has led may be surmised to have fostered the satirical
spirit which has increasingly marked his writings.

As a teacher Veblen was hardly a success with un-
dergraduates, not being gifted with the patience necessary to cope with the average stupidity of American
college students. Among those who took their advanced work with him, however, one finds him regarded, not with love, somewhat with friendliness, but
mainly with a certain awe at the sweep and power of his
mind, and with gratitude for his fertile and stimulating

suggestions. And without exception they display in their own work the influence of their master.

From any external view Veblen has scarcely any history at all. His history is almost exclusively the history of the thoughts that have germinated within his mind as it played over the field of intellectual speculation, over the panorama of history, and over the scene of American life. And it may seem history enough for one man; for those thoughts have been of sufficient force essentially to modify the views of the entire rising generation of American economists. In England economic theory remains predominantly in bondage to the categories of Marshall; whereas in the United States the recently strong grip of Clark, Marshall, and the Austrians has been loosened, and the whole subject is in a state of ferment, marked by the tentative pursuit of new and promising constructive leads. One might list a considerable number of reasons for the situation, but so far as one man can be held accountable, it can hardly be denied that Veblen has been the arch-disturber of the economist's academic peace of mind.

It is not the least interesting aspects of his history that three economists of quite orthodox lineage should have intervened at crucial moments to put the feet of this modern iconoclast of conventional views upon the highroad of achievement. J. B. Clark introduced him to the study of economics. J. Laurence Laughlin rescued him from poverty and obscurity and opened the doors of opportunity. H. J. Davenport extricated him from an unpleasant situation which might suddenly have cut off his career. And it is such as they who are the targets for his most deadly critical shafts.

In proceeding to an exposition of Veblen's work one has necessarily to protect himself with a word of warning. It is at times very difficult to break through his curious rhetoric into the true import of his meaning. He is, for one thing, addicted to the use of words and phrases in senses far removed from their customary uses. In particular, expressions that almost universally carry a derogatory connotation are used with the avowed intention of imputing neither praise nor blame. But one cannot trust his avowed intentions. Moreover, though casting himself in the rôle of scientific observer, he is essentially a satirist, much impressed with the comic or futile aspects of human life. An aloof Olympian humor possesses him. From behind a pose of objective analysis he launches his shafts of humorous exposure or indignant protest against the absurdities, shortcomings, and vices of human nature and human institutions. He is, again, an inveterate and brilliant phrase-maker, and rather continuously sacrifices the objective character of his analysis to the exigencies of striking, even flamboyant, diction. And finally, he attempts to consolidate some rather weak positions by taking a great deal for granted, blandly adopting a position of the shadiest scientific authenticity and arguing from it as though it were not open to question.

One has ever to be on guard against being taken
either by storm or by guile. Veblen may not be read
without the necessity of discounting satire, pose, terminology, and scientific assumptions. What lies be-
neath must be pursued with as much perspicuity as is
available to the task. Through the mere fact of being
himself, Veblen was under the necessity of making his
impressive contribution to economic thought in his own
peculiar personal way. The idiosyncrasies themselves,
enlivening each page as they do, are hardly to be accounted defects. And it is worth some little trouble
to arrive at an accurate comprehension of the fertile
range of ideas which are imbedded in his curious prose.

II

One hears it not infrequently said that Veblen's relation to economic theory is that of a critic only. The
stricture is not one to which the subject of it would
care to assent. The validity of the remark would hinge,
of course, upon what view is taken of the nature of
economic theory. We shall find it necessary somewhat
later to examine the grounds upon which Veblen would
base his claims to be regarded as a properly authenticated spokesman of economic theory. Since, however, it was upon his capacity as critic that his early
reputation and influence were founded, it will be convenient to examine first upon what grounds he dissents

from all systems of theory which have any wide degree of acceptance.[1]

Economic science has been, in Veblen's view, "a body of logically consistent propositions." He is willing to admit that the economists, from Adam Smith down, have been passably good logicians, and he is not disposed to spend much time impugning their excellence in that regard. If "the test of theoretical truth is the congruence of the system with its premises," little can be said in criticism of economists, early or late. Since, however, any system of deductive logic is based upon its premises, the test of a system lies not in its internal congruence, but in the relation of its premises to the facts of the external world which it purports to explain. Veblen's test, it will be seen, is thus the same as that which John Dewey sets up for philosophical systems. The critical examination of any system of economic thought consequently becomes an examination of the premises upon which it is based. But what shall serve as premises to an inquiry into human affairs turns ultimately upon some generally acceptable canons of knowledge which are of a metaphysical character, and which serve as the preconceptions from which the inquiry starts.

In all economic theory down to the middle of the nineteenth century Veblen finds two such ubiquitous

[1] The main body of Veblen's critical position is to be found in a series of essays, published periodically between 1898 and 1909, republished as essays III to XV, inclusive, in *The Place of Science in Modern Civilization and Other Essays* (1919).

canons of truth—(1) a hedonistic psychology, and (2) "an uncritical conviction that there is a meliorative trend in the course of events."[1] The passive rôle played by human nature under the hedonistic view is described in a vivid satirical passage. "The hedonistic conception of man is that of a lightning calculator of pleasures and pains, who oscillates like a homogeneous globule of desire of happiness under the impulse of stimuli that shift him about the area, but leave him intact. He has neither antecedent nor consequent. He is an isolated, definitive human datum, in stable equilibrium except for the buffets of the impinging forces that displace him in one direction or another. Self-imposed in elemental space, he spins symmetrically about his own spiritual axis until the parallelogram of forces bears down upon him, whereat he follows the line of the resultant. When the force of the impact is spent, he comes to rest, a self-contained globule of desire as before."[2] The weakness of the view that man is essentially a passive factor directed in his actions primarily by the impulse to seek pleasurable sensations and to avoid painful ones is seen in the fact that it is belied by all recent psychological investigation. Its importance has not, however, declined, because, though less openly avowed, it has remained implicit in the reasoning of many recent economists, particularly those of the marginal-utility school.

[1] *The Place of Science in Modern Civilization*, p. 150.
[2] *Ibid.*, pp. 73-74.

The fundamental preconception of the meliorative trend in human affairs Veblen regards as a metaphysical conception of theological origin. It represents the common assumption that the world is being directed to some divinely appointed consummation in accordance with the purpose of the Creator. The view was taken over in somewhat attenuated form by eighteenth-century philosophers as a belief in the beneficent working out of immutable laws of Nature. In the speculations of Adam Smith this was the primary preconception, while the hedonistic nature of man was merely one of the means by which Nature works out her purposes. The Utilitarian philosophers, following Bentham, reversed the order of importance, regarding as laws of Nature those uniformities in human action which flow out of man's hedonistic nature. The latter view, of course, leads somewhat away from the conception of a drift toward the realization of a preconceived end. Instituting a sequence of cause and effect running from the nature of man to the phenomena of human life, it necessitated a revision of the principles of morals on the basis of ethical determinism. In this view it transpires that whatever happens is inevitable, and, by a process of interpretation, that whatever is inevitable, being the working out of natural law, is right and good.

When used in the field of economic thought, the hedonistic view permits human nature to be eliminated from the problem. The human factor is abstracted as "the untainted economic man" engaged in the un-

swerving quest of the greatest gain at the least sacrifice. Accepting this view of human nature, the
economists had only to complete their premises with
a statement of the institutions through which the economic system functions. As it happened, at the period
when economic theory was taking shape the most
marked characteristic of economic life was free enterprise, or competition. That this should be regarded
as the "normal" or "natural" form of economic organization was a view reinforced by the prevalent
philosophical belief in Natural Liberty and Natural
Right. The Natural Right philosophy, formulated by
Locke and developed by eighteenth-century thinkers,
was important in economic thought mainly as a defense
of private property and freedom of enterprise. To
serve as a premise for a logical system of economics,
competition must be theoretically perfect, and as such
involves perfect knowledge of the opportunities for
gain, and perfect mobility of human and material factors in response to the stimulus of higher remuneration.

Classical economic science, in Veblen's view, turns
out to be little more than a series of logical deductions
from the premises of perfect competition and hedonistic
human nature. Human nature is constant, and operates
in the economic sphere only by way of pursuing gain
or pleasure in the form of consumable goods and avoiding pain in the form of work or effort. The institutional scheme is fixed, as a competitive system in which
the natural equity of private property is taken for

granted. Thus, by the nature of their preconceptions, "the classical economists knew that the consummation to which, in the nature of things, all things tend, is the frictionless and beneficent competitive system." [1] This competitive ideal becomes the "normal," from the point of view of which all economic phenomena are tested. Normality thus corresponds not to any causal relation of concrete facts, but to an imaginary ideal based upon a set of preconceptions which are largely metaphysical in character.

When abstractions have been made of human nature and of institutions, economic science becomes, as it did in the hands of the Utilitarians, merely a theory of value. Money gains are valued in relation to the pleasures of consumption which they will afford; the irksome effort of labor is endured only for the gain it will bring in the way of consumable goods. Thus, "the theory of value may be stated in terms of the consumable goods that afford the incentive to effort and the expenditures undergone in order to procure them. Between these two there exists a necessary equality." "The theory of value . . . is . . . a theory of cost in terms of discomfort." Money enters into the case only as a common measure for the "hedonistic magnitudes" which enter into the process of valuation. What men overtly seek is pecuniary gain in terms of money. But, in the classical view, money gains to individuals represent goods produced,

[1] *The Place of Science in Modern Civilization*, p. 145.

and goods produced are a social gain. By thus treating acquisition and production as coincident, if not equal, the theory arrives at the simple corollary that the sum of individual gains in terms of money equals the social gain in terms of goods. The equality of pecuniary gains of individuals with social gain and the failure to distinguish between capital as investment and capital as industrial appliances are not, in Veblen's view, tenable ideas. They seem to him merely beliefs flowing out of the preconceptions and current common sense of the times in which they were formulated. They fit nicely, however, into a system which regards "normal" economic activity as the unfettered pursuit of gain under the hedonistic impulse through the mechanism of free and perfect competition. Accepting the premises of the system, the competitive form of economic activity promotes the maximum production of goods, produces the maximum satisfaction of wants, and is thus ethically defensible as the ideally best system.

Since the classical faith has been pretty thoroughly dismantled even by its sympathetic descendants, there would be no point in thus summarizing it were it not for two points which Veblen introduces. In the first place, the validity of this, as of any logical system, lies in the truth of its premises, and the premises here are in some considerable degree out of touch with the facts in the case. In the second place, present-day economic theory is still to some extent under the sway of the conceptions, but more particularly of the method of the

older classical system. Mill and Cairnes undermined
the adequacy of the system as a basis for the political
precept of *laissez-faire*, the former by admitting a qualitative element in the pleasures (utility) to be secured
from goods, the latter by divorcing the system from a
beneficent order of nature and emphasizing the "hypothetical" character of its laws. If goods are "better"
and "worst" and wants "higher" and "lower," human
nature enters into the case as something more than a
receptive agent, and the conclusion of classical economics, that self-interest left to itself tends to produce
the maximum general welfare, disappears. In spite,
however, of this tampering with the simplicity of the
older premises, Mill and Cairnes never quite escape the
necessity of an implicit hedonism, nor do they find it
possible to construct anything more than a logically
congruous system. Their postulates still afford the
standard of normality and the postulates are in a
marked degree questionable both as to human nature
and as to physical fact. The economic "laws" are those
of the normal case, untested by coincidence with matter-of-fact events. Under the hands of these economists, the science advances by a more colorless and
unethical view of normality, but fails to escape the
imprint of the metaphysics which underlay the system
from the start.

Later economists, particularly Marshall, have escaped the gross oversimplification of earlier theory.
Under the influence of the historical school and of

evolutionary conceptions, they at least do lip service to
the importance of institutional changes in shaping economic life. For the most part they recognize the
complexity of human relations and attempt "to make
economic science a theoretical handling of human activity in its economic bearing" instead of a series of logical
deductions from hedonism and competition. But they
are overborne by their classical heritage. For they have
found no way of constructing their body of theory except in terms of "a quiescent normal situation." Their
theory, that is to say, is of a static character. Marshall, for whom Veblen entertains an avowed admiration, is admitted to have attempted to treat economic
life as a development. But, unable to find any method
by which to include all the phenomena of change, he
succeeds merely in constructing "a consummately conceived and self-balanced mechanism." He has brought
economic theory closer to the events of everyday life.
He has relieved normality from any implication of
ethical approval and discarded belief in a beneficent
trend of events. Yet his system is still a system of the
"normal" and normality consists merely in conformity
to the postulates of the system. The postulates include
competition and an implicitly hedonistic view of human
nature, and the analysis runs in terms of pecuniary
acquisition on the implicit assumption that this represents productive service. The framework of the system is a description of the market organization through
which the economic process functions, and a classifica-

tion of the functionaries who promote economic activity and of the rewards they receive. The system is, then, a description and classification of economic functions in a given quiescent situation; that is to say, it is "taxonomic," to use Veblen's favorite derogatory phrase.

With latter-day theorists of the marginal-utility faith, and with his one-time teacher, J. B. Clark, in particular, Veblen is thoroughly impatient. Their psychological premises are, to his mind, an example of gross hedonism, naïvely drawn from early nineteenth-century psychology. A given institutional situation, based upon the natural right of ownership as one of "the primordial and immutable facts of the order of nature," is accepted. Such theory is in form merely a theory of valuation, running in terms of pecuniary motives which are "conceived simply as the immutably correct, God-given notions of the hedonistic calculus." [1] It is wholly static, wholly deductive, wholly unable to deal with the phenomena of change, and carries a bias in favor of the ethical validity of its dogma. As such it represents a reversion to the most indefensible and questionable postulates of the early classical system of which it is a variant. All marginal-utility doctrine is reducible to "a system of competitive acquisition," under conditions so remote from the true economic situation as to give the theory a purely metaphysical interest.

[1] *The Place of Science in Modern Civilization*, p. 245

Nor can Veblen find anything much more favorable
to say of the Historical or the Marxian schools of
thought. The early historical economists, as represented
by Roscher, he considers to have proceeded on a tacit
assumption of Hegelian metaphysics, regarding history
as a self-realizing life process, active, self-determining,
unfolding by inner necessity. The search for the laws
of this spiritual unfolding on its economic side resulted
in nothing better than the view that culture moves in
cycles, together with a few rather vague or obvious
generalizations about cultural sequences. The later
branch, as represented by Wagner, is not occupied with
theoretical work, taking over such doctrines as it needs
from classical economics. For the other branch, as
represented by Schmoller, Veblen entertains a considerable respect, particularly as regards his examination
of the origins of economic institutions. He feels, however, that Schmoller fails to give any adequate scientific
treatment of more recent economic phenomena and of
the cultural influences which have shaped them.

The economic doctrines of Karl Marx are conceived
to be vitiated by much the same defect as classical economics in that they are merely logical deductions from
untenable premises. The postulates of the Marxian
system are drawn from two sources, a materialistic
Hegelianism and the English system of Natural Rights,
neither of which will withstand the test of scientific
examination. Indeed, "the Hegelian philosophical
postulates, without which the Marxism of Marx is

groundless, are for the most part forgotten by the dogmatists of today." [1]   No economist has been more thoroughly torn limb from limb than Marx.   To discredit him was one of the favorite sports of the more orthodox during the later decades of the nineteenth century.   It was almost one of the necessary details of an economist's apprenticeship to have laid low some Marxian fallacy.   The idea is conceivable that this dialectical tilting at Marx was to a large extent responsible for a recrudescence of the defense of the competitive ideal which is apparent during the period.   Veblen is not in any sense unique in having laid him low, as his was perhaps the twentieth dagger.   What marks Veblen's criticism as unique is that he resorts to no counter-offensive of dialectic.   He merely points out the postulates of the system and blandly asks whether anyone in his right mind in the twentieth century could accept them.   That method of attack is double-edged, for it is exactly the same way in which he undermines the position of his orthodox friends who had been most assiduous in the anti-Marxian offensive.

Enough has been said to indicate that Veblen is out of step with practically all types of economic theory which have flowered into systematic expression.   Our tiresomely lengthy exposition of the points at which he has attacked them should at least reveal the technique which marks his offensive strategy.   He does not combat logic with logic.   There is no tactical turning

[1] *The Place of Science in Modern Civilization*, p. 429.

of flanks. The main fortress is taken at the start
by discrediting the preconceptions and postulates upon
which the body of logic rests. The method is disconcerting, to say the least. For it knocks out the
underpinnings of whole systems of thought, and puts
at an overwhelming disadvantage all those whose
knowledge of philosophy, economic institutions, or
modern science is insufficient to permit them to combat Veblen on his own ground. In this sort of controversy Veblen ordinarily enjoys a marked advantage,
due to the wide range of his learning. Economic
theory, of the systematic sort, when traced to its source,
inevitably involves reliance upon some philosophical
concept. A good many economists, however, are not by
training competent to realize the philosophical implications of their own systems of theory. Many, also, are
not at home when dealing with the concepts and method
of the natural sciences, nor intimately conversant with
recent psychological investigation. But these are fields
of knowledge in which Veblen has delved rather extensively. When, therefore, he turns these resources
of knowledge against the foundations of systematic
formulations of theory, the effect is rather deadly.

To this point we have merely indicated the aspects
of various types of economic theory to which Veblen
takes exception, without examining the specific grounds
upon which he bases his exceptions. The categorical
criticisms of modern offshoots of classical economics
we have seen to be, (1) that all involve a hedonistic

psychology, (2) that in general they cling to an attenuated belief in a teleological end and a meliorative trend, (3) that they identify acquisition and production, (4) that they cling to the philosophy of Natural Rights and Natural Law, and (5) that their view of normality involves a view of economic life and institutions out of harmony with the external facts. It will be convenient to let these points rest for the time being, while an examination is made of Veblen's positive views. For Veblen is much more than a critic. He has a substitute for the older approach to economic theory. In formulating his own views he has, nevertheless, always borne in mind the dogma of the systems which he was disposed to confute. In consequence, to indicate the nature of his characteristic approach to the economic process is at the same time to supply the grounds for his critical position. At a later point we can conveniently come back to his charges, as seen in the light of his own position.

III

Veblen's view of what economic science should be is based upon three substantial grounds, the first a conception of human nature, the second, a conception of the nature and method of scientific inquiry, the third, a conception of the nature of the economic process. For his psychology he calls upon the work of recent investigators in that field, with particular reference to William James, William McDougall, Jacques Loeb, and John Dewey. Thus with an engaging appearance of stating a universally accepted truth he proceeds to postulate his entire structure upon this statement: "For mankind as for the higher animals, the life of the species is conditioned by the complement of instinctive proclivities and tropismatic attitudes with which the species is typically endowed. Not only is the continued life of the race dependent on the adequacy of its instinctive proclivities in this way, but the routine and details of its life are also, in the last resort, determined by these instincts." [1]

Instincts are many and various, and each differs characteristically from the rest. They are teleological in character, in that the aims and ends which men find it worth their while consciously to pursue are those which are set by the instinctive proclivities. The mystery surrounding the exact nature of instincts is recognized, and they are permitted to rest as in themselves complex phenomena representing secondary characteristics of the species, hereditary "spiritual traits emerging from a certain concurrence of physiological unit characters." [2] There is thus found in different individuals a wide diversity in the complement or relative activity of instincts, but through this diversity runs "a generically human type of spirtual endowment . . . suitable to the continued life of mankind in society." [3]

[1] *The Instinct of Workmanship*, p. 1.
[2] *Ibid.*, p. 13.
[3] *Ibid.*, pp. 15-16.

The ends of life, then, are set not by rational calculation, but by instinctive proclivities of a relatively stable and persistent sort. Intelligence, or rationality, enters into the case in providing ways and means for accomplishing those ends. It is the logic of ways and means intervening between impulses and their realization. "The ends so sought are many and diverse, and the ways and means . . . are similarly diverse and various, involving endless recourse to expedients, adaptations, and concessive adjustments between several proclivities that are all sufficiently urgent." [1] "The apparatus of ways and means" by which men in society go about achieving their ends "is, substantially all, a matter of tradition out of the past, a legacy of habits of thought." [2] The discipline of daily life, representing action dictated basically by instinctive propensities, takes on the consistency of habit and custom. Habits of action and thought widely current in a social group are institutions. Institutions, while thus fundamentally no more than habits, come to have a prescriptive force and authority in limiting the activity of individuals, whose instinctive ends must be achieved through these established and socially sanctioned channels. The support and perpetuation of the institutions become, in the outcome, the proximate end of groups whose actions have been disciplined by their existence.

Before going more thoroughly into Veblen's treatment of institutions, it will be well to center attention

---

[1] *The Instinct of Workmanship*, p. 7.   [2] *Ibid.*, pp. 6-7.

for a moment upon his view of the nature of scientific
inquiry. His view is, he insists, that of modern science.
Modern science is regarded as inquiry into the unfolding process of changing and developing life. It is,
in short, post-Darwinian evolutionary science of which
biology is the prototype. It is impersonal and matter-
of-fact, concerned only with the run of the facts and
not at all with any imputation of purpose in the life
process, since any such imputation can be nothing more
than a metaphysical bias. Its primary tenet is the
changefulness of all things, and its task is to trace the
process through which change expresses itself. It "con-
structs the life history of a process . . . in which the
run of causation unfolds itself in an unbroken sequence
of cumulative change." [1] The crucial aspect of this
view is that life is a process and change is cumulative,
each situation arising out of that immediately precedent
to it. In this view phenomena are not compressed
within any artificial classification or categories as normal
or natural, with all those things which do not fit into
the classification relegated to the position of abnormal
or disturbing factors. All eventualities are regarded as
equally "natural," the result of the exfoliation of the
cumulative life process. The pre-Darwinian scientific
method, which ran to classifications, natural laws,
specific causation, and a general conception that phenomena tended toward an equilibrium is considered
obsolescent and inadequate to deal with the phenomena

[1] *The Place of Science in Modern Civilization*, p. 16.

of the changeful life process. "Any evolutionary science . . . is a close-knit body of theory. It is a theory of a process, of an unfolding sequence." [1]

In the light of this modern conception of science, the study of human institutions becomes peculiarly important. For, while human nature remains relatively fixed and stable, institutions, or the apparatus through which instinctive ends are realized, are notably transient and changeful. Institutions at any given time constitute the prevailing culture, and as such are an important factor in the process of selective adaptation of human beings to their environment. Institutions, in other words, come by a process of cumulative growth to be a very large part of that environment which determines the selective process. They have perhaps as much to do with determining what types shall survive and what traits shall be dominant as the material circumstances enforced by nature. From whatever cause, whether from changed natural conditions or the pressure of external forces, or from their own cumulative unfolding, institutions constantly change. Veblen's position on this point may best be made clear by a few brief quotations.

Man is "a coherent structure of propensities and habits which seek realization and expression in an unfolding activity." "The activity itself is the substantial fact of the process." Activity will vary according to temperament and circumstances. Desires which inspire

---

[1] *The Place of Science in Modern Civilization*, p. 58.

man's activity "are the products of his hereditary traits and his past experience, cumulatively wrought out under a given body of traditions, conventionalities, and material circumstances. And they afford the point of departure for the next step in the process.. The economic life history of the individual is the cumulative process of adaptation of means to ends that cumulatively change as the process goes on, both the agent and his environment being at any point the outcome of the last process. His methods of life today are enforced upon him by his habits of life carried over from yesterday." "What is true of the individual in this respect is true of the group in which he lives. All economic change is . . . a change in the community's methods of turning material things to account. The change is always in the last resort a change of habits of thought." [1]

Through institutions, human activity comes to be in large part habitual, or, one might put it the other way, that through habitual action institutions come to be. Underneath the constraining force of institutions, by which the group guides or limits the activity of the individual, there continues, however, the pressure of those propensities which are native to mankind. There is no guaranty that the weight of this constraint may not, in a highly developed institutional situation, bear down too hardly upon the underlying human nature,

[1] The quotations are from *The Place of Science in Modern Civilization*, pp. 74, 75.

to the endangerment of the institutions. History is full of the record of "imbecile" institutions, or those fatal to the survival of a given cultural situation, thus setting the scene for a marked, and at times violent, shifting of the institutional scheme.

Enough has been said to indicate that Veblen's work is "cultural analysis." The classical tradition was to take institutions for granted and to reduce human nature to a matter of rational calculation. Veblen insists on a realistic view of human nature so far as modern psychology throws light upon it, and on investigating the origin and nature of the institutions through which the economic side of the life process functions. His work thus lies largely outside the recognized field of economic theory. He insists, however, that it is economic theory, the theory of the process through which economic activity takes place. And he presses the point further, by holding that what is ordinarily included in economic theory, systems of logic and schemes of normality, are no more than obsolescent aspects of a bygone habit of scientific thought. His plan is a genetic study of economic institutions, evolutionary in character and essential to a proper understanding of the economic life of our times.

To make the jump from the general psychological and anthropological analysis with which he starts to a study of economic institutions as such, Veblen is compelled to find some way in which he can separate or isolate these institutions to some degree from the gen-

eral life process of human society. The economic part
of the life process of society is, in Veblen's view, that
part of human activity which is concerned with coping
with external nature to the end of providing for man's
material wants. On this basis it is possible to set up
a classification of human traits and institutions. Those
which assist in furthering the provision for economic
wants are regarded as "generically human," in that they
act to support the life of mankind in society. Those
which hinder this provision act as an obstruction to the
full development of man's ability to cope with his environment, in respect to his material wants. Among
the instinctive propensities of human nature are three
which are definitely assigned to the former class, (1)
the parental bent, (2) the instinct of workmanship,
(3) the bent to "idle curiosity."

The parental bent is used by Veblen to express all
those sentiments that are of an unselfish nature, and
the particular aspect of this bent that lends itself to
his purpose is the sense of solicitude for the welfare
of the group to which the individual belongs. The
instinct of workmanship, unlike other propensities, dictates no ends of its own, inciting to action. It is essentially "a proclivity for taking pains"; its functional
content is the desire to serve the ends of life effectively;
and it thus may be regarded as auxiliary to the other
instincts, which set the ultimate ends. Taken together,
the parental bent and the instinct of workmanship constitute the chief instinctive dispositions conducing to

the material welfare of the race and to its biological survival. The one permits the sinking of individual interests in the larger interests of the group, the other leads to the discovery of progressively more effective means for promoting the material welfare of the group. It is best exhibited in the improvement of technological efficiency, but it may operate in other directions toward ends proximately set by the habitual conventions of the group.

The bent to idle curiosity shares with the instinct of workmanship the peculiarity of setting no ends of action. It is unique, however, in leading to no outcome in a chain of motor activity. It is in a sense a subsidiary and indirect response to stimulus of an "unintended and irrelevant" sort, and it forms its response by the interpretation of the "sequence of activities going on in the observed phenomena." The play of curiosity is inspired by no utilitarian aim and it is thus active only when the more elemental needs have been satisfied. Its importance in cultural development is, however, very great. "The long-term consequences of the common run of curiosity, helped out by such sporadic individuals in whom the idle curiosity runs at a higher tension, count up finally, because cumulatively, into the most substantial cultural achievement of the race— its systematized knowledge and quasi-knowledge of things." [1] It is the instinctive source out of which modern science has developed. So far as curiosity and

[1] *The Instinct of Workmanship*, p. 87.

workmanship concur in promoting knowledge, they ac-
celerate the gains in technology which conduce to more
adequate material provision.   They are hampered in
this by a human propensity to impute some outside
purpose to the course of events and to interpret phenomena in animistic or anthropomorphic terms, running
from primitive animism through magic and theology
to latter-day metaphysics.   Subject to this hindering
contamination, these two bents, guided by the parental instinct, conspire to improve the material lot of
mankind.

It has seemed desirable to display this psychological
stage-setting at some length, as it is an essential part
of Veblen's conceptual apparatus.   We must postpone
the consideration of its validity to a somewhat later
point.   The point to be noted is that the three bents
mentioned are emphasized because of their "generically
human" service in forwarding mankind's material interest.   They are the basis of economic life in society
and the foundation of economic institutions.   The service they render is in improving man's technological
knowledge and skill, and consequent ability to cope with
the material environment by way of shaping it to human
needs and uses.   Over against these bents is set that
unnamed trait which leads men to attribute personality
to impersonal matter, to impute purpose to a mere
process of cumulative causation, and to entertain faith
in the magical efficacy of the supernatural and in the
immutability of passing conventionalities.   This human

trait serves to discourage the growth of matter-of-fact knowledge—that is to say, humanly serviceable knowledge, and primarily technological knowledge. One hesitates to interpret Veblen too confidently on this point, since at times he appears to speak in terms of such a trait, while at other times he appears merely to indicate that certain types of habituation lead to the growth of institutions that operate to contaminate the influence of the instinctive propensities with survival value. In any case, there is presumed to grow up a body of pseudo-knowledge and habits of thought, involving magic, superstition, taboo, tradition, all of which take on an institutional authority and become part of the unfolding sequence of the life process.

Of traits of human nature other than those that have been mentioned, Veblen takes little account. Numerous as they are, they are presumably foreign to his inquiry. We appear, then, to be very near the heart of his whole position. On the one hand are a set of traits and institutions favorable to man's material welfare; on the other hand a set of an unfavorable character. In spite, then, of Veblen's emphasis upon the life process as a matter of cumulative causation, it appears that he has made an abstraction of a considerable part of it. What is left appears to be subjected to a rather unbending classification into two groups, which are presumed to be adequate for explaining the course of man's economic activity. It will need to occupy our attention later, whether an adequate theory of the economic part of the life process of society can be constructed in this way. Do not other traits and other cultural factors, it must be asked, impinge too organically upon the economic process to permit it to be explained in terms of an antithetical dualism of "generically human" and "contaminating" psychological and cultural factors?

Along the lines of this classification runs whatever may be found of moral judgment. Veblen disclaims all intention of judging the process which he purports to describe objectively. Nevertheless, the force of his brilliant satire is forever turned against those contaminating institutions and habits of thought which hinder the working out of the "generically human" ends of life. His pose is to know neither "good" nor "bad," as a scientist. But were he to recognize the distinction, here is where he would find it. The ends which, if not "good," are at least advantageous to survival, are, it should be noted, always expressed in terms of technological proficiency, of bulk of output in weight and tale. He refuses to discuss the justice of distribution and neglects all spiritual traits not bearing upon the production of goods. He has, in consequence, no line of demarcation between instincts and institutions except their effect upon the volume of output.

We have to this point been more attentive to Veblen's psychological, than to his institutional, analysis. It is with the latter, however, that he is particularly concerned. For institutions are the expression of human culture; they arise by a process of cumulative growth; they limit and direct the activities of mankind; and they are in a process of never-ending transition. Characteristically, he takes in hand certain modern institutions, which are parenthetically made synonymous with habits of thought, traces their life history through various stages of human culture, and finally examines their nature and the effects of their operation under the conditions of modern life. His particular tasks are (1) to substantiate his primary thesis that institutions grow out of a process of habituation in relation to man's instinctive traits and to his physical surroundings, (2) to show how this process shapes the terms in which men explain their environment, and (3) to explain modern economic life in terms of the forms of habituation which have shaped its institutions and habits of thought.[1]

It should be said in regard to the following statement of Veblen's main line of analysis that it is only a skeleton account. In treating the work of a writer whose work represents the logical development of certain fairly definite premises, his views may be exposed to view with comparative ease and accuracy in a restricted space. But Veblen is not of that sort and presents a more complicated problem of exposition. For, start-

[1] Veblen's method, as here described, is best illustrated, by *The Instinct of Workmanship* (1914). The description applies also to *The Theory of the Leisure Class* (1899) and *Imperial Germany and the Industrial Revolution* (1915). Elsewhere he deals more particularly with the current situation, and the recent past, taking the background of the modern cultural situation more for granted.

ing from the primary idea that human institutions represent a process of cumulative change in which nothing is stable except certain traits of human nature, he permits himself to roam widely through our knowledge of psychology, anthropology, and the history of human thought and culture in search of the factors relevant to explaining the current economic situation in terms of cultural development. Little more is possible in examining his work than to cling tenaciously to the center of his argument and to expose, in some attenuated fashion, by what method he arrives at his conclusions. It must never be out of mind that he is stating *the theory of a process* of development. As this process bears upon the economic situation, it comes to center about two sets of institutions; on the one hand, those that have to do with the ownership of property, or pecuniary relations; on the other hand, those that have to do with technological methods, or the provision of the material means of life. The dualism contained in this classification runs through the entire analysis of modern economic life. With this essential point kept always in mind, it may be possible to portray Veblen's views with some accuracy, even within the necessary brief limits of space.

His customary procedure is to divide cultural history, so far as it bears upon the economic situation, into four periods—(1) the savage, (2) the barbarian, (3) the handicraft, and (4) the age of the machine process. Being engaged in an economic study, his interest in each of these periods is primarily confined to the effect of the habituation enforced by each of them upon man's efforts to cope with his environment for the satisfaction of his material wants. The range of study is chiefly limited to northwestern Europe and America, and a large erudition in anthropology and history is brought to bear upon it. The savage period is made to include a span of some ten or twelve thousand years from neolithic times down to some indefinite date toward the Middle Ages. Roughly it corresponds to that period of prehistory concerning which we have some substantial knowledge. The barbarian era is typically the Middle Ages and an indefinite preceding period. The handicraft period runs roughly from the Middle Ages to the late eighteenth century in England, and to the middle of the nineteenth century in America and on the Continent. The last period corresponds to that covered by the history of machine industry. Within these periods, a rather sweeping and impressionistic view is given of the type of habituation which prevailed, always with a view to the bearing of the analysis upon the present-day economic situation.

The savage period is conceived to have been predominantly a peaceable culture, chiefly agricultural. It was marked by a steady progress in technological proficiency, hastened by the proclivity of the hybrid northwestern European type for borrowing cultural knowledge. There was comparative freedom from magical or other contaminating lore and a relatively active tendency to acquire matter-of-fact knowledge. Technological knowledge was typically a collective possession, easily accessible to anyone in need of it, and uncontrolled by prescriptive property rights. Under these conditions the selective process was such as to inculcate the parental instinct (a proclivity to forward the ends of the group) and the instinct of workmanship ("a taste for effective work and a distaste for futile effort") as dominant human traits.

The incentive to the accumulation of private property necessarily awaits the time when the state of the industrial arts permits the accumulation of goods above those essential to the current necessities of life. At this stage, property might be accumulated by those in a position to practice fraud upon their own group, an opportunity which accrued chiefly to the priesthood practising "priestly economics"; or by raids upon the accumulation of other groups. Property then is regarded as in origin due to either fraud or force, not to go into the careful treatment which Veblen gives to the subject. The predatory acquisition of property at the expense of other groups begets warlike organization, with chiefs to whom falls much of the booty, and warriors who share a part of it in the way of slaves, ornaments, flocks, and what not. This new institution of property in effect entitles its beneficiaries to a claim upon the usufruct of the industrial arts greater than falls to the lot of the common man. With its coming "self-interest displaces the common good in men's ideals and aspirations," [1] a submersion of the parental bent. The predatory scheme of life leads to the organization of the group on a basis of graded dignity and authority, heading up in a dynastic chief. The economic line of demarcation runs between those who do useful, matter-of-fact work, and those who by reason of control of property are released from that necessity to the pursuits of war, religion, statecraft, and the like. Under the predatory scheme of graded dignity, consumption is affected by emulation of one's superiors. The result is that workmanship and technology are contaminated by being set to supply many conventional articles whose only use is to display, what has come to be meritorious, a control over property and an abstention from useful work. The result of this emulative resort to "conspicuous consumption" is not to improve the material well-being of the run of the group, but merely to facilitate the expenditure of effort upon the production of humanly useless goods for the use of those who have prescriptive rights upon the usufruct of the community's stock of technological knowledge.

The main cultural consequence of the predatory life, so far as concerns economic development, is the settled institution of private property, carrying in its train a set of consequences inimical to material welfare, as in the inversion of the parental bent, the growth of invidious distinctions based upon property, the guidance of consumption into channels of conspicuous waste, and

[1] *The Instinct of Workmanship*, p. 160.

the consequent contamination of the instinct of workmanship.   This habit of life involves other activities
inimical to economic welfare, such, for example, as the
pursuit of warlike aims and the encouragement of supernatural beliefs and magical practices which impede
the accumulation of useful matter-of-fact knowledge.

The predatory stage is of central importance in
Veblen's interpretation of economic development.   For
it is conceived to have given rise to a cumulative growth
of institutions based upon the property idea, and the
habits of thought thus inculcated remain among the
dominant features of the present situation.   In particular the economic process comes to be guided primarily
by the pecuniary motive of private acquisition rather
than by care for the material needs of the group.   Social
esteem comes to be based upon control over property
and freedom from economically useful work.   Consumption is guided by the desire for social esteem and
consequently takes conspicuously useless forms.   At
the same time there remain those socially inferior
classes, mainly occupied with matter-of-fact workmanship.   But even their habits of thought are somewhat
turned away from useful ends under the discipline of
the predatory life, graded dignity, and property rights.
They absorb the sentiments of religion and dynastic
loyalty, and their consumption is affected by imitation
of the socially esteemed.   Their welfare is checked by
the fact that the usufruct of their knowledge is held
by the propertied classes and their skill goes into the

fabrication of useless articles of consumption, instruments of warfare, priestly accessories, and the like.

As Veblen presents it, this type of habituation "contaminates" the instinctive propensities which serve the "generically human" ends of life. The phrase does not imply criticism, presumably. He is concerned with building up a theory of the cumulative growth of institutions by a process of habituation. It is not of the essence of the theory that the institutions which evolve should in the long run have a high survival value from the point of view of the group or race. They are mere accretions developing with the passage of time under the influence of habits of life, and the institutional structure may come in time to bear down hardly upon the persistent instinctive proclivities and may diverge widely from serving the material interests of mankind faithfully.

The handicraft period is deemed to have arisen with the coming of a settled quasi-peaceable state near the end of the Middle Ages. Accompanied by the break-up of feudalism, this area of transition was marked by the emergence of a masterless man, the growth of trade, and the rise of individual initiative in commercial and industrial enterprise. With the hard-and-fast lines of class distinction thus impaired, the situation favored a larger expression of the instinct of workmanship. Under the handicraft discipline this bent was associated with the motive of pecuniary gain. That part of the population which fell under the discipline inevitably

associated the accumulation of property with the production of material objects. The institution of property, originating in fraud and force, then protected by
law and custom, comes in this phase to be associated
with productive effort. Under the situation of peaceable ownership and handicraft industry two lines of
mental habituation are predominant; as owners men
are engaged in the quest for profit, or gain through
bargaining; as workmen, in the development and
effective use of technological knowledge. Leaving out
of account the landed interest, this period is marked
by the growing importance of a class subjected simultaneously to this dual discipline. We have, then, workmanship compounded with ownership or the pecuniary
culture; and the differential, emulative, invidious character of the latter does not, as in the previous stage,
severely handicap the former.

The advancement of technological knowledge, under
peaceful conditions and the pecuniary stimulus, was
wide and rapid. It entailed a growing habit of matter-
of-fact attention to material phenomena and a growing
attention to material cause and effect. It thus served
to minister more fully to the material needs of life,
while carrying in its train a varied set of cultural consequences. It undermined theological beliefs. It
promoted rapid advance in the natural sciences. It
helped to undermine dynastic loyalty and thus aided
in the movement to constitutional government. It led
to the philosophical and scientific belief in natural law,

with which were associated the doctrines of Natural
Rights and Natural Liberty. These two doctrines were
particularly characteristic of the handicraft habituation.
And in particular the natural right of ownership became inculcated in law and custom and common sense
through the obvious connection between productive
labor and the accumulation of property. The most
important aspect of the period was, however, the outlet it gave for the instinct of workmanship. "Creative
workmanship, fortified in ever-growing measure by the
conception of serviceability to human use, works its
way gradually into the central place in the theoretical
speculations of the time, so that by the close of the era
it dominates all intellectual enterprise in the thought-
ful portions of Christendom."[1] It was, indeed, the
repercussion of this situation which led to the extensive
revision of the institutional framework under new
theories of civil and legal relations. "Differential
rights, duties, and privileges give the point of departure
in this mediæval system of civil relations; whereas in
the system worked out under the auspices of the handicraft industry the denial of differential advantage,
whether class or individual, is the beginning of wisdom
and the substance of common sense."[2] Such was the
spirit of the system of Natural Rights and Natural
Liberty, as born out of handicraft.

The modern economic era arose out of the handicraft

[1] *The Instinct of Workmanship*, p. 285.
[2] *Ibid.*, p. 294.

period through a change in technological methods, in the shape of power machinery. The discovery of new methods may be attributed to the habits of thought incident to the greater absorption in matter-of-fact knowledge under the handicraft discipline. The bent of workmanship had full and adequate expression under that discipline, leading to a rapid cumulative growth of technological expedients. The instinct of idle curiosity, the force of which had in earlier times largely spent itself in formulating systems of knowledge in animistic or anthropomorphic terms, turned under the material-istic preoccupations of the period to the explanation of material phenomena in materialistic terms, in terms of cause and effect. And thus was born the modern scien-tific spirit, tainted indeed with lingering teleological views of the universe, but sufficiently pure to lend itself to the dominant trend toward technological advance.

The modern period in economic development lends itself to a variety of designations, according to the point of view from which it is viewed. It may be regarded as the age of the factory system, or of large-scale en-terprise, or of capitalism, or of the credit economy. Technologically, it is "the era of the machine process." It is in the light of the machine process that Veblen carries out his analysis of modern civilization.[1] It is

---

[1] The best example of Veblen's analysis of current economic insti-tutions is to be found in *The Theory of Business Enterprise* (1904). The views there expressed are amended or extended in later books, *The Nature of Peace* (1917), *The Vested Interests* (1919), *The Engineers and the Price System* (1921), and *Absentee Ownership* (1923).

the machine that gives the scope and method for modern industry. The pace is set for the rest of the industrial system by the machine industries; "the scope of the process is larger than the machine." The machine process makes of the industrial system a highly complicated, completely integrated mechanism. Physical production has become an endless sequence of processes, and it is controlled by a continuing series of interstitial adjustments between the various branches and sub-processes of industry. Industry, as such, is governed by the necessity for accuracy and quantitative precision. "By virtue of this concatenation of processes the modern industrial system at large bears the character of a comprehensive, balanced mechanical process."[1] From the point of view of the material welfare of the race the function of this system is to supply goods in abundance, and in the present high state of development of the industrial arts this function could be adequately fulfilled.

It happens, however, that in the operation of the system discretion lies in the hands of business men. The motive of business enterprise is not maximum production of useful goods; it is pecuniary gain. "The aim and usual outcome is the accumulation of wealth." "The economic welfare of the community at large is best served by a facile and uninterrupted interplay of the various processes which make up the industrial system at large; but the pecuniary interests of the business

[1] *The Theory of Business Enterprise*, p. 16.

men in whose hands lies the discretion in the matter are
not necessarily best served by an unbroken maintenance
of the industrial balance." [1]   We have, then, arrived
finally at the fundamental theme of Veblen's whole
scheme of analysis, the antithesis between "business"
and "industry."   Out of this antithesis arises almost
every opinion which he holds as to the modern economic
situation.

IV

One of the consequences of the revolution in industry was the gradual drift of the industrial system into
the complicated concatenation of physical processes,
already mentioned.   Another important outcome was
the fairly rapid division of those concerned in the operation of the system into two fairly distinct classes—
on the one hand, those who carry on the physical
processes of production, engineers, technicians, scientists,
workmen, and, on the other hand, those who, through
the prescriptive rights of ownership, exercise control
over the processes.   Since control is exercised with an
eye to maximizing their gains in terms of money, it
may be said that "industry is carried on for the sake
of business, and not conversely." [2]   The functions of
business enterprise in organizing comprehensive industrial processes Veblen dismisses with the remark that

[1] *The Theory of Business Enterprise*, p. 27.
[2] *Ibid.*, p. 26.

they have received adequate theoretical treatment and their good results in that direction are a "matter of common notoriety." His view is that the treatment accorded the *entrepreneur* in economic theory relates to an early stage of the machine era when owners commonly supervised the operation of their plants and were "master technologists" as well as business men. Regarding that stage as obsolescent, he purports to deal with the more recent phase of investment for profit, when the supervision of physical production is consigned to technical experts while the business man directs his attention wholly to financial matters. He is interested in examining business enterprise solely from the point of view of the dissociation, or conflict, of interests between the community and business men.

The business man's opportunity for profit arises out of the interdependence of all the parts of the industrial system. The adjustment between the parts is carried on through the agency of the price system, necessitating a continuous process of purchase and sale. It is at the point of these "interstitial adjustments" involving purchase and sale that the great gains of business enterprise are made. For Veblen entertains no theory that competition is ubiquitously active throughout the system, reducing or tending to reduce profits everywhere to a minimum. His view is that the principle of price-making is "what the traffic will bear." The business world to him is an affair of widespread collusion, where great corporations, trusts, trade agreements, established clienteles, and all manner of semi-monopolistic enterprises and practices are matters of course, not mere occasional excrescences upon the pure surface of a competitive order. "It is very doubtful if there are any successful business ventures within the range of the modern industries from which the monopoly element is wholly absent. . . . The endeavor of all such enterprises that look to a permanent continuance of their business is to establish as much of a monopoly as may be." [1] It is thus from some power to interrupt the free flow of materials from one part of the industrial system to another that business profits typically arise. The net result, beyond causing a flow of income into the pockets of the fortunate, is a lowering of the efficiency of the system and a reduced volume of material goods flowing to "the underlying population." [2] The relation of business men to industry, so far as they are concerned with the physical output, may then be shortly described as "sabotage," or "conscientious withdrawal of efficiency." [3]

Not only does Veblen assume a high degree of collusive control of industry; he attempts to demonstrate the impossibility of free competition in the machine industries. The earlier stages of the machine era he concedes to have been marked by sharp competition, so long as the cheapening of goods through improved

[1] *The Theory of Business Enterprise*, p. 54.
[2] A recurring phrase in *Absentee Ownership*.
[3] Phrases recurring throughout *The Engineers and the Price System*, *The Vested Interests*, and *Absentee Ownership*.

methods of production led to the opening up of new markets which could absorb the increased output. This period he conceives to have been passed, so far as England was concerned, about the middle of the nineteenth century, and to have been put into the limbo of past situations by the entrance of machine methods into Germany and the United States. When markets no longer could be expanded to carry off the additional output as rapidly as technological improvement could increase it, a situation arose which foretold the death of active price competition. To competition under this situation is attributed in large part the chronic depression which marked business traffic during the last quarter of the nineteenth century. The causes of depression go deeper than this, but this was an important factor and led, under the exigencies of business enterprise as set by the price system, to a movement toward combination and collusion designed to insure profits through a restriction of output. The trouble with the modern industrial system, from the point of view of business men, is that it has become "inordinately productive." Consequently the essential element in business success is to keep the product of industry under adequate control, a complete reversal of the earlier handicraft situation when "unsophisticated productive efficiency was the prime element of business success."

The two dominant aspects of modern life, business and industry, lead to a curious cultural dualism by reason of the different habits of thought engendered under

divergent habits of life. The concern of business men
and those groups whose interests are allied to theirs is
with pecuniary gain. Their transactions are almost
wholly in terms of money measurement; their power
is based upon the differential advantage arising out of
large property holdings; and their whole manner of
thinking is shaped by their pecuniary preoccupations.
The institution of property, around which their interests
center, "pervades and dominates the affairs of civilized
peoples more freely and widely than any other single
ground of action."[1] The current views as to the proper
limits, rights, and responsibilities of ownership are "the
outgrowth of the traditions, experiences, and speculations of past generations," as embodied in the philosophy of Natural Rights. The natural right of ownership
is still the prevailing belief of the business community
and is firmly imbedded in law and custom, though
the situation which gave rise to it is no more than a
historical memory. The law as it stands is designed
primarily for the protection of property rights and
conspires to make easy the way for pecuniary manipulation and profit.

But a large proportion of the populace are exposed
in only a secondary way to the discipline of pecuniary
habits of thought. These are the ones whose daily
work brings them under the standardizing, materialistic
sway of the machine. "The discipline of the machine
process . . . inculcates a habit of apprehending and

[1] *The Theory of Business Enterprise*, p. 70.

explaining facts in terms of material cause and effect.
. . . Its metaphysics is materialism and its point of
view is that of causal sequence." [1] The cultural growth
dominated by the machine industry "is of a skeptical,
matter-of-fact complexion, materialistic, unmoral, un-
patriotic, undevout." [2] Subject to some residue of tradition, the machine discipline "inculcates thinking in
terms of opaque, impersonal cause and effect, to the
neglect of those norms of validity that rest on usage
and on the conventional standards handed down by
usage." [3] The classes affected by this discipline are
primarily the industrial workers, including also engineers, technical experts, students of material sciences
—in fact, all those who are "required to administer the
laws of causal sequence that run through material phenomena." It is the activity and energy of this group
that have brought the industrial arts to the state of
efficiency where business strategy is compelled to cir-
cumvent or hinder the output of goods. Veblen, it will
be seen, thus eschews the familiar explanation of technical advance in terms of business competition, and
explains it in terms of the bent of workmanship and
the discipline of materialistic habits of thought.

The habits of thought induced by this discipline
traverse the conventional eighteenth-century truths of
natural law, natural rights, and natural liberty. They
engender a "weakening sense of conviction, allegiance,

[1] *The Theory of Business Enterprise*, pp. 66-67.
[2] *Ibid.*, p. 372.
[3] *Ibid.*, p. 310.

or piety toward the received institutions," particularly the institution of property as at present maintained. The trade-union movement Veblen regards as displaying to some degree, the modern socialist movement to a marked degree, the effects of this discipline. They are, "however crudely and blindly, endeavoring, under the compulsion of the machine process, to construct an institutional scheme on the lines imposed by the new exigencies given by the machine process." [1]

The present situation, then, is that there exists a *de facto* habituation to the machine process out of which arises the latter-day common sense of important groups of the community. This common sense runs to the view that the industrial system should be directed to the supplying of goods abundantly for the benefit of the community. Over against this is a *de jure* situation, grounded in an obsolete philosophy, the practical effect of which is to protect the differential advantage incident to ownership, and to protect business men in their practices of deriving gain from a sabotage upon the industrial system.

Whether the views of one side or the other are right or wrong, is, in Veblen's view, entirely beside the point. The crude and unvarnished truth is that the situation exists and that it has arisen by a process of cumulative institutional change, unrelated to any ethical norms of permanent validity. So far as giving expression to the instinct of workmanship is concerned, it is in the

[1] *The Theory of Business Enterprise*, p. 336.

field of industry that the opportunity is most freely offered. Here, too, is seen the reëmergence of the parental bent, concerned for the welfare of the group. And here is found also the declining sway of animistic and teleological ways of thinking, and of emulative practices so strongly ground into human nature by centuries of habituation and selection. On the side of business, however, still rests the weight of institutional authority. Out of this situation, somewhat dramatically displayed, the economic process will move on to its next phase.

It would carry us far beyond the limits of our space to attempt to present the infinite detail with which Veblen embroiders the argument or to recall the mass of facts which he brings to bear upon it. Yet the high quality of his work is best seen in the luxuriant exfoliation from his central ideas, as the beauty of a tree is in its leaves and flowers and rounded contour. Admitting the imperfection of the picture thus portrayed, we must be content merely to sketch in briefly a few of the limbs springing out of the main trunk. Very much of Veblen's work has consisted in an examination of the manifestations of the institution of property as it manifests itself in the machine era under modern forms of ownership and business enterprise. To his view of these novel modern developments of property rights attention may now be directed.

It is not always possible to say exactly what Veblen's position is. In the course of his years of writing he

has changed his views to a considerable degree. In his
earliest work he spoke of the economic system as a competitive system. By the time of *Business Enterprise*
(1904), he took the view, as we have seen, that in the
high state of efficiency of the industrial arts active
price competition was fatal to business enterprise, and
that the function of such enterprise was primarily to
exact a profit by interfering at some point with the
smooth articulation of the productive process. But he
then viewed the collusion directed to that end as taking
place in many industries, in a rather scattered and separate way. By the time of *Absentee Ownership* (1923),
he sees, or foresees, a sort of integrated collusion of
the "key industries" dominated by the power of the
great financial, or banking, interests. It is collusion
on this upper level that slows down the productive
process most directly, because the "key industries" by
controlling the supply of essential materials or services
such as steel, fuel, transportation, and so on can set
the pace for the rest of the industrial system. Throughout the secondary fields of manufacturing and merchandising a considerable degree of competition is
admitted, not in regard to price, but to advertising and
salesmanship. Even on this level a businesslike cur-
tailment of supply is essential to business success, but
much of the gains that might otherwise accrue drift
off into increased selling costs at the expense of "the
underlying population." Agriculture is the sole remnant of the former competitive system, and the ab-

sence of effective collusion in this important field places it at the mercy of the upper branches of business enterprise.

In dealing with the phenomenon of credit Veblen admits with a passing nod the occasional truth of the view that it favorably affects industrial production by transferring funds from less competent to more competent users. But he does not at all acquiesce in the usual favorable version of the effects of credit. To business enterprise it represents a differential competitive advantage, as against those who cannot secure it, by permitting an increased size and rate of turnover. It is thus a competitive weapon which ceases to retain any power when universally resorted to. As increased purchasing power, its primary effect is to raise prices and produce speculative inflation of values, with only secondary and remote effect upon industrial production. Credit is obtainable not only against physical property, but on securities which are themselves merely evidences of indebtedness. Loans of the latter sort, being nothing more than a duplication of credit upon the same underlying material items, can have no direct effect except to inflate values. Loans are thus a significant and important fact in business traffic, but their effect on industry is indirect. "Funds of whatever character are a pecuniary fact, not an industrial one; they serve the distribution of the control of industry, not its materially productive work."[1]

[1] *The Theory of Business Enterprise*, p. 104.

Rising values due to credit extension increase the money values of the underlying plant and of industrial securities, which thereby serve as the basis of further credit. Thus is generated a cumulative growth of credit. Basing his analysis from this point on modern methods in corporation finance, Veblen perceives that rising prices increase money income and that the current practice is to capitalize a business on the basis of its presumptive earning capacity. Such capitalization is strictly an inflation of the money value of a business, not an increase in industrial capacity. Since debenture securities of one sort or another are commonly issued equal to or in excess of the value of the plant, such value as attaches to the voting stocks is merely the capitalization of a company's good-will, or intangible assets in the way of established business relations, franchises, trade-marks, patent rights, exclusive control of raw material, or some other differential business advantage which brings in income. These intangible assets from the business man's point of view are as much capital as his plant, though they are not serviceable to the community. They represent merely the modern method by which, under the law of private property, income is diverted into the pockets of those holding exclusive privileges to retard industrial production. A curious result of modern methods of finance is that the discretionary control of industrial operation is in the hands of the owners of the intangible assets. The material instruments of industry have a pecuniary equivalent only in the debenture securities which carry no share in control. Such securities (evidences of debt) can serve as the basis of credit, which in turn swells capital values. The whole round of credit and capitalization constitutes a very complicated situation in which the line between credit and capital, debt and property, is very indistinct. Certainly, under modern conditions, business capital ("capitalized presumptive earning capacity") bears a very loose relationship to industrial plant.

Out of his analysis of credit and capitalization, Veblen devises a theory of economic cycles. The cumulative increase of credit, values, profits, and capitalization goes on until in some enterprises there appears a discrepancy between capitalization and anticipated earnings. Creditors, fearing their collateral to be inadequate, demand payment, and the interlocked character of indebtedness necessitates a widespread liquidation of credit, resulting in reduced earnings and capitalization, widespread insolvency and reorganization, shifting ownership of property, and business depression. Here again the effect on industrial plant and production is indirect. What has happened has been merely a movement, or manipulation, of money values incidental to the business practice of acquiring money gains. Most of the phenomena of cyclical fluctuations Veblen traces to the business man's psychology, whereby he pursues monetary values exclusively and under a superstitious belief that the money unit is a stable quantity. Tech-

nology enters into the situation to insure the maintenance of a period of depression, because more efficient
methods of production put older enterprises, loaded
down with heavy fixed charges and high costs, in a
position where they find it difficult to earn a "reasonable profit." It is this disconcerting effect of increasing industrial efficiency that has made competition
obnoxious, if not fatal, to business enterprise. It has
stimulated the modern movement to combination and
collusion with a view to stabilizing the sources of profit.

As we have attempted to show, Veblen explains the
fact that the discretionary control of the industrial system is permitted to rest in the hands of business men,
who obstruct its efficient operation for purposes of
pecuniary gain, as a holdover of certain habits of
thought from the eighteenth century. The Western
World has to a great extent continued to believe in the
natural right of property, which was a product of handicraft habituation. It has not clearly discerned the
element of sabotage in business enterprise; it has even
identified the business man's gain with the community's
welfare. And the character of machine industry has
led to the differentiation of a large and influential part
of the community whose habituation is entirely in
pecuniary concepts, and whose interest is to maintain
the legal precepts in regard to property. Veblen, as
we have seen, displays the activities of this class in
anything but a favorable light. Discretion is in the
hands of "absentee owners" whose right to control

rests only upon possession of the country's "intangible assets" which are made possible by our laws of property. They are the "kept classes" enjoying "free income" which arises from activities disserviceable to the community's material welfare. The country-town merchants bleed the farmers. The manufacturers bleed the country merchants. Employers bleed the workers. The key industries in collusion with the bankers bleed everybody. In effect, the "One Big Union of the interests" has become possessed of "the community's joint stock of technological knowledge and efficiency," the usufruct of which goes to the "kept classes" to be spent in "an indefinitely extensible consumption of superfluities." Meanwhile, "the underlying population," the farmers and industrial workers, fail to receive the benefits which the high present efficiency of the industrial system would permit, were it organized to serve the welfare of the community instead of the acquisitive ambitions of absentee owners.

As the phrases quoted would indicate, Veblen's analysis runs to a very incisive and biting criticism of the control of the industrial system by absentee owners whose object is profit. Examining successively various aspects of modern economic life, the farmers, small-town merchandising, the labor movement, the control of credit, salesmanship, monopoly, and international politics, he sees an industrial system amply able to supply material abundance torn by the struggle for pecuniary acquisition. In this struggle, ascendency for the moment is with the interests that are in a position to control essential services by collusive exercise of the rights of ownership. The advantages derivable from the increased efficiency in technology are curbed from pecuniary motives, and such increase in physical production as is permitted is sidetracked into the pockets of the dominant business interests, to find an outlet in consumption on no higher principle than that of conspicuous waste. And the reason for this absurd miscarriage of industrial efficiency is nothing more tangible than the holding over of obsolete habits of thought from an antecedent cultural situation, as exhibited in the legal position of ownership and the psychology of the business man.

Meantime, as has been said, large sections of the population are being subjected to the matter-of-fact discipline of the machine process, with resulting habits of thought inimical to the standards of right action prevalent in the business community. "The popular feeling of incongruity and uselessness in the current run of law and custom under the rule of these time-worn preconceptions is visibly gaining ground and gathering consistency, even in so well-ordered a republic as America." [1] Out of this newer type of habituation some reconstruction of the institutional framework is inevitable. "Such wear and tear of institutions is unavoidable where circumstances change; and it is through the altered personal equation of those elements of the

[1] *The Vested Interests*, p. 179.

population which are most directly exposed to the changing circumstances that the wear and tear of institutions may be expected to take effect. To these untidy creatures of the New Order common honesty appears to mean vaguely something else, perhaps something more exacting, than what was 'nominated in the bond' at the time when the free bargain and self-help were written into the normal constitution of Christendom by the handicraft industry and the petty trade. And why should it not?" [1]

Just what form the next step in institutional change will or should take Veblen does not feel called upon to say. He is mainly content to clarify the diverging habits of thought in regard to economic conduct and leave the future to work itself out on the principle that "any resulting revision of the principles of conduct will come in as a drift of habituation rather than a dispassionately reasoned adaptation of conduct to the circumstances of the case." [2] He is not, however, averse to a little prophesying. In *Business Enterprise* (1904) he stated that "the full dominion of business enterprise is necessarily a transient dominion"; [3] and thought it due either to give way before some new form of organization, perhaps some form of socialism, arising out of the disciplinary effects of the machine process, or to be crushed by the mounting weight of power politics and armament for purposes of national ag-

[1] Concluding passage of *The Vested Interests*, p. 183.
[2] *Absentee Ownership*, p. 19.
[3] *Ibid.*, p. 400.

grandisement. In *Absentee Ownership* (1923) he finds business interests still firmly in control of both industry and politics, and foresees within the calculable future no diminution of that control. "The outlook should accordingly be that the businesslike control of the industrial system in detail should presently reach, if it has not already reached, and should speedily pass beyond that critical point of chronic derangement in the aggregate beyond which a continued pursuit of the same strategy or the same businesslike principles will result in a progressively widening margin of deficiency in the aggregate material output and a progressive shrinkage of the available means of life." [1] The limits of tolerance passed, there will some time probably result a gradual or abrupt institutional change, long overdue, designed to restrict the prerogatives of ownership and release the potential productive power of the industrial system. In the nature of the case institutional changes are always overdue, or, to use a current sociological phrase, there is a "cultural lag." For, "the growth of custom follows after the facts of experience which give rise to it. . . . In this sense, therefore, any established order of law and custom is out of date, in some degree. The code of right and honest living is always in arrears." [2]

What direction change *ought* to take, Veblen has usually been careful to avoid hazarding. He does not

---

[1] Concluding passage of *Absentee Ownership*, p. 445.
[2] *Absentee Ownership*, p. 18.

put on the mantle of the reformer. He does not speak of "progress," but only of "cumulative change." But he definitely, if only implicitly, takes sides in the current conflict between industrial efficiency and business enterprise. His work is decidedly an *exposé* of the deficiencies of business control. Moreover, he regards modern evolutionary science as an offshoot of the habit of dealing with material phenomena in a matter-of-fact way in terms of a process, a habit which he traces to the machine process. As he criticizes economic science and other systems of knowledge from the standpoint of "modern science," it is not unfair to say that he is in a sense the spokesman of industry, as against business. He is, in effect, arguing for some revised form of control, by which the potential productiveness of the industrial system may be relieved of the incubus of the present debilitating business control for pecuniary ends. In *The Engineers and the Price System* he goes some distance in outlining somewhat vaguely a desirable form of economic control, with discretion resting in the hands of a hierarchy of engineers, scientists, and technical experts. His *idée fixe* is, one might say, that the material welfare of the community could be greatly increased by proper control, but he consistently refuses to say that the community *ought* to adopt such control. For manners and morals are but of the day.

It appears to be Veblen's view that the present institutional situation is one designed to thwart the expression of those instinctive propensities which serve the

"generically human" ends of the race.   Under the
acquisitive struggle for "something for nothing," the
parental bent toward serving the ends of the group is
inverted into a metaphysical theory of the coincidence
of private acquisition and public welfare.   The instinct
of workmanship, though offered considerable scope in
industrial occupations, is thwarted as an auxiliary to the
parental bent, restricted by business sabotage, and sub-
verted to the fabrication of useless articles of consumption.   The high state of efficiency of the industrial arts
is, however, evidence of the activity of this propensity.
Were it now permitted, by a revised control of industry, to act more in conjunction with the parental bent,
modern industry would represent a situation more
favorable to the expression of man's most humanly useful instinctive proclivities; instead of their being, as
now, subordinated to the proximate end of perpetuating a set of established but antiquated institutional
furniture.   "In point of native bent and capacities European mankind is still the same as the neolithic European
population once was, some ten or twelve thousand years
ago. . . . The scheme of law and custom which now
governs civilized life under modern industrial conditions is still made up out of the same spiritual forces
that have made the outcome in the past, early and late.
It is only that the material circumstances which condition the growth and working of this established
scheme of law and custom in recent times are dif-

ferent."[1] In his more dyspeptic moments Veblen is not averse to drawing a picture of the obstructive character of this modern scheme of law and custom, in which mankind would appear to be headed straight for the abyss.

In the attempt to cling to the central aspects of Veblen's thinking, it has been impossible to do justice to the sweep of his mind as it plays over the modern scene. With brilliant, if unsupported, generalizations, he comments upon the economic position of farmers, wage-earners, merchants, manufacturers, and bankers; upon the economic effects of advertising, salesmanship, monopoly, and the control of credit; and upon the allocation of economic power. He examines the field of international politics, in *The Nature of Peace*, and traces statesmanship, patriotism, and competitive nationalism back to the institution of property and to the principles of business enterprise. He looks into current standards of consumption in *The Theory of the Leisure Class* and lumps them largely into the category of "conspicuous waste," based upon invidious distinctions in point of property. And in *The Higher Learning in America* the control of education by men of property is pungently characterized.

Always and everywhere the analysis comes back to the institution of property, to its origins, to the habits of thought by which it is supported, to its submersion of the "generically human" ends of life, and to the dis-

[1] *Absentee Ownership*, p. 41.

sension and distress to which, under modern conditions, it inevitably leads. And always there rise in opposition the habits of thought inculcated by the machine process, involving with ironical certainty the necessity that mankind shall pass through a period of institutional adjustment by stormy paths to one knows not what *dénouement*.

v

We have by now perhaps secured a sufficiently integrated view of the more essential elements of Veblen's scheme of thought. Having come so far, we may profitably cast up a few accounts, or at least raise some of the questions that linger in the mind.

His primary preconception, as has been said, is that no study is scientific which is not made from the evolutionary point of view. Biology is in his view the prototype of all science. Other sciences are admitted to the fellowship of "modern science" only to the degree to which they engage in the sort of genetic studies which the evolutionary principle has enforced upon biology and other sciences dealing with organic materials.[1] This, in itself, is a highly controversial dictum, and it is assuredly a hardy position to take which reads much of physics and chemistry, mechanics and astronomy, botany and zoölogy, out of the scientific

---

[1] For the development of this thesis, see the title essay in *The Place of Science in Modern Civilization*.

fold. It is hardly a tenable position, that scientific observation by way of description, classification, and generalization has become necessarily obsolete and archaic because of the evolutionary principle. In this, as in so many of his dicta, Veblen appears intent upon startling a dozing world out of its lethargy by elevating a neglected half-truth into the whole truth.

The point of establishing the supremacy of the evolutionary approach in the natural sciences is thereby to establish the exclusive authenticity of that approach to the scientific study of society. Veblen insists upon a thoroughgoing analogy between biology and the social sciences. And he refuses to regard society from any other angle than that of its process of "becoming." It is as though we were to condemn comparative anatomy to exclusion from medical schools as both unscientific and useless. He takes no pains to prove that his position is well taken, merely blandly assuming it as indisputable. His purpose, of course, is to demonstrate the shortcomings of the analogy common to most economic theory between physics or mechanics and economics. He assumes for this purpose that society is a form of organic life comparable to a biological organism, and contends unforgetably that living and growing types of organic life are not amenable to explanation in the terms used for explaining inert matter. The mere device of adopting the evolutionary approach tends at the very beginning to cast doubt upon the "static" and "dynamic" analysis of orthodox theory.

And, though one should not go the whole journey with Veblen, he is compelled to take into consideration the partial and incomplete character of most economic theory, and its inadequacy as a basis for any scheme of social philosophy or of social policy. One may, then, question whether, in introducing the evolutionary approach to economics, Veblen did not claim too much for it. It may be reasonably supposed that much important scientific investigation is possible from quite other approaches. It can, however, hardly be questioned that his approach has leavened the whole lump of contemporary economic thinking, and that it has raised problems and suggested methods which continually eluded the attempts of Marshall, Clark, and others to come to grips with them while using the classical technique.

Veblen, as appeared at an earlier point, traces the origin of the modern point of view in science—that is, the evolutionary view of a cumulative life process uncolored by teleological or animistic assumptions—to the discipline of the machine process. It may be noted in passing that his uncritical assumption of this as the only tenable viewpoint raises a rather fine-spun logical difficulty. By his own interpretation of the life process this discipline and this viewpoint are in the nature of the case fortuitous and transitory, doomed like all antecedent habits of thought to impermanence. Or, if not, he is in the position of regarding as final and ultimate the machine process and the materialistic evolutionary viewpoint, as the destined end of the age-long process of change; which would make him guilty of a form of the teleology of which he is so consistently critical. The point is no doubt unimportant to the point of quibbling. It is merely interesting to note that one finds no modest doubts expressed concerning the possible perishability of his own point of view.

In approaching the present significance of Veblen's scheme of thought it would hardly appear necessary to do more than recall his critical position in the briefest way. Lingering notions of purpose or a meliorative trend in economic life are derided as metaphysical hold-overs. The ideas of "natural laws" and "normality" in economic phenomena are relegated to outer darkness as representing both obsolete philosophical beliefs and obsolete scientific conceptions. The hedonistic view of human nature is conceived to be untenable in the light of modern psychology. The normalized institutional situation which serves as a postulate of economic theory is conceived to be out of touch with current facts. For, in the first place, the economic system is no longer mainly competitive, because the logic of business enterprise demands collusive action to control and reap profits from physical production in view of the "inordinately productive" character of modern technology. And, in the second place, acquisition can no longer be identified with production, nor capital with instruments of production; since acquisition is commonly promoted by sabotage upon production, while capital is in current significance the "capitalized putative earning-capacity" of differential sources of gain, only loosely when at all related to industrial plant.   Having thus summarily disposed of the postulates and preconceptions, Veblen is in a position to relegate to footnotes or parentheses, as obsolete or absurd, the normative systems of value and distribution with which economic theorists have been mainly concerned.

Veblen's criticism thus cuts into every essential postulate and conclusion of the neo-classical and marginal systems of economic thought.   No one can read him and retain quite so simple an acceptance of any systematized economic faith.   It is by the deadly character of this critical attack that Veblen has thrown the whole subject of economic theory in the United States into such utter confusion.   But what he has substituted is in no sense adequate to place economic theory upon a sound new footing.   What he develops is a theory of the growth of economic institutions.   But he does it within the framework of a rather rigid set of categories, neglecting even to mention numerous human traits and social forces which are or have been of equal force with those he mentions in shaping social development and setting the economic scene.   He does not, moreover, throw much light upon the problems with which economists have been struggling, the problems of value and distribution.   With a certain, one would say conscious and deliberate, contrariety, he has gone out of his way to dig up and expose to view every real or putative fact which would operate to discredit the methods and conclusions of the "orthodox" economists. He is the prophet of "friction" and "disturbing factors." Exhaustively and brilliantly he has provided the antithesis to almost every economic thesis. He has been engaged in pushing his antitheses to extremes. What can one say to the views that business is primarily sabotage; that national establishments are solely for protecting property rights; that religion is important chiefly as obstructing production; that almost the sole effect of credit is monetary inflation; that consumption is almost entirely based on invidious display; or that the law of the conservation of energy derives from double-entry bookkeeping? Into most of these views, as of his others, there enters the sting of a partial truth; but the part is displayed as the whole. It might at times be almost thought that his sole ambition was to demonstrate that a more plausible case might be made out in terms running directly contrary to the generally acceptable canons of truth, whether in economic theory or in the practical phases of economic life. But if, in pushing his antitheses to extremes, he reduces himself occasionally to absurdity and fails to come to grips with many problems, it cannot be denied that the delightful play of his skepticism is infinitely enlightening and stimulating.

The one-sidedness of his analysis appears in the bias which leads him to imply, if not avow, that economic salvation lies in releasing the potentialities of technical proficiency for purposes of the physical production of goods. As a negation of the blessings to be found in the present economic organization, the argument has some force. But he does not demonstrate that social efficiency or the community's material welfare can be organized on a basis of technical skill alone. Nor does he grapple with the problems of economic guidance and direction, which are certainly as essential economic functions as technical and physical effort. Reducing business principles and the price system to obstructive absurdities, he has nothing to offer in their stead.

He appears to accept uncritically Mill's "economic principle" that the greater material gain is preferable to the smaller, with its corollary that that is the most desirable system of economic organization which will maximize material output. In short, he knows no canon of welfare except maximum output of goods, certainly a very narrow view of the "generically human" ends of life. This narrowness of view to which his scheme of thought eventually leads lies implicit in it from the start. By selecting out of the human mind those traits and out of history those institutional situations which appear to him to affect material welfare favorably or adversely, he artificially excludes psychological and institutional factors of undoubted influence in shaping the life process of society. One may grant him the desirability of deriving an understanding of the modern economic situation through a study of its derivation from the past, and still question whether, in terms of his own purpose, he has not built upon too narrow a principle of selection to construct a tenable theory of the economic life process.

Veblen's scheme for attaining welfare is as dubitable as his idea of the content of welfare. With no more concrete suggestion than a vague plan for the supervision of the economic system by technical experts, he succeeds merely in evading the problem of economic guidance and the problems of value and distribution, which lie within the sweep of the price system. He thinks the "mutual defeat" inherent in the present economic order should be escaped, in the interest of material welfare and race survival. But no intelligible theory of social ends, no adequate account of social forces, and no tenable scheme of social control are anywhere advanced.

Assuming for the moment that Veblen is to be taken seriously as a "modern scientist," certain further comments appear called for. His avowed purpose is to give a highly objective, matter-of-fact explanation of economic institutions in terms of the process by which they have developed, and an unbiased account of the operative effects of current institutions. Were the materials available for such an evolutionary study, and an intellect competent to cope with them, there might be some hope of achieving such a purpose with a relative approach to a scientific ideal of objectivity. But Veblen is undeterred by the paucity of material for his task, nor even, it would appear, aware of it. Armed with an enormous erudition in anthropology, universal history, psychology, natural science, and corporation finance, he proceeds blithely to the performance of an impossible task, nothing daunted at undertaking the labors of Hercules. One cannot fail to raise certain questions as to the methods of performance.

It is not obvious, for example, how modern economic institutions can be scientifically explained without a very wide and complicated survey of cultural history, an almost encyclopedic presentation of factors that have entered into the process of "cumulative causation." It may be asked whether Veblen has not merely evaded the difficulties of his task by forcing his analysis within categories too rigid and formulas too simple and abstract. Can we assume that the dominant traits of human nature were fixed by the few thousand years of neolithic discipline of a putatively peaceable sort, rather than by hundreds of thousands of earlier years? Can we adequately interpret modern economic life in terms of a simplified antithesis between the obstructive and invidious principle of ownership and the humanly useful principle of workmanship? Can we regard modern economic institutions as the outgrowth of two or three instinctive propensities and the one long-lived institution of property, under changing conditions of material environment? Does not this method of analysis make abstractions of many factors relevant to the unfolding of the life process, and thereby invalidate the results? Does not Veblen make loose long-range arguments from disputable prehistoric data to the facts of modern life, and does he not, on the other hand, impute modern habits of thought to people living under more primitive conditions? Is he scientifically justified in measuring, and implicitly judging, the outcome of institutions by their purely economic effects? Is his analysis of modern economic life not vitiated and made partial and incomplete by forcing facts into the framework of his own rigid artificial categories? Such are some of the many questions that arise in pondering over the problem of Mr. Veblen, even when he is given the advantage of having his performance weighed in the scales of his own method and balanced against his own avowed purpose.

One can hardly escape the conclusion that, whatever else it may be, his work is not science. To attempt to do what Veblen attempts in a truly scientific manner would involve labors too monumental to be practicable, or even thinkable, for any man. One will arrive more directly and accurately at the heart of the matter if he drops the fiction that Veblen is a scientist. His task is carried out with none of the cold objectivity which, in his own view, distinguishes the scientific spirit. With consummate skill in selecting and coloring his facts he has succeeded in building up his central antithesis to its consummation between business and industry, between obstructive and invidious acquisition and humanly useful production. With his tongue in his cheek and under cover of a sophistical scientific pose he has accomplished

a covert ethical damnation of the dominant modern
economic institutions. It is the eye of a philosopher
that he casts over the mundane scene; an eye trying
to descry, not meaning, but only broad lines of causation in the muddled course of history, trying to see as
clearly as may be into the heart of modern economic
life. Much that he sees appears futile and ignoble and
imbecile, nor does his somewhat jaundiced sight lend
any temptation to gild the scene. Regarded in this
light as some composite form of cosmic philosopher,
shrewd observer, and bitter critic, Veblen still retains
the signs of undoubted genius—not, indeed, of the
man of science, but of some more human gift of impressionistic art, strongly expressing a brilliant and
baffling personality.

If, then, so many questions arise and so many strictures spring to the mind concerning Veblen's work, it
may be asked wherein lie his importance and significance
in the field of economic theory. The force of his critical attack upon established systems of theory has been
sufficiently noted. Its disintegrating effect has been
enormous. Anyone familiar with the theorizing of a
generation ago will know that it predominantly followed the classical method of deductive logic. Such
controversy as existed was chiefly confined to amending
or clarifying the postulates, and to defining concepts,
particularly those of capital and rent. The search was
for the controlling laws of the normal case, which
would explain prices and distributive shares, subject to

minor corrections. In the minds of many economists
Veblen has thoroughly discredited the usefulness or
the scientific validity of that type of analysis. The
problem which worried Marshall, but which he could
not subdue, the changefulness of human institutions,
Veblen places at the center of his scheme of thought.
If, as he postulates, institutional change is "normal,"
then all forms of normality postulated upon the fixity
of institutions disappear. If one accept that position,
then the whole character of his social theory must de-
part from the customary types of economic speculation.

The Veblenian idea that has been widely accepted
among the younger generation of economists is that
economic life is part of an evolutionary process, and
that the function of economic theory is to throw light
upon the process. His view differs from Hegel's in many
ways, but characteristically in supposing no destined
end to which the process moves. It differs from that
of the historical school in seeking no laws of progress.
It attempts to wed economic science to something
analogous to genetic studies in biology. Veblen is not,
of course, unique in being a student of the development
of economic institutions. On one side, his work has
points of resemblance with that of Sombart, Ashley,
and the Webbs. But he is unique in the particular
way in which he introduces human nature into the social
process. Economic life appears to him merely an ex-
hibition of the play of human motives. To psychology
he must go for an understanding of the basic and

hereditary propensities of the human animal. Human
activity, though basically instinctive, is to a considerable degree habitual, as molded by the institutions which
condition it. Institutions, then, are important because
of the way in which they bear upon human nature and
shape the course of human action. Since human nature
is of the nature of the problem, Veblen says in essence,
let us see what psychologists have to say about it. They
say it is fairly stable? They say activity is largely instinctive or habitual? Then let us ask the anthropolo-
gists how it expresses itself under primitive forms of
social organization. Let us see from history how it expressed itself at various points of time and under various conditions. Habits of action and habits of thought
seem to have undergone radical changes? Then let
us appeal to science for a theory of developing organic
life. They attribute it to natural selection and a cumulative change of environment? Let us then examine
developing forms of human activity in the light of
that doctrine.

Not in that sequence, probably, but somewhat of
that sort, were the questions that Veblen must have
asked himself. He was anxious to escape the bounds
of customary economic thought and to appeal to many
sources of knowledge for light upon the problems of
human action with which economic science is concerned.
And it is this undoubtedly that has made him "a light,
set upon a hilltop," guiding the thought of many who
were wondering, however vaguely, whether the meth-

ods of economic science were not somehow out of step with the progress of knowledge in other fields.

The outstanding characteristic of this novel and arresting approach is its power to raise new questions and problems. If it be said that human nature is of the essence of economic activity, one must find out what human nature is like. If it be averred that human activity is largely habitual, habits must be run down to their sources in human nature and material environment. If habitual action is constrained upon individuals by the prescriptive force of established institutions, it must be asked how well these conventional practices are designed to promote the material welfare of the community. If it be admitted that present institutions are the outcome of a cumulative process of past events, the tangled lines of derivation become interesting. Within the wider social sweep of such problems, the possibility of isolating the economic elements demands attention, if it be desired to explain economic institutions and economic behavior, as such. If institutions are changeful, is the process amenable to intelligent control? And what are the origin and nature of the conceptions of welfare for purposes of which control would be desirable?

Such questions, and innumerable others, lie inherent in the evolutionary, psychological, institutional approach of Veblen to economic theory. Attacked by the economist, they carry him beyond all the conventional frontiers of his field of labor. They defeat all attempts to carve out a specifically "economic" sphere within which the economist can work in isolation. Or, if he be limited in his field of endeavor, they form a framework of problems toward the solution of which his particular problem is an item in a large coöperative intellectual enterprise. Such new problems Veblen has set for economists. He has also attempted to solve a good many of them. Any careful estimate of his work demands that a sharp distinction be made between the approach he has devised and the questions he has raised, on the one hand, and the methods he has used and the conclusions he has reached, on the other.

It is with regard to the latter that the obvious criticisms, of the sort that have been recounted, arise. Such criticism is only to say that Veblen is not sufficiently the superman to solve all the problems he has set himself. His blindness perhaps lies in attempting so heroic a rôle. Yet it is in this field that he displays much of the acuteness and originality of his mind. One need think only of a few typical pronouncements—the sharp distinction between the pecuniary and the materially productive aspects of economic life; the motives of invidious distinction in point of ownership which underlie the current concern with acquisition, current standards of consumption, and the aversion to labor; the contributions to the psychology of labor and of business enterprise. With remarkable acumen he has essayed to explain economic behavior, current and past, in terms of the human nature and the institutional situations which have conditioned it. He has at once thrown light upon the nature of man and upon the nature of the institutions within the bounds of which his activity takes place; and by the same strokes of the pen he has cast doubt upon the validity of equilibrated structures of prices built upon subjective foundations of "real costs" and "utilities."   In doing so he is usually plausible, often convincing, and always vivid and striking. That many of his views are debatable reflects the curious range of learning on which they are based, not possessed by his readers, and reflects as well his flair for sweeping, if dubitable, generalizations. That he seems at times manifestly absurd is to admit that he is very, very human. With nothing less than omniscience could Veblen have carried his method through to generally acceptable conclusions.

If this method has had some influence, and his specific views more, upon contemporary economic thinking, one must still go back to his general approach to find the dominant source of his influence. That human activity, including economic activity, may be most profitably approached from the angle of an evolutionary process; that economic studies must deal with real human beings, not with a rationalized human nature; that institutions are decisive factors in shaping human behavior; that to study the run of the facts, not to normalize them, is the function of the economist; and that the technological and the pecuniary aspects of economic life must be strictly distinguished from each other in economic analysis—these ideas form the frame-work within which increasing numbers of economists are defining their problems. They attract men whose methods are as the opposite pole to his methods, whose work is as restricted, painstaking, and scientifically ac-curate as his is sweeping, universal, and impressionistic. These ideas represent a formula sufficiently broad to include the most varied types of economic investigation. At the same time they suggest an endless array of attractive intellectual problems. To such facts must be credited the spread of Veblen's influence and the out-cropping of Veblenian notions in the most unlikely quarters, not only among economists, but among the devotees of the social sciences at large.

Moreover, the superb effrontery of his criticism and the brilliant heterodoxy of his analysis of current eco-nomic life have served as a mental shock which has jarred the younger generation of economists out of the rut of traditional habits of thought before they were too deeply settled in them. Had he been a less ex-treme and less spectacular iconoclast, Veblen would probably have had more followers, but less influence. As things stand, there are not many who will follow him all the way either in his interpretation of history, or in his analysis of current economic life, or in the adoption of his method. But there are many who owe to him their views of the nature of the economic process and their starting-point from which to investigate its problems. He has made economic heterodoxy more

prevalent, and at the same time less culpable. For
lesser heterodoxies fade into insignificance beside his
monstrous heterodoxy, and their perpetration almost
ceases to cause comment. So far has this situation developed in the United States, indeed, that it is almost
orthodox to be heterodox, and to be orthodox in the
older sense is almost to be queer. In other words, economic thought is running strongly down other channels than those set by the classical tradition.

One is in danger of crediting Veblen with too much.
It lies beyond our present purpose to deal with the
varied forces that have given new turns to economic
theory in the twentieth century. Many of them are,
as Veblen would say, contained in the material environment. The only point that need be made here is that
Veblen is the one individual who, more than any other
in recent years, has given force and direction to economic speculation in the United States. He has loaded
his shells with ideas garnered from widely scattered
fields of knowledge, thereupon making economists
acutely aware of them by exploding them like shrapnel
over their unhelmeted heads. It would perhaps be too
long a task to search for all the sources of knowledge
from which he has supplied his armory of ideas. As
has been indicated, his knowledge of history, anthropology, and philosophy is wide. His acquaintance with
the history of economic thought is exhaustive. His
interpretation of present-day economic life is guided by
an extensive knowledge of business practice. He is well

acquainted with psychological research down, at least, to the vogue of William McDougall. His views on psychology and epistemology run somewhat parallel to those of John Dewey, and one would judge that he was largely indebted to him. He is, however, the disciple of no one, and his knowledge in many fields is but raw material to be passed through the processes of his mind. And in his mind this raw material is all blended to emerge as his large scheme of interpreting economic institutions as part of the evolutionary process of cumulative causation. If one part of his scheme of thought is more fundamental than the rest, it is the evolutionary postulate.

All the philosophical and practical implications of Veblen's scheme of thought are not quite apparent. At times, for example, he appears to be completely a determinist, regarding man as but the buffeted creature of his instincts and his environment. Yet the element of rationality, or intelligence, is never quite ruled out. There remains a lingering suggestion that by taking thought man can intelligently control his environment for humanly useful ends.[1] But such an

[1] For example, he wrote near the end of the war that "The paramount question just now is, what to do to save the civilized nations from irretrievable disaster and what further may be accomplished by taking thought so that no similar epoch of calamities shall be put in train for the next generation"—*The Vested Interests*, p. 13. A similar sentiment runs through *An Inquiry into the Nature of Peace and the Terms of Its Perpetuation* (1917) and *The Engineers and the Price System* (1921). When regarded in a time sequence, Veblen's work appears to take on a less objective and more purposeful tone during the war, and, it may be surmised, as an emotional reaction to it.

outcome is not inevitable, since human behavior may be too strongly shaped by "imbecile institutions," to the detriment or destruction of civilization as we know it. One may read into Veblen a complete fatalism. Or one may find in him the lesson that we must understand our social institutions thoroughly, the more intelligently to control them for the common good. Since America is not temperamentally given to fatalism, it is probably in the latter sense that he is generally understood. But he falls sufficiently short of lucidity or frankness to give rise to something analogous to the Hegelian right and left.

The attitude of economists toward Veblen's work is marked by great diversity of opinion. In the opinion of some he has thoroughly demolished older types of theory and cleared the way for a new and truly scientific economics. Others feel that, without entirely discrediting the neo-classical methods, he has displayed their limitations and opened up new domains in which theorists may profitably employ their time. A third and more conservative group will admit only that he has stripped away some of the less essential parts of the older type of theory, and regard most of his work as not economic theory, whatever else it may be. One may learn a good deal about an economist's general habit of thought merely by his reaction to Veblen. And the wide variety of such reactions is sufficient evidence to the confusion which today exists, when the question of the scope and method of economics will elicit a most heterogeneous and uncrystallized set of answers.

On the whole, Veblen's followers are not greatly concerned over the future of economic theory. Anxiety on that score is more particularly reserved for the contemporary representatives of the classical tradition, who wish to see economic truth reduced to a logically articulated system of laws and principles. To those who work under the influence of Veblenian ideas, it appears not to be a defect that their tasks are of a varied and fragmentary character. Their aim is not a logical system, but a knowledge of the facts of economic life. And this they conceive themselves to be achieving by a gradual process of patient scientific investigation. It is a kind of work that can be done quite divorced from any scheme of systematic theory. It is somewhat a process of reducing Veblen's grandiose cosmic ideas to a bill of particulars. In short, Veblen's organon of thought is being applied to the study of the economic order in a wide range of ways which he did not himself envisage.

Even among those who read Veblen sympathetically there will be found little agreement concerning the relative importance of his various contributions to economic thought. Some will give precedence to his critical accomplishments; others to the evolutionary point of view; others to his genetic-historical treatment of institutions; others to his analysis of present-day economic institutions; and others, finally, to his introduction of a realistic psychology into economics. One is not called upon to choose between them here. In point of influence, the idea that economic life must be studied from the point of view of process, not of normality, would seem to have gained the widest currency, together with the related idea that a knowledge of the process is to be gained only through a realistic study of institutions and a realistic view of human nature.

Whatever may be the deficiencies of Veblen in the scientific rôle which he assumed, the effect of his work has been to stimulate some of the best scientific work of the present century in the field of the social sciences. Economists are engaged more exclusively in describing and interpreting the run of the facts. The "economic man" and competitive normality are in danger of obsolescence through disuse. Economic science is less committed to the discovery of hypothetical economic laws, and more committed to a realistic explanation of economic behavior and of the processes of the economic order. The most various factors have led to this change of direction. But no single individual has had a larger hand in it than Veblen.

We may now leave him in peace, remote and aloof in his Olympian privacy, whence may his stinging phrases continue to puncture our cherished illusions or to goad our lethargic minds.

Alfred Marshall

Alfred Marshall

I

DURING the generation that has passed since the appearance of his *Principles of Economics*, in 1890, Professor Alfred Marshall has occupied a position of practically undisputed preëminence among English-speaking economists. His name is linked reverently with the giants of the past, Adam Smith, Ricardo, and John Stuart Mill. Falling in more unregenerate days than Ricardo or Mill, his theoretical system has never been blessed with such general acceptance as theirs in their respective generations. The diverse approaches which have characterized the scientific study of economic life since 1870 have caused most of his system to fall foul of the doctrines of one economist or another. So far, however, as there is today any generally accepted body of economic doctrines, it is largely what Marshall made it. For a generation the more accredited economists have been largely engaged in modifying, interpreting, extending, and in general embroidering Marshall's economics. And even for the dissenters and nonconformists, Marshall has been very generally the point of departure. In a study of contemporary economic theory, he stands out as perhaps our most important figure. Though he is dead, his work still lives and flourishes.

Marshall came of good middle-class family, of modest means and pious habits, his father being employed as cashier at the Bank of England. The boy's early evidence of high mental faculties secured him a place in the Merchant Taylors School in London, where his education was largely in the classics. His interest, however, turned gradually in the direction of mathematics, so that upon completion of his secondary schooling he refused a classical scholarship at Oxford and turned to Cambridge and mathematics. Graduating in 1865 with high honors, he became a lecturer in mathematics, with the intention of pursuing his further studies in the field of physics. During his school and university period his intention had been eventually to take holy orders in the Anglican Church. Of devout evangelical parentage, his own religious feeling was strong and his mind intermittently turned to the thought of foreign missionary work as his proper field. From an early age, therefore, his mind was divided between religious and humanitarian zeal and a strong bent for abstract intellectual pursuits.

Marshall's associations at Cambridge after his graduation threw him into the society of a group of men interested in philosophical studies, a group which included T. H. Green, F. D. Maurice, W. K. Clifford, and Henry Sidgwick. Pursuing for the time this new philosophical interest, he became engrossed in Kant and a little later fell much under the influence of Hegel's philosophy of history. His mental confusion was much increased by contact with Darwin's *Origin of Species* and the works of the utilitarian philosophers. A mental crisis followed the impingement of these new ideas upon his established religious convictions. His interest in mathematical and physical science gave way to "a sudden rise of deep interest in the philosophical foundation of knowledge, especially in relation to theology," as he has himself recorded. Out of the confusion of this period there developed in Marshall's mind the attitude of intellectual agnosticism combined with a sort of religious humanitarianism so characteristic of the better minds of that disturbed generation.

Intellectually unsatisfied by the metaphysical and scientific studies that had undermined his theological preconceptions, he directed his attention to the field of social ethics. Much disturbed over the ethical justification of existing forms of social institutions, he came under the influence of Mill's economic writing, and of Bentham and Spencer. In the study of how the material lot of the common man might be lifted above the poverty and depravity which he saw about him, he found an outlet for his religious zeal, and his interest and attention swung sharply in that direction. It is possible to see, then, what manner of young man it was who ceased his mathematical lectures in 1868 and took up a new lectureship in the Moral Sciences, where his weight listed the ship sharply to the side of political economy. A brilliant mathematician, a young philosopher carrying a somewhat undigested load of German metaphysics, Utilitarianism, and Darwinism; a humanitarian with religious feelings but no creed, eager to lighten the burdens of mankind, but sobered by the barriers revealed to him by the Ricardian political economy—one sees the background of the man who was to be to his students sage and pastor as well as scientist; whose objective scientific approach was to give economics a renewed public standing; whose sympathy for social reform was to rout its enemies; whose high gifts were to be as zealously devoted to his intellectual mistress as any artist's to his muse.

Except for eight years, from 1877 to 1885, when he taught at Bristol and Oxford, Marshall's life was spent entirely at Cambridge. He held the professorship of political economy from 1885 until his retirement in 1908 and, until his death in 1924, continued his independent work in his old surroundings. One result of his work at Cambridge was to make it so far the superior center of economic training in England that, until the rise of the London School of Economics, it attracted for a generation a large proportion of the best brains of the country that contemplated economic studies. From the stream of his students have come most of the more brilliant writers on economics throughout the Kingdom. The result has been to create a Marshall tradition in England very strange to observers from distraught countries unblessed by such academic unanimity. Though his supremacy is perhaps not comparable to that of Mill during the 'fifties and 'sixties of the last century, one can hardly differ radically with Marshall in the circles where economic theory is taken seriously and still be regarded as thoroughly intelligent.

In addition to his duties as teacher, administrator, and writer, Marshall was frequently called upon for expert evidence before royal commissions, particularly in relation to problems of currency and fiscal policy. In government reports and in his numerous contributions to periodicals is to be found his best work in the field of current economic problems. As our attention is necessarily confined to the more general outlines of his theoretical system, it will be impossible to examine his methods or conclusions in regard to the problems upon which he prepared formal reports, but it may be briefly said that these documents stand as models, the envy and the despair of other economists charged with bringing a theoretical organon to bear upon problems of current policy.[1]

Marshall's books, unfortunately, do not round out

---

[1] The preceding biographical details have been mainly taken from Mr. J. M. Keynes' excellent article in *Memorials of Alfred Marshall,* edited by Professor A. C. Pigou. The same volume contains many of Marshall's shorter writings and letters. His documentary reports have been published under the title, *Official Papers of Alfred Marshall,* edited by Mr. J. M. Keynes.

in any systematic fashion the whole of his views.[1] His
work has been marred from first to last by his inability
to work to a preconceived plan and by his unwillingness
to publish anything until it was as perfect as he could
make it. The broad survey of economic life of which
the *Principles* was conceived to be the introductory
volume was never completed. The other volumes
came near the end of his life and are composed of
materials which he had been collecting for a lifetime.
Expanding as they did under his hands, much was
crowded out for which he would have wished a place,
and he was left at his death with the material for three
further studies he had intended to make on conditions
affecting employment, the economic functions of government, and the economic conditions of progress. It
remains true, however, that in the eyes of many the
Principles is the greatest text of economic theory that
has been written. It is in this volume that his genius
is best displayed and on it his reputation chiefly rests.
With it we shall be chiefly concerned, and with his other
writings only in so far as they throw light upon the
approach and the system there displayed.

To understand the direction taken by Marshall in
his theoretical work one must lay it against the background of the time in which it was shaping. His starting-point, as we have seen, was Mill's version of

---

[1] The books that embody the greater part of his life's work are
Principles of Economics (1890), *Industry and Trade* (1919), and
Money, Credit, and Commerce (1923). The *Principles* has been fre-
quently revised and is still a current text.

Ricardian political economy. This version was, of course, compounded of diverse elements. There was a cost-of-production theory of value based upon competitive action; a theory of distribution in which laws of wages, rent, and profits were arrived at by diverse principles; a background of hedonistic psychology and utilitarian ethics; and over it all an atmosphere of humanitarian sympathy which was no part of the theoretical system. The Malthusian theory of population added to the wages-fund theory indicated a future far from bright for the working classes, the effects of competition on profits were conceived to hold the capitalist-employer in check, and the landlord appeared to be residuary legatee of the benefits of industrial progress. The system was obviously not one of "economic harmonies," though it gave rise to harmonic variations in the hands of some of its interpreters. But so long as the postulates upon which it was based were unquestioned—the institutions of private property and free enterprise and the hedonistic postulate of rational self-interest—its doctrines carried at least the implication of being laws of nature.

At the time of Marshall's induction into economic studies, Ricardian economics was just upon the eve of its decline from the authoritative position which it had held for nearly half a century. Karl Marx was appealing to Ricardianism to support quite unorthodox conclusions. Mill foreswore the wages-fund theory. Jevons' version of Benthamism and exposition of a subjective theory of value undermined the accepted value theory and split the deductive economists into armed camps. The German historical school became known to English thinkers through Cliffe Leslie, and took issue with English economists along their entire front. The apologetics of Cairnes and Keynes revealed the abstract and hypothetical character of the science, and weakened more than they rehabilitated it. Walker's new wage theory added to the confusion and Arnold Toynbee's lectures gave a demonstration of the uses of the historical method. The evolutionary principle was casting doubt upon the mechanical analogies in which economic analysis was framed. Other less academic events were undermining the Ricardian structure. Labor organizations were growing in power, oblivious of the theoretical demonstrations of their futility. The progress of working-class numbers and prosperity placed the Malthusian theory of population under a cloud of doubt. The need for protective factory laws cast doubt upon the virtues of the policy of *laissez-faire*. Ricardo's long-run views concerning rents and profits were belied by events. In their travail of controversy the economists ceased to enjoy the confidence of statesmen, and their theories, or doctrines, or laws, by virtue of their mutual incompatibility, lost the prestige of general acceptability. Under this wave of events the Ricardian political economy was being submerged. And such was the situation during the twenty years before 1890 when Marshall was forging into shape the outlines of his system of economic theory.

Marshall started his career as an economist with some knowledge of economic theory in which the laws of value were the central problem, and with a technical knowledge of mathematics. It is natural, then, that his first phase should have been marked by the application of mathematical analysis to the laws of value. This mathematical bent was stimulated by the appearance of Jevons' *Theory of Political Economy* in 1871, in which Jevons used a mathematical equipment to overthrow the Ricardian cost theory of value and to substitute his own theory of final utility. Marshall, better versed in mathematical technique, had been working along somewhat similar lines, though to rather different ends. Under the influence of Cournot and von Thünen he had been experimenting in a mathematical way with final or marginal increments, and shares with Jevons the credit for that type of analysis.

Though interested in Jevons' method, he was not impressed by the facile manner in which economic science was converted into a mere mathematical application of the hedonistic calculus. He was much impressed by the complexity of actual economic life and felt that economic science must furnish a competent tool for dealing with concrete facts and problems. The theories of the German historical economists interested him, and the writings of the socialists found him a sympathetic reader. But his mind refused to accept the dogma of either, and he applied his most earnest efforts to studying, understanding, and interpreting the economic life of his time. As time went on he became more engrossed in economic history and the problems of economic organization which did not lend themselves to mathematical treatment. His mathematics had, however, assisted him in elaborating with much originality the theory of money and of foreign trade. His work in this field, though not published until 1923, was disseminated much earlier and furnished the starting-point for much of the work of later mathematical economists. In particular, however, his mathematics were of assistance in shaping his characteristic views as to value and distribution; and, no matter how heavily overlaid with illustrative material, his *Principles* bears the imprint of his early bent for "pure" theory.

II

There is the touch of novelty in the opening words of the *Principles:* "Political economy, or Economics, is a study of mankind in the ordinary business of life; it examines that part of individual and social action which is most closely connected with the attainment and with the use of the material requisites of well-being." [1] This is very different from Mill's definition, "the science of wealth," and shows the drift of Marshall's intention,

[1] *Principles of Economics*, p. 1. All references are to the eighth edition.

to develop a science of human behavior in society, so far as it is affected by economic environment and motives.

Two great sets of influences are conceived to have been the more important formative agencies in history, the economic and the religious. Of these, the economic influences, the daily tasks of making a living, have been .of the greater importance in shaping the existing institutions and modes of thought and action. The primary task of the economist, then, is to study the behavior of men within the bounds of the institutions under which they actually live. He must "collect facts, arrange and interpret them, and . . . draw inferences from them" in order "to reach thereby a knowledge of the interdependence of economic phenomena." [1] In this task it is useless to attempt the attainment of generalizations of universal validity. For institutions change and the behavior of men is shaped largely by the institutions under which they live. Economic generalizations, or laws, are thus mutable, applicable only under given conditions, and inevitably subject to modification with the passage of time.

Starting as he does with a historic sense of the changefulness of human institutions, Marshall suffers under no "delusions of grandeur" concerning the universality or permanence of any generalizations which the economist may discover. But if everything that economic theorists may do is to be swept down the current

[1] *Principles of Economics*, p. 29.

of obsolescence and into the sea of oblivion, any excuse
for their existence may appear dubitable. It does not
so appear to him. For the purpose of economic studies
is twofold: first, to satisfy the desire for knowledge for
its own sake; and second, to throw light upon the social
problems of the present, to discover the foundations
of their solution, and to furnish guidance for the intelligent control of the forces of change. Bertrand
Russell has somewhere said that the one divine attribute
of man is his desire to know, and Veblen has stamped
his approval upon the spirit of "idle curiosity" as the
proper state of mind for the scientist. It is not so with
Marshall. He does desire to understand economic organization and processes, but for a purpose. There remains in him some remnant of the young missionary
who would show the light to the heathen, so that he
could write, "the dominant aim of economics in the
present generation is to contribute to a solution of social
problems." [1]

The practical character of his aims is indicated by
his enumeration of the questions to which economists
must address themselves, which will be given in abbreviated form.[2] Of a general character there are these:
What are the causes affecting the consumption, production, distribution, and exchange of wealth; the organization of industry and trade; the money market; wholesale and retail dealing; foreign trade; the relations of

[1] *Principles of Economics,* p. 42, margin.
[2] See *Ibid.,* pp. 40-42.

employers and employed? How are all these related
and what are their ultimate tendencies? How far does
price measure desirability? How far does increase of
the wealth of any class promote general well-being?
How far is industrial efficiency impaired by the inadequate income of any class? How complete is economic
freedom in any place, rank of society, or branch of industry? Does economic freedom tend to produce
monopolies? How will various classes be affected by
the operation of economic freedom, mediately and ultimately? What will be the burden and incidence of any
system of taxes? Such are the general questions that
the economist must attempt to answer.

His work, however, is animated by the desire to assist
in the solution of more specific problems by furnishing
the information upon which an intelligent solution may
be based: How may we increase the good and diminish
the evil under economic freedom, and how far can we
eliminate injustice? Is a limitation of the rights of
property and free enterprise advisable in the interest
of more equal distribution of wealth? Would such
limitation decrease the aggregate of wealth? Could
wealth be more largely distributed to the poor and their
labor lightened without stifling the progress of industry? How ought the burdens of taxation to be distributed? Are existing forms of division of labor satisfactory? Must large classes of people be occupied at
unelevating work? Is a system of coöperative industry
feasible? What are the proper limitations upon the

economic activity of individuals, groups, and states? Are existing rights of property necessary? Are prevailing methods of using wealth justifiable? Can social opinion exert adequate control over individual action in lieu of a dubitably successful intervention of government? Are the duties of nations like those of individuals in economic matters?

Such questions indicate how Marshall's mind ran from "what is" to "what ought to be." It has seemed advisable to introduce them at some length. For Marshall is attempting to construct an organon of thought applicable to economic problems of all kinds, to lay bare the deeper foundations of economic and social progress. No estimate of what he does is possible without a knowledge of what he essays to do. His first task is to make clear the character of the forces that are at work in the current economic organization of society.

In the contemporary world Marshall conceives the most fundamental characteristic of economic life to be *Economic Freedom*, or *Free Enterprise*. The connotation of these terms he thinks preferable to *Competition*, since they carry more the sense of independence, deliberate choice, and forethought in human affairs, and less the evil savor of deliberate selfishness which has grown up about the latter term.[1] No ethical connotations are to be read into the terms. Indeed, he considers the evils which accompanied the Industrial

---

[1] In spite of this preliminary distinction, Marshall drifts into the indiscriminate use of *competition* and *economic freedom*.

Revolution and contemporary industrial abuses too patent to permit anyone to suppose that economic freedom involves any automatic or natural check upon the distressing results of the operation of the baser side of human nature. A conceivably better society would result if people were inclined to engage in "unselfish work for the public good." But economic activity is commonly self-regarding and "in the responsible conduct of affairs, it is worse than folly to ignore the imperfections which still cling to human nature."[1] From the start it is obvious that we are to be treated to no system of economic harmonies. Elsewhere Marshall has written, "There is no general economic principle which supports the notion that industry will necessarily flourish best or that life will be happiest and healthiest, when each man is allowed to manage his own concerns as he thinks best."[2]

In seeking to discern uniformities of human behavior, some recourse must be had to the motives upon which men act. There are, Marshall concedes, a variety of motives to human action, and love, hatred, avarice, or fear beget their destined results. It is, indeed, this variety of motives that complicates the task of the economist, for he "deals with the ever-changing and subtle forces of human nature."[3] So far, however, as economic motives do not lend themselves to measurement, they escape from scientific treatment. The su-

[1] *Principles of Economics*, p. 9.
[2] *Industry and Trade*, p. 736.
[3] *Principles of Economics*, p. 14.

preme difficulty of the economist, as scientist, is to reduce motives to some common denominator of measurement. Marshall, in facing this difficulty, perceives
that there is one large group of motives, in fact the pre-
dominant group, which can be tamed to his hand. That
is the group of steady motives which can be measured
in terms of money. Since so large a part of the life of
man centers about the pursuit of a livelihood or of gain,
his motives and incentives in that direction must be in
some degree reducible to the common denominator of
economic activity, money. Thus, as economic scientist,
one must for the most part make abstractions of those
aspects of life into which money does not enter.

Within the field thus chosen, Marshall thinks a certain scientific accuracy may be hoped for. What one
may expect, at least, to find is the direction which human activity will tend to take under the play of forces
that operate in a variable and interdependent price system. Economic science is incomparable to the physical
sciences due to the less tangible character of its data,
the less explicit character of its generalizations, and
the larger margin of error, due to neglected causes of
action, which must be corrected before it is applicable
to the solution of concrete problems. It has, however,
an advantage over other social sciences. For the steady
motives measurable in money constitute a body of data
that can be worked with relative scientific accuracy. It
is this fact that justifies making of economics a separate
field of scientific study.

The starting-point, then, is human motives as proximately reflected in their money measurements—that is, in the price system. Marshall dissociates himself from the Utilitarian idea that motives are capable of direct measurement. He deplores the tendency of economists to talk in terms of pleasure and pain as ultimates, discards the notion that "utility" is directly measurable, and in particular objects to the loading of a hedonistic system of ethics upon the back of economic analysis. The effort to approach his work unimpeded by any philosophical bias is apparent. It will be necessary at a later point to examine the degree to which this attempt is successful.

No attempt is made to give a simple explanation of human nature, and the self-regarding, ratiocinating "economic man" is definitely disavowed. It is considered, indeed, a matter of relative unimportance why a particular individual comes into the market, whether from avarice, love of comfort, family affection, social pride, or philanthropy. For the economist is concerned in particular with the study of society in the large, and with the actions of the individual only in so far as they affect the larger problems of group life. When, indeed, one looks at individuals alone, measurement of motives by money is rendered practically hopeless by the fact that money possesses a different value for different individuals, due principally to the inequality in the distribution of wealth and income. "But in fact economists, like all other students of social science, are concerned with individuals chiefly as members of the social organism." [1] Economic measurements are thus group measurements, and the groups are presumably of sufficient size and cut across differences of income with sufficient regularity to give some degree of validity to a scientific treatment of them in pecuniary terms.

Marshall makes no attempt to give any clarity to his conception of the "social organism." He nowhere elaborates the biological analogy. He does not, like Professor Clark, boldly proclaim a harmonious functioning of the parts of this mythical being. But, in a somewhat disembodied and transcendental state, the concept of the social whole broods over the scene. It is, however, upon the parts, not the whole, that the limelight is thrown, upon the major groups into which men are divided as functioning members of a producing organization. And behind the groups lie the hosts of individuals in indistinct perspective; their habits and passions largely obliterated; exposed to view principally with regard to their acquisitive motives alone, and so far as their goods or services are for sale for a price; not, Marshall tells us, "economic men," but certainly men obscured except as to their acquisitive characteristics.

The analysis thus starts with a set of institutions epitomized as free enterprise. It runs forward from the motives of individuals to the constitution of producing and income-receiving groups. It runs backward

[1] *Principles of Economics*, p. 25.

from the groups to the lives and fortunes of individuals. It attempts to uncover the relations and interactions of human forces which determine the goods to be produced, the prices of those goods, the organization under which they are produced, and the rewards to producers considered as members of groups or classes. Obviously, there is no novelty as to scope. As two generations of economists had been doing, he is seeking for the laws of value and distribution. The novelty lies in the thoroughness with which a scientific technique is brought to bear on the problem, in the wider sweep of imagination over the forces at work, in the thoroughness of the investigation, and in the humble tentativeness of his conclusions.

Marshall is concerned that his analysis of economic forces shall be scientific. What has been said will reveal his personal preconceptions concerning the nature of scientific investigation. Its function, as he sees it, is to disclose the regularities which run through the phenomena examined. He is, therefore, foresworn to find regularities in economic activity. The regular action of forces, he thinks, can be discerned only where the forces are measurable. In economic affairs there is only one standard of measurement, money. He therefore at the outset confines himself to the examination of such economic forces as are reducible to money measurement. He thus in effect limits the *scientific* investigation of economic life to the study of prices. Admitting the importance of the less ponderable and measurable aspects of life bearing upon the economic situation, he may not permit them to intrude into his scientific conclusions except in so far as they demonstrably affect prices.

In taking this view of science he is plainly influenced by the customary nineteenth-century view of physical scientists, that the function of the scientist is to reduce the world to law and order. He is too sophisticated to attempt to reduce economic phenomena to terms of mechanics. His knowledge of economic history, his acceptance of the evolutionary viewpoint, and his knowledge of human life in general debar him from approaching his problem so simply. But it must still be admitted that the concepts of physics and mechanics rather than those of biology are the ones that most affect his viewpoint and method as he approaches the scientific investigation of economic phenomena.

Beside his scientific preconception, the influence which undoubtedly affects his work in the greatest degree is his respect for the work of the economists who had preceded him, particularly that of Ricardo and Mill. He has not their confidence in the universality of the doctrines he expounds. He conceives his work to be an analysis of the forces at work at the particular time at which he lives and under the particular circumstances which obtain in the Western World. His central problems are nevertheless derived from them and his method is a refinement of theirs.

With his attention centered on the price problem and

his aim defined as the establishment of regularities, his task takes the form of establishing the *normal* action of the forces which fix prices. Normality, he is careful to point out, is a concept which has no meaning except in relation to a given set of circumstances. It connotes for him no sense of universality, no derivation from immutable laws of nature. Those things are normal which may be expected to flow from a given situation, under given conditions, and under the impulse of given forces. He is then faced with the necessity of defining the conditions upon which his view of normality is based.

The problem of defining these conditions in the midst of the changefulness of human affairs he finds most harassing. Keenly aware of the rapidity of change in the field of industry, he is averse to reasoning upon assumptions of a static condition. But to reach any theoretical conclusions at all, in the absence of experimental facilities, he is compelled to use assumptions of some sort and to engage in some deductive reasoning. His dilemma arises out of the two major aspects of his mind, the historic sense of change and the scientist's desire to uncover regularities. The resulting method is a compromise. He conducts his argument on the basis of a modified static state, in which change is going on, but no change of sufficient force to upset the validity of his general assumptions. For example, capital (the productive wealth of society, excluding land) and population are permitted to increase, but at approximately the same rate. Business enterprises grow and decay, but in a regular sort of way which reveals certain firms as "representative." Forms of business organization may change, but there are to be no revolutionary changes in technique. We are, in short, to be led warily through a quasi-static, or a steadily progressive world, as close to the real world as the necessities of deductive reasoning permit, as far from it as they demand.

It is of some considerable importance to secure a firm grasp upon Marshall's position at this point. It is extremely slippery and elusive. He is frankly skeptical of the value of reasoning from static assumptions to their foreordained conclusions. The world envisaged is too unreal and the conclusions too simple. "In this (the real) world, therefore, every plain and simple doctrine as to the relations between cost of production, demand, and value is necessarily false; and the greater the appearance of lucidity which is given to it by skillful exposition, the more mischievous it is." [1] With so simple but sweeping a gesture he knocks such static systems as Clark's into a cocked hat. His avowed use for static analysis is not to disclose static laws, but purely as a method of approach. He conceives that the operation of one force at a time can be viewed while other forces are impounded for the time being in *cæteris paribus*. The separate examination of the normal action of various forces in a static environment will, it is presumed, place us in a position to discern the central forces at

---

[1] *Principles of Economics*, p. 368.

work amid the complicated and changeful phenomena of the real world.

The task undertaken in the *Principles* is principally "qualitative analysis" of this sort—that is to say, analysis of the kind of forces at work in economic life. Marshall conceives that such analysis will form the basis for later "quantitative analysis," by statistical methods, of the relative strength and importance of the various forces at work. But he does not stop with the isolation of forces. The main argument of the *Principles* consists of a consummately conceived combination of forces designed to show how prices would be adjusted in the long run, were the forces to operate under conditions sufficiently stable to permit them to achieve their destined results. The analysis does not, therefore, pretend to make a complete contact with reality, since "this volume is concerned mainly with normal conditions; and these are sometimes described as Statical." [1]

And in the course of his argument he has reference constantly to fairly definite postulates upon which his reasoning is based. One hesitates to construct a list of the premises of his theory, since they are not in every case openly avowed. Moreover, he does not hesitate to shift or amend them in order to bring out the various aspects of whatever problem he is engaged in examining. The following are, however, suggested as his basic assumptions: (1) Property rights remain approximately in their present position. (2) Freedom

[1] *Principles of Economics*, p. 366, note.

of enterprise, or competition, continues to be the pre-dominant aspect of economic organization. (3) No marked innovations in technique or organization occur. (4) Capital and population increase slowly and at relatively the same rate, and both are mobile, though slowly, in response to the stimulus of increased gain. (5) Economic activity is motivated by the pursuit of happiness through the satisfaction of human wants, and is limited by the growing distastefulness of continued labor; and conduct in general is predicated upon a reasonably consistent pursuit of economic gain. (6) Buyers and sellers are reasonably well informed concerning the state of the market, present and prospective, and neither are hampered by an appreciable inequality in their bargaining power.

The most that can be said is that these postulates serve as the foundation for whatever part of Marshall's economics takes systematic form. And that is the part with which we shall mainly concern ourselves. They run like a thread through the shining beads of apt and realistic illustration. Whatever is pictured as normal grows out of them. Whatever broad principles are developed are their offspring. If our interpretation is correct, Marshall's theoretical structure is thus of a quasi-static character. It is applicable to the real world to the extent that its assumptions represent the true state of affairs. The central argument develops the laws of value and distribution out of the action of economic forces under conditions that are normal by definition. There is then woven into the fabric of the argument a discussion of the immeasurable forces of change which limit or nullify the action of those forces. It is suggested that, to understand Marshall properly, a very close eye must be kept upon what is the central argument, what is illustration, and what is limitation.

This somewhat extended account of Marshall's problem, preconceptions, and method has seemed essential to a proper understanding of his exposition of economic doctrines. Our attention will now be centered upon the coherent or systematic parts of his work, somewhat to the neglect of the illuminating excursions which he makes into problems of the day. Any brief treatment of his theory incurs the risk of attributing to him views more precise, categorical, or dogmatic than he would care to assent to. One may only hope to avoid any gross misrepresentation, since it will be impossible to do justice to the qualifications and modifications with which his broader conclusions are overlaid.

III

It may facilitate the further exposition of Marshall's economic scheme of things to state in advance his central position. The heart of his theoretical scheme is found in the theory of value, as set forth in Book V of the *Principles*. In the earlier parts of the volume he is working up to this, and in the later parts away from it, by way of applying the laws of value to the distribution of income. The values of things are conceived to be purely relative, expressing the ratios which they bear to one another under the process of exchange. The modern system of marketing causes values to be expressed as money prices and it is with these that the analysis is mainly concerned. Prices are fixed by the play of the forces of demand and supply. The tendency of prices is toward a point of stable equilibrium between demand and supply. At such a point of equilibrium prices coincide with the cost of production, and any deviation from this normal price sets in motion forces to restore it. Day to day market prices are affected by a variety of influences which cause them to vary from the normal prices, but their tendency is to oscillate about them. Normal prices are thus the result of influences operating over a relatively long period of time.

In Marshall's opinion, recourse to the mere phrase, demand and supply, throws no light on the value problem. The explanation of values is to be found only by explaining the long-run forces which determine the demand and the supply, respectively. The operation of these forces must be displayed by the method of deductive reasoning, since the economist is debarred from the scientific methods of isolation and experimentation. The results are valid only in so far as they proceed from premises that correspond to conditions in the real world, and of necessity all general laws of value are applicable to particular cases only by allowance for a margin of error due to causes not allowed for in the general reasoning.

The theory of distribution is an application of the laws of value to particular classes of phenomena. The incomes which are received by various classes of people, when viewed from a certain angle, are the prices paid by business men for the use of the various factors of production. The prices of the factors of production are controlled, like the prices of commodities, by the play of demand and supply. And a true understanding of distributive shares that accrue to the members of various producing classes is dependent upon an extended view of the long-run forces which govern the demand for and the supply of the various factors of production. Marshall is thus seen to be attempting to establish a fundamental unity throughout the sphere of economic life. He is displaying groups of attractive and repellent forces, whose normal action under competitive conditions will result in a sort of solar system of counterpoise and balance, marked by a "fundamental symmetry."

The system thus displayed is advanced neither as good nor as inevitable, but merely as the normal result of economic freedom under relatively stable conditions. In human affairs, the conditions may be modified and the results changed by combined action of groups or of the state, and the normal tendencies under economic freedom exist by no indefeasible laws of nature nor by dictates of natural justice. With so brief an indication of the direction of the argument, we may examine it more in detail.

The aim and end of economic production is, Marshall conceives, to satisfy the wants of people, viewed as consumers. There is, however, no simple explanation of wants. Once the elementary demand for the necessities of life is satisfied, wants are aroused by the nature of one's work and by a multitude of social relationships, so complicated as to elude analysis. Since wants are so dependent upon activities, it is absurd to make a theory of consumption the scientific basis of economics, as some economists have attempted. On the other hand, the demand for goods for consumption is so vital a part of the economic process that it requires to be carefully examined.

The power of goods to satisfy wants may be expressed by the term "utility." The term labors under the disability of having to do service both for the anticipation which stirs to activity and for the satisfaction which results from it. But a rough equivalence may be assumed between the anticipated and realized satisfaction. For individuals at a given time, the utility of a thing diminishes with any increase in the stock of it. In other words, the primary law of demand is the familiar law of diminishing utility. The individual is conceived to carry in his mind a schedule of demand prices, running to lower figures as the number of units increases. The actual income available for expenditure, together with differences of taste, will cause different individuals to have different demand schedules. Any one individual will attempt to allot his demands in such a way as to keep the marginal expenditure for his entire range of purchases in some sort of balance. But since utility is not directly measurable and since human beings are not divinely rational, it cannot be assumed that individual incomes are so spent as to procure their possessors the maximum possible satisfaction. There seems, indeed, to be a tendency in that direction, but for purposes of scientific analysis it is futile to try to go behind the patent fact of what is offered in terms of money to some putative absolute standard of utility. The purchaser is, of course, faced by the antecedent existence of a system of prices, so that individual demand schedules operate consciously only in the immediate neighborhood of established prices. On the side of demand, the strategic parties in the adjustment of prices are those persons who are contemplating marginal purchases in the region of the existing price.

The analysis of the demands of individuals leads to the general market rule that "the amount demanded increases with a fall in price" and diminishes with a rise in price. Assuming the existence of a going price before one has explained it, the most that can be said is that "the price will measure the marginal utility of the commodity to each purchaser individually." [1] There is no warrant for the notion that a price expresses the marginal utility of a thing to society, as Jevons, and

---

[1] *Principles of Economics*, p. 100.

later Clark, would have it. This, in Marshall's view, involves an acceptance of a hedonistic philosophy and a view of society unwarranted in any scientific view of economic relations.

The demand analysis of the marginal utility school of economists is thus followed with some qualifications up to the fatal point at which they attempt to leap the yawning chasm between the individual and society. To Marshall, that transition means departing from a solid world of reality into the speculative bogs of metaphysics. For economists after Jevons, the decision as to whether there is or is not such a thing as social marginal utility was a crucial point. The controversy that raged over this article of faith doubtless lives still in the minds of our elders. The "nays" have had it their way for the most part, though the idea may occasionally be encountered in popular manuals, usually in a mutilated or sterilized form. The controversy was not without importance, since the opposed views lay back of two diverse approaches to social policy. For the logical outgrowth, as perceived in Clark, of the concept of social marginal utility was a thoroughgoing defense of the competitive system and a public policy directed to the maintenance of that system; while its denial withdrew the chief latter-day theoretical prop of economic "harmonics" and necessitated a search for a basis of public policy toward business on grounds less doctrinaire and more pragmatic. The action of Marshall in ranging himself with the dissenters must rank as perhaps the major blow to the application of marginal utility analysis to the social whole. And it would appear that it placed economic analysis more firmly on a realistic basis, though destroying some of the pleasure of the metaphysically minded.

The analysis of demand along lines of diminishing and marginal utility appears to Marshall an illuminating method when dealing with a narrow range of time. He finds it disappointing, however, not to say useless, when searching for some scientific mechanism for the prediction of demand. The element of time frustrates him at this point, as we shall see it harrowing his scientific efforts elsewhere. Wants he sees to be elastic in relation to price. The responsiveness of demand to a rise or fall in price is part of the general law of demand. But the complicating factors are the uncertain degree of responsiveness and the uncertain direction of future demand. Statistical analysis can demonstrate to some extent the effect of price changes on demand in the past. But even here it is impossible to allow for all influences on demand outside of price changes. Nor can the effects of a change of price of one commodity upon the demand for others be at all accurately measured. Elasticity differs for every commodity and for every class of consumers. So that a proper interpretation of elasticity in the past is almost as difficult as predicting it for the future. But were one fairly sure about the past, the prediction of future demand faces certain fundamental difficulties. Changes of all sorts, in the value of money, in general prosperity, in taste or fashion, in character of products, and the like make the prediction of consumer demand over any extended period of time most difficult. Such difficulties as these, and many others, Marshall parades before the eye; not with any counsel of despair, but with the warning that, until our statistical information is much improved, demand will defy scientific treatment. Here, as elsewhere, he illustrates his characteristic of never glossing over difficulties, but of always displaying his limitations.

It is apparent to Marshall that he has made but little headway toward a scientific study of demand. He leaves that as a field for statistical investigation in the future. The result of this incorrigibility of demand data is that most of the subsequent analysis is confined to the study of supply. It is easy to see why this should be so. Demand takes one at once into the presence of human wants, which have ever played a game of blind man's buff with economists; unless, indeed, they are prepared to make assumptions so abstract and sweeping as those of Clark. Supply, on the other hand, leads into the field of money-costs which can be grappled with. And, if human elements are as important in the field of business enterprise as elsewhere, they can at least be laid at one side with more grace, and attention fixed more immediately upon less slippery data.

Marshall thinks it obvious that if one is looking for a mere explanation of "market-prices" at any given time, the answer is simple. When a supply of goods is actually in existence or "in sight," the price will be such as to remove the whole supply from the market, and, assuming a body of buyers and sellers well posted on the situation, a single price will rule for all units of the stock. In this case, supply is the passive factor and the state of demand the active factor in fixing the price. It is merely a question of how low the price will have to go to bring into the market enough buyers to carry off the whole available stock of goods.

When, however, economic activity is viewed as a process extending over a period of time, the supply of goods must be regarded, not as a *stock*, but as a *flow* of goods. An adequate economic analysis must explain the forces regulating this flow. As the flow extends over an indefinite period of time and as time introduces elements of change, the most difficult part of price analysis lies in coping with the element of time. Marshall attempts to tame this element by analyzing prices in relation to three periods of time: (1) short periods, in which the existing productive capacity undergoes no change; (2) long periods, of sufficient length to permit the production and use of a new supply of the factors of production; (3) very long periods, in which the secular trend of prices is affected by long-time changes in population, capital, technique, wants, and the like. Attention is concentrated upon the second of these, and the main argument of the *Principles* is devoted to interpreting and limiting the doctrine that, in *the long run*, price corresponds to the cost of production. The search, then, is primarily for the "normal" elements of cost which enter into the "normal" long-run price.

Before entering into that, however, it will be well to look into prices as determined in short periods. Production under modern conditions does not run smoothly, due principally to the disturbing influence of the credit system upon prices. During periods of industrial activity, assuming a fixed stock of appliances and labor, increased output will probably proceed at increased cost. But at the same time traders' demand is liable to increase because of advancing prices, without regard to the more remote effects of advancing prices upon consumers' demand. On the other hand, in periods of slack business, the desires of business men to cover some part of their fixed charges may lead them to produce goods at prices insufficient to cover both prime and supplementary costs. The result is that, looking at the flow of goods in short periods only, prices may be much greater or much less than the costs of production. Demand is the more active influence in fixing prices, while the bottom limit is fixed by prime costs. Even in the slackest periods, however, prices will seldom reach the level of prime costs, since the distaste of business men for "spoiling the market" will cause them voluntarily to limit production with the effect of bolstering up prices. Looking at short periods, then, it can be said that prices represent an unstable equilibrium of demand and supply; that demand is the more active factor; and that supply has little reference to costs of production. The phenomena that Marshall treats in relation to short periods are largely based upon changes in the purchasing power of money due to cyclical fluctuations of business. But, as he has determined largely to exclude that range of phenomena from his introductory treatment of economic activity, the analysis is not carried far.

Upon his analysis of the conditions which determine the supply of commodities over a period of time, Marshall lavishes great care. The analysis is not one that can be reduced to simple terms, and only its broader aspects can be examined here. Production of commodities proceeds upon the incentive of prospective gain from supplying them to the market. Consequently, they will only be permanently produced where the prospective price is sufficient to cover the costs to the *entrepreneur*, including a gain to himself sufficient to stimulate his activity. Whatever the vagaries of prices in short periods, in the long run prices must compensate all costs, both prime and supplementary.

Costs, however, vary according to the amount of a commodity produced. And many different enterprises are engaged in producing the same commodity. This latter difficulty Marshall tames to his scheme of normality by assuming that there is a normally efficient form of enterprise for producing any given commodity, and that the normal assiduity of *entrepreneurs* in pursuit of gain will cause the bulk of production to fall into the hands of enterprises of this "representative" sort. While some firms will be producing at greater and some at less cost than the representative firm, it is presumed that the costs of the latter are the significant factor in fixing the price at which goods will be offered for sale.

For purposes of establishing the nature of the equilibrium of demand and supply, Marshall has tentatively to assume a quiescent situation—that is to say, a continuing stability of the conditions of demand and supply. The problem of the variance of costs in the face of differing amounts is thus for the time being eliminated from the problem. Under these conditions there will be found to be a certain demand for any particular commodity at any stated price. At the same time there will be a potential supply of goods which will be produced at any given price. In other words, there will be demand schedules and supply schedules, which can be graphically expressed as demand curves and supply curves. Under the assumption that at some point unit cost increases with increase of supply, there must mathematically be a point at which these curves cut each other. In other words, there must be a point at which, under all the given conditions, the amount demanded and the amount offered are equal.

Marshall presents this position as one of stable equilibrium. For any change of price will set in motion forces tending to restore the price fixed. An upward movement will cut off some demand, make the supply

redundant, and lead to a lowering of price. A downward movement will cut off some supply, stimulate
bidding, and raise the price. As has been explicitly
stated, Marshall's analysis to this point applies only
to a quiescent situation. This situation he creates in
order to make perfectly clear the nature of stable
equilibrium. It is not conceived as a realistic portrayal
of the pricing process, but as a demonstration of the
forces at work. It is particularly designed to demonstrate the intimate relation between demand, price, and
supply, and to make plain the idea that, while prices
in the stated situation are cost prices, what cost prices
will be, depends upon the amount produced, and that
in turn depends upon the amount demanded, which
in turn depends upon the prices at which any particular
volume can be supplied. In other words, the factors
in the situation are mutually determining one another.

The price representing this equilibrium is the normal price in the sense that it is the one which would
be established if the existing conditions remained sufficiently stable to permit it to be reached. Marshall,
however, after carefully dealing with normal equilibrium statically, admits the forces of change into the
picture. Changes affecting either demand or supply
will, of course, change the equilibrium amounts and
prices. The normal equilibrium price to which actual
prices tend is consequently a changing amount, moving
with the shifting point of equilibrium.

In attempting to apply this conception to the actual

world of affairs, Marshall is compelled to assume that changes are sufficiently gradual to permit actual prices to approximate the normal prices. Otherwise it would be impossible to say that actual prices oscillate about them, and the idea of normal price would retain only a metaphysical interest for anyone. The most obvious question that arises is whether under modern conditions such stability can be assumed as an essential part of a theory of prices. Other questions, of course, arise concerning the reality of such conceptions as demand and supply schedules. And a little later it will be necessary to ask whether costs are of such a character as to permit them to be treated as normal constituents of prices.

It is plain that what are costs to business men are incomes from the point of view of the recipients. The theory of normal price, therefore, demands a theory of normal incomes. The search for an explanation of commodity prices thus leads step by step back to the normal prices of the various factors of production. When that has been done the laws of interest, wages, profits, and rent will have emerged, and the whole process of distribution will have been subsumed under the theory of value. The examination of this further extension of the theory may be postponed while the intricacies of value theory are further explored.

Assuming the validity of the demonstration that the forces of supply and demand tend to meet at a point of stable equilibrium, it is obviously at this point that

the process of price changes can be best observed.
Here one finds in delicate counterpoise three factors—
demand, supply, price. Any change in any one of
these will affect the others, as moving one of three
marbles in the bottom of a bowl will move the other
two. It is at this point, marginal for both demand and
supply, that Marshall examines the principle of substitution. At the margin the least keen wants are
brought to bear upon the price. Wants of this class
are most liable to shift, and any shifting of demand
at the margin affects the price and the supply. On the
other hand, at the margin is expressed the lowest price
at which "representative" firms are induced to bring
into the market a given aggregate of any commodity.
Whether the amount demanded be great or small, the
force of competition will tend to enlarge supply up
to the point where there is no further financial incentive
to production. Cost price will change with different
aggregates of production, so that the state of demand
is always influencing the cost price at which goods can
be supplied.

There is always an incentive to individual firms to
keep their costs as low as possible. Consequently, business enterprise will be constantly on the alert to combine
the factors of production in the most efficient manner.
The principle of substitution will cause the various
agents to be applied up to a margin of indifference,
as between the use of a little more of one agent or
another. Consequently, any agent of production will

be valued by a business man in relation to the efficiency of the last units used in adding to the value of his total product. This brings Marshall within speaking distance of a marginal productivity theory of distribution. But he is careful not to commit himself to such a doctrine. The income of various classes of factors is regarded as tending to equal the value-product of marginal units of each class, but this fact has no causal significance. "Marginal uses and costs do not govern value, but are governed, together with value, by the general relations of demand and supply."[1] Productivity at the margin is not the cause of anything, but the effect of wider market forces.

Marshall's most careful and extended analysis is applied to establishing the theory of equilibrium price for single commodities. He was no doubt impelled to emphasize this part of his analysis through the controversies which were so keenly fought, during the years of its growth, between the marginal utility and cost theories of value. It was his eclectic treatment which, in England at least, effectually ended that controversy.

He does not, however, stop with this analysis of separate prices. Working with his favorite device of marginal units, he proceeds to develop the intricate way in which the demand for different commodities is related. And he develops much more fully the way in which, under competitive conditions, the supply of

[1] *Principles of Economics*, p. 410.

various kinds of goods is regulated by the alternative uses to which the factors of production might be put. When this complicated analysis is complete, the result emerges that not only is there an equilibrium for the price of each commodity, but that the whole economic process tends to a state of equilibrium. The careful examination by consumers of their wants, and by *entrepreneurs* of their costs, and the gravitation of the various factors of production into the most gainful occupation insure a situation so delicately integrated that a change in any one place sends its reverberations throughout the entire economic system and sets in motion forces to readjust the equilibrium.

If one were to go no deeper than monetary expressions, this situation would represent a wholly circular concatenation of phenomena, prices being compounded out of costs and costs themselves being prices. Marshall, however, breaks the circle by appealing to the "real" forces underlying what may be called the solar equilibrium of the whole economic system. These real forces are conceived to be, on the one hand, the human motive of the desire for the utilities contained in goods and, on the other hand, the motive of distaste for labor, as related to the existing technology and the existing material resources. The whole complicated balance or counterpoise in which the price system is held is conceived to be based fundamentally upon the action of these "real" forces. Marshall thus comes back to his starting-point—that is to say, that economic analysis is an examination of the operation of human motives, so far as they are scientifically measurable in monetary terms.

Plainly, the motives which he considers ultimate are of a very simple sort, and of a distinctly hedonistic complexion. And the process of price-making, as he displays it, is no less obviously dependent upon a very thoroughgoing pursuit of monetary gain under highly competitive conditions. It is this persistent tracing of human activity back to the desire for consumption, limited ultimately by the irksomeness of labor, that lends force to the impression that Marshall did not succeed in avoiding a hedonistic type of value theory, however strongly and explicitly he may have avowed his freedom. It appears to be only the ethics, not the theory of human motivation of hedonism that he succeeded in avoiding.

In so brief an exposition of the theory of value, its details and ramifications have had to be neglected. Two or three further aspects of it must be noted before the theory of distribution is taken up. In the first place, Marshall notes that the long-run trend of normal price will differ radically for different commodities, with quite diverse social results. It may properly be assumed that the trend of affairs is toward increasing population, increasing accumulated wealth, increasing production. In this situation, the trend of normal prices will depend largely upon the way in which larger production affects the costs of production. In agriculture, in old countries, the law of diminishing returns will cause an upward price tendency for products of the land, in the absence of offsetting influences in the shape of improved methods or the opening of new lands in other countries. Over a wide range of industries, however, increased production will induce great economies in the way of improved transportation facilities and the like. Consequently, while the short-run effect of increased demand is sure to be higher prices, its long-run effect in many instances will be lower prices. To some extent the economies of improved organization will be offset by the increasing cost of products derived from the land, and no general rule is devisable to cover price trends in general. It is a matter for investigation of the forces affecting the trend of prices for each commodity severally.

The fact that long-run price trends run in diverging directions is adduced as an argument against the doctrine that competitive prices afford a maximum of satisfaction to the community. Government bounties, for example, on commodities responding to the law of increasing returns might decrease prices and benefit consumers far more than they cost the state. Adding this to the fact that equal sums of money represent unequal utility to different persons, Marshall effectively demolishes the *prima-facie* case for an unregulated competitive system.

A further possible consequence of the action of increasing returns due to internal economics is that economic freedom may lead to the concentration of an industry into a few large establishments which can combine to exercise monopolistic control. Marshall admits this possibility and in a later volume[1] undertakes to see how far it has proceeded in modern life. Where this condition arises, his theory of normal prices is patently inapplicable. He sketches the outlines of a theory of monopoly value, and raises some questions of public policy in relation to monopolies. This digression into the field of monopoly is not permitted, however, to unseat normal value from its primacy. The primary assumption of competition is buttressed by an extended analysis of marketing conditions, leading to the conclusion that competition is unlikely to be widely displaced by monopolistic combinations. So far as monopoly is inevitable, it represents an aspect of the development of society not amenable to any laws arrived at by his present quasi-statical method of analysis.

Turning to another aspect of value, Marshall looks at the consequences to the consumer of the manner in which prices are determined. If demand schedules are based upon the law of diminishing utility and prices arise out of the influence of these aggregated demand schedules in relation to supply, the utility of a commodity to all except those just induced to buy is something more than the price paid for it. This constitutes a consumers' surplus, and if one could get a statistical display of demand schedules, its money amount might

[1] *Industry and Trade*, Book III.

be determined. Marshall here runs very close to the
Jevonian idea that utility is a measurable quantity. He
handles the notion very gingerly and deftly, however.
He permits its operation to commence only from a
base line of the necessities of life, and permits it to be
applied only to one thing at one time and in the region
of the customary price. He does not enter it as evidence of the beneficence of the competitive system and,
in short, uses it merely to demonstrate the nature of
the advantages accruing to purchasers.

The wide implications of the theory of normal value
are displayed by Marshall in an impressive series of
illustrative excursions. The forces at work are passed
in review one at a time, presented in different combinations, turned around, and held up to the light. These
illustrations are certainly one of the most valuable parts
of his work. They give a clinical demonstration of the
uses of deductive logic in the parts of economic analysis
where the data must be handled by logical methods as,
for example, in problems of taxation. It is in these
short excursions that Marshall is at his best. In them
he shows the force of his own belief that deductive
reasoning in economic theory should be confined to
short chains dealing with data sufficiently precise to
be manageable. What he demonstrates in this part of
his work is not a body of doctrine, but a method.
Nevertheless, his illustrations are selected largely
within the range of assumptions that support the doctrine of normal value, and about that doctrine all his

other material clusters, and from it his short chains of reasoning are pendant.

IV

When one turns from Marshall's treatment of value, or price, to that of the distribution of income, he is not entering a new field, but is turning to the application of value theory to special sets of circumstances. As has been pointed out above, normal commodity prices are compounded out of costs, costs are the prices of agents of production, and these prices are the distributive shares. So far, then, as distribution is treated on theoretical lines, the analysis proceeds to examine the conditions of supply and demand out of which arises the normal or long-run price of each factor. This long-time analysis is supplemented by examining aspects of distribution which arise during shorter periods. The whole subject is overlaid with an admirable discussion of the effects of economic changes on the lives and fortunes of mankind, designed less to uphold the theoretical structure than to illuminate the effects of change upon the organic social whole and upon the classes of which it is composed.

The factors of production for the services of which a price must be paid are classified as land, or the gifts of nature, labor, capital, or all productive wealth excepting land, and organization plus organizing ability. This classification runs along customary lines, differing

in a marked degree from that of earlier economists of
the classical line only in the definite inclusion of organizing ability or enterprise.   Correlative to these factors are the incomes—rent, wages, interest, and profits.
To regard these forms of income and their variants
from a national standpoint for the sake of simplicity,
Marshall notes that the annual sum of them represents
the total annual income, or national dividend.[1]   Under
modern conditions the economic system produces a substantial and growing surplus of products over the absolute necessities of life.   The problem of distribution
is to discover what forces determine the division of this
surplus between the various factors that have coöper-
ated in its production, and, in the long run, what forces
determine the demand for and the supply of the factors
themselves.

The demand for the factors of production is proximately the business man's demand for their services in
the processes of production, except in the case of business organization and ability, where the demand is a
more indirect social demand.   The effort of business
men is to apply each factor as far as they profitably can,
and to combine the various factors, by the principle of
substitution at the margin, in such a way as to offer no
further incentive to substituting one for another.   The
relative amounts of the various factors that are demanded are thus determined by business men's calcula-

[1] Allowance having been made, of course, for duplications and for
striking a balance between payments coming from and going to other
countries.

tions, based upon watching the effect of the marginal units of various factors upon the value of their products. The application of any factor to the profitable margin will mean that the marginal increment of each factor will secure as its reward the equivalent of its addition to the value of the total product. Competition will broaden this tendency to the end that the reward of every increment of a given factor will receive the same reward as the marginal one, so far as all are interchangeable or of equal efficiency.

To this point Marshall's analysis proceeds upon the same lines as those upon which J. B. Clark builds his whole theory of wages and interest. But Marshall refuses to make it into a theory of distribution. To do so, he conceives, would be mere circular argument. For the prevailing wage-rates determine the point at which labor becomes marginal, and this untenable circle emerges, that marginal product governs wages while wages govern the margin. Clark, it will be remembered, escaped from the circle by setting up a concept of social value in which the final term of reference was a "final hour of social labor." Under that scheme of thought competitive values are the result of social appraisal, under which every man gets what he produces and therefore what he deserves. Marshall, eschewing the concept of social value, is thereby debarred from the comfortable and plausible theory of marginal productivity as the *cause* of distributive shares. He would seem to have proved, one might say conclusively, that such a theory is inseparable from the concept of social value, an idea that some later economists appear not always to have thoroughly comprehended. He has, too, relieved himself of the necessity of encumbering his view of distribution with any ethical implications of justice. In his view, then, the tendency of agents to be rewarded according to the net product of marginal increments merely "throws into clear light the action of one of the causes that govern wages" or other shares; that is to say, it helps to explain the demand.

In short periods, when the supply of factors of production can be taken as practically fixed in amount, the demand for them will be the principal factor in determining their remuneration. Pay will be a function of relative scarcity. "The more there are, the less they get," is a patent, if bitter, truth. More important, from Marshall's point of view, are the causes which determine the supply of productive agents over an extended period of time. The remuneration of the agents exercises a reflex influence upon the supply of them, except in the case of land or natural agents. It is the fixity of the supply of land (in an old country), together with the fact that it has no cost of production, that dictates the necessity of creating separate categories of income from land and capital. Looking at labor and capital, the trend of the argument runs to the end that in the long run the supply of them will be governed by the cost of producing them. To reach this conclusion involves, as it did in the case of commodity prices, a resort to the quasi-static assumptions. "If there is no violent change in the arts of production and in the general economic condition of society, the supply of each agent will be closely governed by its cost of production." [1] Thus we are brought back to the sphere of normality, as it works out where the passage of time is permitted to expand the scale of economic life without greatly affecting its processes; where business men may confidently anticipate the course of events over a term of years; and where fathers can safely predict the future demand for the services of their infant sons. So far as conditions do not ally themselves to this stable situation, income, of course, fails to fall into Marshall's normal scheme of things and, indeed, eludes the grasp of the theorist. If change is too incessant and radical to permit the postulating of any normal trend, then values and incomes are what they are, and their causes are a skein to be untangled by other than logical processes.

The run of the general argument to this point may be indicated by two quotations. "The national dividend is at once the aggregate net product of, and the sole source of payment for, all the agents of production within the country. It is distributed among them, generally speaking, in proportion to the need which people have of their several services—*i.e.*, not the *total* need, but the *marginal* need. By this is meant the need at that point at which people are indifferent whether they

[1] *Principles of Economics*, p. 537.

purchase a little more of the services (or the fruits of the services) of one agent, or devote their further resources to purchasing the services (or the fruits of the services) of other agents. Other things being equal, each agent is likely to increase the faster, the greater the share which it gets, unless indeed it is not capable of being increased at all. But every such increase will do something toward filling up the more urgent needs for that agent, and will thus lessen the marginal need for it, and lower the price at which it can find a market. This reflex action may be slow. But if there is no violent change . . . the supply of each agent will be closely governed by its cost of production." [1] "Wages tend to equal the net product of labour; its marginal productivity rules the demand for it; and, on the other side, wages tend to a close though indirect and intricate relation with the cost of rearing, training, and sustaining the energy of efficient labour. The various elements of the problem mutually determine (in the sense of governing) one another; and incidentally this secures that supply price and demand price tend to equality; wages are not governed by demand price or by supply price, but by the whole set of causes which govern demand and supply." [2]

With Marshall, this concise theory of distribution is the magnetic center about which actual phenomena irregularly gravitate, disturbed from their proper orbits

[1] *Principles of Economics,* pp. 536-537. The quotation runs together nonconsecutive sentences.

[2] *Ibid.,* p. 532.

by innumerable conflicting attractions and mutual collisions. The electrons of no atom ever moved more unpredictably about its nucleus than Marshall's realistic examples of the forces affecting the supply of productive agents gravitate about his theoretical center. We can do no more than glance rapidly at the major aspects of each type of income.

In the case of land, there is no cost of production, and, in settled countries, the supply is fixed. Much of the productive capacity of long-used land must be regarded as the result of capital invested in maintaining the soil, and the income from that investment really attaches to the capital, not to the land. The principal attributes of land are its extension in space and its annuity of sun, rain, and air, plus whatever remains of its original properties of fertility. Rent may, however, for convenience be reckoned as the income from land including the improvements imbedded in the soil. The first fact about rent is that the products of the soil are valued in the market through the play of demand and supply. The second important fact is that the cultivation of land responds to the law of diminishing returns. Out of these two facts arise the main principles applicable to the fixing of rent. Increments of labor and capital will be applied to land up to the marginal point where further application will not pay for itself. Land will be transferred from one use to another in response to the opportunity for an increased gain, giving a tendency for land to be worked in its most remunerative uses. The demand for, supply, and price of various crops are mutually determining the uses to which land will be put, the margin of intensive cultivation, and the poorest lands that will be used. Out of this play of forces emerges the allocation of land to its various uses, which change with the lapse of time.

Keeping in mind the fixity of the supply of land and its relative scarcity, the active factor in determining the uses of land and the production of various crops is the relative demand. When carried to the margin of cultivation as fixed by the market valuation of its products, land is cultivated at a cost which equals the return to the marginal "doses" of labor and capital multiplied by the number of "doses" applied. But the value of the crop, except on marginal land, is something more than this, and since all other agents in producing the crop have been remunerated, this "something more" is a true surplus, attributable to the land. It is like other forms of income in that its amount is determined by all the conditions that govern the demand for and supply of the products of the land. It differs from them, however, in that its amount has no reflex influence on the supply of land, so that there is no long-run tendency for rent to adjust itself to the normal cost of producing the agent out of which it arises.

The value of land is, then, unrelated to its cost of production. Its value is primarily a capitalization of the annual value of the surplus which it is likely to afford, modified by whatever other influences affect the advantages of land ownership, such as social esteem or systems of taxation. Looked at, however, from the viewpoint of the individual landowner, land is not noticeably different from capital, for free capital can be interchangeably invested in either land or the appliances of industry, and in either case the income will be regarded as a rate of interest on the investment. This analysis is brought by Marshall to bear upon the long-standing controversy over Ricardo's dictum that "rent does not enter into the cost of production." When it has left Marshall's hands, the whole controversy has become a matter of words. It is a case of "yes and no," of distinguishing between the social and private points of view. Viewed as the result of a social process of the valuation of products, rent cannot be considered as a factor in cost, since it arises out of a surplus of market value over costs to the cultivator. Viewed as a rate of return to the landowner on the capitalized value of the land, it is indistinguishable from interest, and to the renting farmer represents one of the charges which the market price must cover.

Nothing less than Marshall's careful analysis on this point could make plain his entire concept. He has said elsewhere, "It is *wisest not* to say that 'Rent does not enter into the cost of production': for that will confuse many people. But it is *wicked* to say that 'Rent *does* enter into the cost of production', because that is *sure* to be applied in such a way as to lead to the denial of subtle truths, which, in spite of their being subtle, are of the very highest importance scientifically and also in relation to the practical well-being of the world."[1] The classical phrase he considers "an indisputably bad one," and his desire is to place the analysis of rent upon a new scientific basis, divorced from that controversial phrase. He insists upon the social aspects of land, in which the fixity of amount is the crucial point, and his analysis is pointed toward a solution of the proper social policy toward land in a developing society. In this view rent appears as a surplus, the amount of which is determined (1) by the excess of the market price over the cost of production, (2) by all the forces that affect market demand, (3) by all the forces that affect the supply of each crop (under the principle of substitution combined with diminishing returns on a fixed area). The way in which this idea of surplus is applicable to other distributive shares will be noted a little later.

The fundamental facts that create the form of income called "interest" are, as conceived by Marshall, that payment is offered for the use of capital because a gain is anticipated from its use; and, second, that capital is scarce enough to require a payment for its use because of "the preference which the great mass of humanity have for present over deferred gratifications." In other words, the demand for capital is based

[1] *Memorials of Alfred Marshall*, p. 436.

upon its *productiveness*, the supply upon the *prospective* action of individuals, or, more remotely, upon all the causes that induce people to save more or less from their incomes. Gross interest includes charges for risks incurred, and earnings of management, which must be subtracted to get at net interest. The difficulty in expressing interest as a ratio of the value of capital arises out of the fact that capital invested in the concrete appliances of industry, in factories, mills, and machines, may earn amounts related to their cost in very different proportions from that borne by the existing interest rate to amounts of free capital available for investment. Marshall attempts to escape this difficulty by appealing again to the device of long and short periods. The income from capital in concrete form may, during short periods, bear no distinct relation to the costs of the concrete appliances. For the time being their earnings are thus comparable to the earnings of land. The stock of them is for short periods relatively fixed, and their earnings are dependent upon the valuation placed upon their products in the market. Viewed thus, these earnings are properly not interest, but "quasi-rent." They can be expressed as a "rate" of interest only when they have been capitalized at the present rate.

In a longer view, however, as in the case of commodity prices, the situation is rather different. Unlike land, industrial equipment may be multiplied. As new savings flow into new instruments and as replacement capital (sinking funds) is reinvested, they tend to flow into concrete forms of which the earnings are high, and away from forms where earnings are low, and thus to equalize the earnings from various forms of invested capital. "It is therefore not unreasonable to assume for the present that the owners of capital in general have been able in the main to adapt its form to the normal conditions of the time, so as to derive as good a *net* income from their investments in one way as another."[1] This assumption is obviously an essential underpinning of the whole theory of normal value, for if there are no normal earnings of capital there are, of course, no normal costs of production. The analysis explicitly assumes that the value of money is stable and rules out of account the effects of periods of commercial inflation and depression. The static character of the analysis thus comes once more prominently into view.

The earnings of capital are, then, seen in these three aspects: (1) The current rate of interest is a temporary equilibration of all present demands for, and present supply of, "free" capital available for new investment. (2) Capital already invested is during its lifetime relatively fixed as to amount, and its earnings may bear no fixed ratio to the cost of the equipment, and are thus of the nature of rent, or quasi-rent. (3) In long periods, the tendency is for all forms of capital to produce a normal rate of return, though this normal rate is not a fixed ratio, but shifts under the

---

[1] *Principles of Economics*, p. 592.

influence of changing conditions. The normal rate arises out of all the influences which determine the supply of capital and the demand for it, but it tends to correspond to the additional amount of value-product attributable to the capital applied at the margin of production. The forms which capital will take are determined, assuming an established field of technological knowledge, by the operation of the principle of substitution, which is "a special and limited application of the law of the survival of the fittest"; while the tendency of the earnings of capital to a normal rate follows from the business man's incentive to press the use of each agent of production to the margin of profit. Normal interest thus constitutes a special example of normal price.

The formula of value when applied to the remuneration of labor introduces at once a number of complicating features. For simplicity, labor has been used as an inclusive term, as though it were a general fund of labor units. There is, however, in Marshall's view, no such fund for the units of which a general rate of wages can be found. In fact, there are numerous grades of labor in the modern world, and these strata tend to perpetuate themselves. As the wage-determining forces fix a different level of pay for each grade, no such notion as a "general rate of wages" can be maintained. Even within a given grade, the quality of work differs from man to man, so that the only tendency of wages to equality even there is that of what

are called "efficiency wages." Marshall parts company with Jevons and Clark by insisting upon many
grades of labor and many rates of wages. He also dissociates himself from the division of labor into four
"noncompeting groups," as developed by Cairnes from
a hint of Mill's, thinking groups to be more numerous
but less crystallized than that division indicated. The
formula of value is, then, to be applied not in the
sense of the demand for labor as a whole and its supply
as a whole, but to the demand for each grade and the
supply of that grade.

On the side of demand, the general analysis applied in the case of capital fits the situation, so that "the
wages of every class of labour tend to be equal to the
net products, due to the additional labour of the marginal labourer of that class." [1] This is not a theory
of wages, but merely, "throws into clear light the action
of one of the causes that govern wages." In periods
sufficiently short to permit the supply of labor to be
regarded as fixed, the demand for it, acting through
the calculations of employers, is the active factor in
determining wages. In such short periods wages, being
adjusted by the current market situation without reference to the cost of producing laborers, are, like interest
on capital, to be regarded as quasi-rent.

It is, however, in the analysis of the forces affecting
the supply of labor that Marshall finds most prominent
the peculiar features bearing upon the value of labor.

[1] *Principles of Economics*, p. 518.

One cannot here follow through the maze of influences which he displays as affecting the supply of workers. There is the biological tendency of the race to multiply rapidly. There are the checks upon fecundity arising out of accepted "standards of comfort" and "standards of life" in one class and another. Capacity for foresight is a limiting factor, least in evidence among the very poor. Family affection, the facilities for education, and the opportunities for technical training affect the supply of labor in various grades. Mobility is hampered by the necessity of the laborer's delivering his person as well as his labor at a certain point. The length of time that can be devoted to preparation in youth affects the numbers in the various grades, and this depends upon the means, knowledge, and foresight of parents. The social situation in which people find themselves defines their aims and ambitions, and determines in great measure the course of labor supply for the next generation. Changes in industry upset previous calculations and result in maladjustments of the supply of various kinds of labor to the needs of industry. Present necessity weakens the bargaining power of the lower grades of labor. Great masses of laborers are caught in the vicious cumulative circle of poverty leading to weakness and inefficiency leading to deeper poverty. Only in the study of deep-seated social forces of this sort may one perceive the clues to the supply of labor as a whole and to the supply of each grade. It is in the pursuit of these clues that

Marshall is seen at his best as a marvelously acute student of the social forces that are shaping the world. It is here, too, that one observes the philanthropic spirit in which he searches for some solution to the more grievous ills of humanity.

All this, however, groups itself about the theoretical system. The inquiry centers itself about the price of labor, and the delving into the social situation is pursuant to an explanation of the supply side of a particular factor of production. Somehow, to support the theory of value, wages must adjust themselves to a long-run normal rate for each grade, related to the cost of producing the laborers. Very haltingly and uncertainly, Marshall proceeds to propound a doctrine of normal wages, much overlaid with modifications necessitated by the difficulty of explaining the supply of labor as a response to economic causes. Economic causes, he says, do play a part in regulating the growth of numbers as a whole as well as in each various grade. "But this influence on the numbers of the population as a whole is largely indirect; and is exerted by way of the ethical, social, and domestic habits of life. For these habits are themselves influenced by economic causes deeply, though slowly." [1]

The response of the supply of labor to the demand for it is, however, fairly ready where standards of comfort are low and where income is largely spent upon the necessaries of life. Where unhindered by conscious

[1] *Principles of Economics*, p. 218.

defense of standards of comfort or of activity, fecundity is increased by any rise in the rewards of labor. This combination of low standards of living with the physiological capacity for rapid procreation makes the reward for labor in large sections of the world correspond rather closely to the distressing "iron law of wages." Even "in the Western World the earnings that are got by efficient labor are not much above the lowest that are needed to cover the expenses of rearing and training efficient workers, and of sustaining and bringing into activity their full energies." [1]

The "deliberate adjustment of the supply of expensively trained labor to the demand for it is most clearly seen in the choice made by the parents of occupations for their children, and in their efforts to raise their children into a higher grade than their own." [2] The adjustment is hindered because deliberate calculations hold but a secondary place as compared with other influences on the birth rate, and because of rapid changes in industry. Marshall concludes, however, that in the long run "there is a constant tendency toward a position of normal equilibrium, in which the supply of each of these agents shall stand in such a relation to the demand for its services, as to give those who have provided the supply a sufficient reward for their efforts and sacrifices. If the economic conditions of the country remained stationary sufficiently long, this tendency would realize itself in such an adjustment of supply

---

[1] *Principles of Economics*, p. 531.　　　[2] *Ibid.*, p. 570.

to demand, that both machines and human beings would earn generally an amount that corresponded fairly with their cost of rearing and training." [1] So much for a static view of wages. "As it is, the economic conditions of the country are constantly changing, and the point of adjustment of normal demand and supply in relation to labour is constantly being shifted." [2]

One may well ask whether at this point Marshall's notion of normality in a rapidly changing world does not become so tenuous as to have nothing but a metaphysical authenticity. Statically viewed, the forces at work today are toward a labor adjustment a generation hence. But a generation hence the situation will have so greatly changed that the market adjustment of wages may bear hardly the slightest resemblance to that which drew out the existing supply of labor. Leaving the validity of the analysis of static or steadily progressive forces unchallenged, one may wonder whether the discerned tendency of wages to equal the cost of production is not so far from explaining actual wages as to make the long-run doctrine of little scientific value. Earlier economists had based a "natural" rate of wages upon an assumed perfect mobility of labor. Marshall, unwilling to remove difficulties so cavalierly, has reduced mobility to slow adjustment. By so doing, what is "normal" must change incessantly, and it is possible to be in doubt as to whether his treatment of the social forces affecting the supply of labor

[1] *Principles of Economics*, p. 577.   [2] *Ibid.*, p. 577.

might not have been more effective and more realistic, had he not been constrained by the exigencies of his theory of value to shape them to a given conclusion.

It is not necessary to give any detailed account of the theory of profits, since the reasoning is not essentially different from that concerned with other factors of production. The forms of business organization are shaped by the play of social forces, and establish themselves upon the principle of substitution, or "survival of the fittest." This is not to say that the forms surviving are fittest to benefit their environment, but merely best fitted to thrive in it. In various industries the type of organization best suited to the situation will emerge as the result of the incentive to press each type to the margin of advantage. The opportunity for profit is the incentive which lies back of the forms of industrial organization. Profits as such are, however, an additional instance of the equilibrium of demand and supply, in this case between the demand for business ability of every grade and the supply of it. In this view, all "wages of management" from foremen to managing directors or owners are classed as profits, and the pay of each grade proceeds by the same principles as those governing wages.

The rewards of owners, however, involve certain peculiarities. For, while owners or employers or managing directors are the instruments through which the demand for other agents expresses itself, the demand for forms of industrial organization and business ability

emerges in a very indirect way through the competitive
process. The supply of ability comes in part from
native gifts, in part from education and training, and
it distributes itself as between one industry and another on the basis of the incentives offered. The profits
of enterprise in short periods fluctuate widely, and may,
like other types of income, be classed as quasi-rent, but
for long periods there must be assumed to be a normal
rate of profits available to each type and grade of business ability, such as to lure into each industry its appropriate share of ability. The prospective normal profit
is indeed what leads to the distribution of business
ability as between various alternative enterprises. Thus
viewed, "the whole of the normal profits enter into
the true or long-period supply price," [1] constituting a
part of the normal long-run costs of production. In
one sense, the rewards of exceptional business ability
are to be regarded as a surplus or quasi-rent, since the
supply is limited or fixed. Since, however, exceptional
profits are a part of the lure of ability into various
fields, they are one of the determining forces in fixing
the normal profits in each industry, and to that extent are to be included in the normal supply price of
commodities.

So pitifully brief a treatment of profits is here included, not to do justice to Marshall's long and admirable discussion of the problems of business organization, but merely to display his conclusion that there is a

[1] *Principles of Economics*, p. 619.

"fundamental unity underlying the causes that determine profits and normal wages." [1] The question raised
in regard to wages again comes to the mind in another
form—whether the analysis of profits along static lines
can lead to the conclusion that in a changing world
actual profits do oscillate about any equilibrium of
normal rates of profit. As it stands, the theory is a
logical theory of profits in a competitive world where
business men intelligently pursue their interests under
conditions sufficiently static to make the results achieved
approximate those anticipated. Marshall does not indeed concur with some economists who have deduced
a tendency of competitive profits to a common level.
He allows different normal rates in relation to the
type of organization, the risks involved, and the character of ability required. But attempting to approach
reality, he appears to distort it by confining the figure
of reality within the rigid corset of normality. Perhaps the most that Marshall himself would say for the
theory is that it is as close as one can get to a scientific
generalization concerning the ultimate effects of the
forces at work, in the absence of an adequate statistical
display of the facts of matter.

v

It is perhaps time to cast a sweeping gaze over the
complicated mechanism of theory that we have been

[1] *Principles of Economics*, p. 623.

examining. Primarily it has been an analysis of prices under competitive, but not too perfectly competitive, conditions. But it has escaped the closed circle of reasoning which entangles economists who refuse to step outside the price system into the shadow-land of human motives. Prices are nowhere explained merely in terms of the other prices out of which they are compounded. They are treated as indirect measures of human motives; they constitute an interrelated and mutually dependent system; and the system represents a rough picture of the equilibrium of the opposed human incentives to activity and inactivity.

There lies implicit in the exposition the notion of the mutual dependence of every price upon every other which Walras in 1871, and Cassel more latterly, have displayed with mathematical clarity by series of simultaneous equations. But the real explanation of prices resides in the "unknowns," in all private tastes and incentives and abilities of individuals as affected by the social environment, the technological knowledge, and the supply of materials which are the heritage of the race. The apparent unpredictableness of human actions melts away before certain observed regularities of response to the lure of the coin of the realm, regarded as the symbol of material welfare. Viewed as operating in a steadily progressive world, this lure leads to a normal adjustment of the production of commodities, the relative prices at which they exchange, and the rewards of the agents whose efforts are instrumental to production—the whole being "correlated by a number of mutual interactions so complicated that it is impossible to comprehend the whole in a single statement."[1]

As Marshall summarizes the mechanism of his system, the theory of value traces "a continuous thread running through and connecting the applications of the general theory of the equilibrium of demand and supply to different periods of time; from those so short that cost of production could exercise no direct influence on value, to those so long that the supply of the appliances of production could be fairly well adjusted to the indirect demand for them, which is derived from the direct demand for the commodities which they produce."[2] The theory of distribution applies the value theory to the various agents of production. It is "concerned with another thread of continuity, which lies transversely to the thread connecting different periods of time. It connects the various agents and appliances for production, material and human; and establishes a fundamental unity between them, in spite of their important differences of outward feature."[3]

This body of theory, extending, modifying, and developing the classical doctrines, constitutes the main doctrinal content of the neo-classical school of economic theory, of which Marshall may be considered the founder. Like the classical writers, Marshall centers

[1] *Principles of Economics*, p. 545. The phrase is wrested from the context.
[2] *Ibid.*, p. 660   [3] *Ibid.*, p. 660.

his analysis about the problem of exchange values. In spite, however, of his reverent attitude toward Ricardo and Mill, his more sweeping inquiry into the complicated processes of economic life gives his doctrinal scheme the appearance of being much less mechanical and much more lifelike than theirs. Nevertheless, their concepts and methods are so definitely his points of departure that he is properly to be considered in the legitimate line of descent from them. It must still be acknowledged that his work is marked by an originality and independence which make him much more than a disciple. The vital center of his system of thought consists of an extension of the notion of the equilibrium of demand and supply, to the end of demonstrating the complete interdependence of the price system, and the fundamental unity in principle of all economic values. The whole economic order is made to appear as a sort of "solar system of balance and counterpoise," held together in a "fundamental symmetry."

In displaying this picture of economic symmetry, Marshall's principal tool is marginal analysis, particularly the principle of substitution at the margin. With the aid of this tool he accomplishes a convincing presentation of the forces which regulate the demand for commodities and the supply of them; which elicit the supply and adjust the uses of the various factors of production; and which determine the prices of commodities and the incomes of persons. The all-embracing unity of his thought is most clearly apparent in the enlightening idea that the agents of production are simultaneously rivals for employment and the field of employment for other agents. It is apparent, also, in the conception of the national dividend as at once the total product of a country and the total source of demand for products.

Such enlightening conceptions, combined with the meticulous exactitude of Marshall's thinking, may be supposed to account for the enthusiasm which the *Principles* elicited upon its first appearance. The volume appeared to resolve current controversies and to give a new certainty and scientific authenticity to economic theory. The controversy between marginal utility and cost-of-production theories of value was resolved to the satisfaction of most economists, when the two theories were combined within the confines of a single system of thought without destroying its logical congruity. An equally effective peace was made between the partisans of inductive and deductive method, by combining the most exact reasoning with a comprehensive survey of the facts of the economic process.

Moreover, the criticisms of the historical school were further hushed by a willing assent to its views upon the changefulness of social institutions and modes of life. In all Marshall's work, the influence of the historical economists is evident in the analysis of the institutions and customs that constitute the living body of the economic system. As they leave his hand, economic theories are applicable only to the particular stage of development at which a civilization finds itself. They are valid only in so far as they are based upon premises that represent the actual situation. Economic laws are thus not of universal validity, but are applicable only to the behavior of human beings as it is shaped by the particular social environment in which they live.

In other ways Marshall attempted to raise his work above the scene of current controversies. He tried to free himself from the bondage of the hedonistic ethics of Utilitarianism, and to get away from any arbitrary assumptions concerning human nature. It was to this latter end that he conceived the device of using money as an objective measure of otherwise unmeasurable human motives.

It was, moreover, the attempt to achieve a more realistic organon of economic thought than had previously been achieved that led to the painstaking treatment of the element of time, which earlier economists had avoided by assuming the universal, unobstructed mobility of capital and labor in response to a pecuniary stimulus. The time analysis constitutes some of Marshall's most illuminating work. One finds in it his characteristic treatment of long and short periods; the discounting of future pleasures as the basis of many types of economic action; the shading of all incomes into manifestations of the principle of rent; the treatment of diminishing, constant, and increasing returns, and of prime and supplementary costs; and a new conception of the meaning of normality.

The characteristics of Marshall's work which have just been mentioned illustrate not only his drive after realism, but also the eclectic view which raised him above the controversies of his day and led him to seek from whatever source the terms in which to formulate a theory of the functioning of the economic system. Inevitably, what he gained in realism he lost in mechanical precision. He may not be translated into brief doctrines and authoritative precepts for political action, as was Ricardo's fate. But, conversely, his theoretical position is less assailable. The guarded postulates from which he reasons do not succumb to mere skeptical derision. If they are defective, the defects can only be made visible to the understanding by one sufficiently aware of the objective processes of economic life to present a more convincing portrayal of their nature. The critic, in other words, needs a more intimate acquaintance with economic life than Marshall himself had.

While explicitly defending most of the doctrines of the classical economists, when properly interpreted, it is apparent that Marshall departed from them widely and vitally at many points. They were content, on the whole to develop logical systems in which the actual organization of industry and the character of human motives were simplified and abstracted to serve as somewhat shaky and at times naïve premises. The results of their work served to throw into clear light much that was obscure in the operation of economic forces. But their so-called "natural laws" were of a highly hypothetical sort, for the most part of a static character, not closely fitted to one another, and of doubtful applicability to concrete problems. Marshall introduced at least a change of emphasis which led him far away from them. He was interested much less in logical systems than in a true conception of the forces actually at work. In attempting to be realistic, he refused to be bound by hard and fast concepts. The world of industry was searched for facts and the facts were fitted into concepts much more vague than had been customary. Using on the whole a conventional terminology, he develops it, and changes its content. He makes economic concepts at once more complicated and more lifelike. On the other hand, he runs a thread of unity through his analysis, in the shape of the equilibrium of forces, which integrates the laws of value and distribution into a balanced whole, as they had not been before.

The masterly manner of his achievement made the appearance of the *Principles* perhaps the most important event in economic theory after Ricardo's *Political Economy*. It is commonly said to mark the beginning of a new epoch in economic thought. Certainly it ended an epoch, the epoch of the ascendency of Ricardian economics and of its decline under the march of events and the combined attacks of the historical and marginal schools. Whether it marked the beginning of a new epoch and the ascendency of a new "school" is not a question to which any answer would find general assent.

The *Principles* is still current coin to some, debased currency to others, and a museum exhibit to still others. In England, the Marshall tradition is still paramount, based as much, perhaps, upon the influence of a great teacher as upon his writings. To some extent his analysis has been developed and extended and modified, particularly by Professor Pigou and others at Cambridge University. He has been the inspiration of men engaged in widely varied fields of work, in mathematical economics, in economic history, in the statistical approach to economic problems, and in the general grappling with theoretical and practical problems of economic life. To many he is the Master, and to all an inspiring workman in his field.

In the United States, his theoretical work has been assailed more generally along its entire front; on the one hand, by the more devout believers in marginal utility analysis, the disciples of Professor Clark and of the Austrian "psychological" school; and on the other hand by writers who have little use for theoretical "systems." Critics of the first sort have carried on a petty warfare over "concepts" far removed from the larger issues that were in Marshall's mind; while the others, headed by Veblen, have questioned the general assumptions upon which his system is built, and, indeed, the whole desirability of constructing a logical system. The exposition of economic theory in the United States is at present too chaotically diverse to permit any precise generalizing. But one might hazard the statement that a large part of it owes more to Marshall than to anyone else. Unfortunately, however, his influence has been primarily in the shaping of theoretical formulations and not, as in England, in furnishing the inspiration, background, and technique for attacking practical problems. We have had his books, but not the man.

Any close examination of Marshall will disclose a curious discrepancy between his professed intentions and his accomplished fact. Regarding economic theory as merely a tool for handling amassed data and for cutting through to the heart of problems, he expresses a strong distaste for "long chains of reasoning." Yet it is a very long chain by which he carries economic forces through to a position of equilibrium. Adopting static or steadily progressive assumptions merely as a "method" for throwing light on one force at a time, he carries them through as the basis of a highly integrated body of theory. No one has explained the shortcomings of static method more carefully than he, and been more aware of the changing character of economic institutions than he appears at times to be. Yet, in spite of his belief that social change is biological, not dynamic, in character, his entire theoretical structure, leading up to what is normal in the long run, is dependent upon a halting of all changes in the *kind* of forces at work, and in the proportions, though not the amounts, of population and wealth.

He allows, indeed, for change in this sense, that what is to be regarded as normal may shift periodically, one might say daily or momentarily. But if, as has been true in the past century, the technique of industry is revolutionized and the relative importance of trades violently altered within each generation, it would appear to be not true that actual prices and income shares oscillate about a normal which represents cost of production. In that case, his long-period analysis would appear to be a work of supererogation, though one made no objection to his short-period conclusions. And yet it is in dealing with the element of Time that he is often most stimulating and illuminating, particularly when he is engaged in what one might call genetic studies concerning the supply of labor and capital.

Marshall lays himself open to criticism on another score. He was trained in the Utilitarian philosophy of hedonism, and his first edition treats of human motives largely in the phraseology of that philosophy and from its point of view. In subsequent revisions, under the influence doubtless of later psychological studies, he attempted to remove all traces of "Hedonics" and hedonistic ethics, one would say not with entire success. He does not state nor demonstrate, but does work in the terms of the major premise of Utilitarianism—that "to procure the greatest possible sum of satisfactions for all is right, or reasonable, or the *summum bonum* or *faciendum*," in Professor Edge-

worth's phrase.[1] He does not, like J. S. Mill in his
earlier phase, consider rational self-interest guided by
the desire for wealth and the love of ease a sufficient
assumption on which to base economic deductions.   In
spite, however, of an overt recognition of habit and of
other motives than self-interest, his general reasoning
in reality is based upon an individualistic psychology in
which men pursue satisfaction, economize effort, and
balance alternatives rather rationally and consistently.
He is, one feels, a good deal of a Benthamite, unawares
or in spite of himself.   The influence of Utilitarianism
on his concepts is unmistakable.   How far he dissented
will remain a matter of opinion, based largely on the
relative weight given to one or another part of his work.

Further, his system, for short periods as well as long,
depends upon active competition, though not upon a
perfect market.   He admits the tendency to monopoly
under conditions of increasing returns, and frankly
admits the inapplicability of his doctrines in that case;
indeed, he traces the outlines of an alternative theory
of monopoly value.   He believed, of course, in the
actual dominance of competition as the chief regulator
of economic relations.   He could hardly be expected
to be aware, during his earlier years, of the extent to
which combinations large and small, corporations, trusts,
trade associations, open-price associations, and every
manner of ingenious agreement, as well as trade unions
and government intervention, would come to limit price

[1] In *The Economic Journal*, vol. v, p. 587.

competition in the United States, and to a lesser degree in England. Probably he never understood it very thoroughly. The present generation really is only beginning to understand it.

It should be emphasized, however, that Marshall was exceedingly modest about the permanence of his doctrines. He belonged to a generation in which it was believed that competition could be taken for granted. He wrote for that generation. And, being wise in his own generation, he made no claim to be framing enduring doctrines. He saw the world changing about him, and in his later years practically wrote the epitaph to his own system. During the World War he wrote: "A thousand years hence 1920-70 will, I expect be *the* time for historians. It drives me wild to think of it. I believe it will make my poor *Principles*, with a lot of poor comrades, into waste paper. The more I think of it, the less I can guess what the world will be like fifty years hence." [1] Such insight and courageous renunciation in so old a man mark the stature of his mind—in marked contrast to the traditional repetition by lesser minds of dogmas that are at the least obsolescent.

How are we to judge a man who has thus concurred in his doom and signed his own death-warrant? "Judge not" is perhaps the best motto. Shall one, then, try simply to "explain" him? To do so in simple terms would violate the memory of his belief in the com-

[1] *Memorials of Alfred Marshall*, p. 490.

plexity of causes. An adequate explanation could proceed only on a complete insight into his mind and a large knowledge of his social *milieu*. Yet if one recall the group of influences that played upon him, as displayed at an earlier point in this essay, a sound appreciation may be gained as to why his thought took the turn it did. From Mill and Ricardo come his approach to economic analysis, and his doctrinal points of departure; from von Thünen and Cournot and a mathematical education, his early method; from an avid historical interest his appreciation of the infinitely complex pattern of social life and of the evanescence of the institutional framework of society; from Utilitarianism, a view of psychology and of ethics; from Jevons and the Austrians, certain clues as to method and content; from close investigation of business practice, an intimate knowledge of the functioning of the economic organization; from the times in which he lived, a set of problems awaiting solution; from a religious nature and a warm heart, a purpose and aim; from the developing natural sciences, something of his method and conceptions; from the totality of his surroundings, whatever the ineffable atmosphere was that gave the tone and character to Victorian England. Any such list can be little more than a hint at the sort of influences that played upon him. What he wrote was his own, individual and characteristic; but it carried the trace of many men and many influences which link him to his generation.

It can hardly be said that Marshall has "settled" any of the knotty problems of economic theory. In 1892 he could evoke "reverent and abiding admiration" from a disciple [1] for combining cost and utility analysis, historical and mathematical approaches, inductive and deductive method; for achieving unity in the theories of value and distribution; and for ending a twenty years' chaos of controversy, during which the "contrariety" of thought had threatened to discredit economics as a scientific field of knowledge. Yet today, there is hardly a single concept, assumption, or doctrine of his system that is not under attack, from one quarter or another. The contrariety of scholars seems to be perennial. And as the phases of the moon pass into the process of the years, time seems endlessly to alter the organization of man's activities, and the nature of his problems, and, indeed, the very terms and concepts in which he describes his activities and attacks his problems.

Marshall's work is not, however, ready for the *requiem* and "taps." It is imbedded in most of the economic theory upon which the present generation of students is being raised. It continues to influence our thought upon the operation of economic forces, as they affect prices, wages, currency, tariffs, taxation, poverty, and any number of other subjects of perennial interest. It probably will continue to do so until it is thought that competition has become too tenuous to be

---

[1] L. L. Price in *The Economic Journal*, vol. ii, p. 34.

regarded as a principal regulator of economic activity;
or until an adequate psychology disposes of logical systems with unstable psychological underpinnings; or
until change is generally thought to be too rapid to
permit generalizations for long periods, or until it is
thought that the social process is not explainable in
individualistic terms and by mechanical analogies. How
far these alternative views are at present valid are
largely the issues about which the present controversies
in economic thought have developed.

It may be possible to place the implications of Marshall's system in a stronger light by raising certain questions: Can the term "utility" do service for both
"desire" and "satisfaction"? Does he not tacitly assume a high degree of rationality in men as a basis of
his reasoning? Can money serve at once as a measure
of motive and a measure of satisfaction, even for
homogeneous groups? Can any approximation to
equality between money costs and "real" costs be properly assumed? Can the equilibrium of prices be assumed to represent roughly an equilibrium of "real"
forces, of human desires and human distaste for further effort? Is competition the principal regulator of
economic activity? Are the processes of change sufficiently regular to permit even a rough equality between
prices and money costs? Can a system developed by
deductive reasoning be made compatible with his views
on the biological character of social change? Is modern
business properly to be treated from the point of view

of production rather than of acquisition? Does the conception of normal equilibrium of supply and demand furnish an adequate basis for investigating modern economic problems, even those of prices and incomes? Is the "representative firm" adequate for explaining the relation between costs and prices? Are there not innumerable incomes based upon privilege or special advantage of one sort or another that do not fall within the conventional categories? Is the idea of normal profits and normal wages tenable in the modern world? Are the ideas of equilibrium and of normality applicable in any scientific sense to the life of society?

And so one could go on multiplying questions. Chiefly they center around a few large issues: whether Marshall holds tenable views concerning human nature; whether he has tamed the elements of time and change; whether his view of economic organization is adequate for a correct explanation of prices and income; whether economic motives are sufficiently isolable to be amenable to scientific measurement; and in what terms social processes shall be scientifically described. It is not our purpose to enter any answers to such questions. Obviously a simple answer of "yes" or "no" is often impossible; for some lead off into controversial fields of psychology, philosophy, and ethics, not to say manners and æsthetics and all manner of imponderable things; while others lead into the "unseen" or "unknowns" of social organization and social processes. Marshall picks a wary path along the edge of the bogs of philosophy and over the roots of disconcerting facts. Whether he does not occasionally muddy his feet or stumble, it may be left to each to judge for himself.

It really is of secondary importance how permanent or how "true" his theoretical system is. It is of much more moment that Marshall's intellectual powers, amounting to genius, should have been brought to bear upon an analysis of the functioning of the economic system. Time may, as he apprehended, render his theories obsolete. But time cannot change the fact that his insight has illuminated many problems; or that his scientific integrity has been the model and the inspiration of a new generation of economists; or that his humane spirit has speeded the search for ways and means to cope with the pressing problems of modern economic life. It may well be that that part of his work with which this study has been chiefly concerned may be its most evanescent element, and that its other parts, his insights, the example of his patient analysis, and his tradition may be the more enduring.

The scope of the present inquiry has made it necessary to confine the analysis of Marshall's work to what is contained in the *Principles* and in various articles and addresses related in subject-matter. The picture thus created would doubtless have been corrected, at least as to emphasis, had it been possible to accord to *Industry and Trade* and *Money, Credit, and Commerce* the attention that their importance would justify. Two aspects of Marshall's work they amplify:

(1) theoretical treatment is extended to questions of currency and international trade; and (2) the institutional framework of economic organization is historically and descriptively developed. The theoretical treatment of financial and trade relations is hardly comparable, in point of workmanship and suggestiveness, to the more general treatment of values in the *Principles,* due doubtless to Marshall's advanced age when he drew together these strands of his work. The long delay in publishing this part of his work has robbed it of its true freshness and originality, for Marshall's distinctive thought along these lines had passed into economic literature long before it was separately published. Important for an understanding of his position along the entire economic front, it adds but little to an understanding of his general viewpoint and theoretical approach, which it has been our purpose to display.

Turning from its avowedly theoretical portions, we find his later work largely occupied with historical and descriptive material. *Industry and Trade* is almost wholly so occupied. It is, as the preface states, a thoroughly realistic "study of industrial technique and business organization, and of their influences on the conditions of various classes and nations." It may be regarded as a contribution to, or an interpretation of, economic history, and as a contribution to an understanding of business and industrial organization in our own time. The fact that Marshall's later work runs so strongly in this direction reinforces his belief that economics is not a body of dogma, but a technique for dealing with economic data. In this view, dogma may be a hindrance to the labors of the economist, but a thorough understanding of the operation of the economic system is an essential part of his equipment. In the light of this later trend and of the avowed tentativeness of his theoretical structure, Marshall becomes closely allied to those economists who emphasize the "historical" or the "institutional" or the "genetic" approach to economic studies. He never, however, disavows or turns his back upon the hypothetical method of his classical masters, and his interpretation of the economic process permits him to store much of his wine in their bottles.

Later economists may not find it possible to do their most fruitful work within the confines of Marshall's systematic exposition of theory. He himself foresaw its shortcomings for coping with the problems of a new age. They will, nevertheless, work in his spirit and with his blessing if, in their theoretical tasks, they continue the attempt to forge instruments of thought for handling economic data, to the end of assisting in the solution of the economic problems with which the world is faced. No one could approve himself to Marshall who would make of economic theory a scholarly preoccupation for "closet" philosophers. In his view, "the work of the economist is 'to disentangle the interwoven effects of complex causes'; and . . . for this, general reasoning is essential, but a wide and thorough study of facts is equally essential, and . . . a combination of the two sides of the work is *alone* economics *proper*." [1] By illustrating this dictum, by rescuing economics from barren controversy and formal logic, and by inspiring much of the best work in economics during the past generation, he established himself as the greatest of modern economists. That the sweep of events is weakening the foundations of his formal system of thought does not lessen the enduring value of his labors and his example.

[1] *Memorials of Alfred Marshall*, p. 473.

John A. Hobson

John A. Hobson

JOHN A. HOBSON is a contemporary representative of a long line of dissenters who have
from time to time protested vigorously against the
doctrines of the dominant systems of economic theory.
He is, however, much more than a mere dissident. For
he has an alternative body of theory to propound. And
he has at the same time a concrete plan for the modification of the present economic organization, the implicit
defense of which is in his mind the chief defect of
economic theory.

A brief survey of the relation of economic dissent
to classical economic theory will assist in placing Mr.
Hobson in relation to current thought. Ricardian economics constituted the prevailing economic faith in England during much of the nineteenth century. Its most
important relation to the life of the times was that it
furnished the basis for a reasoned defense of a political
policy of governmental non-interference. The fact that
such a policy was highly acceptable to the powerful
new classes of capitalists and industrialists was undoubtedly a considerable factor in determining that it should

become the dominant economic faith. The growth of English trade and wealth under the policy of free trade furnished presumptive evidence that the tenets of the faith were sound.

The carefully guarded statements of the economists, who were generally aware of the nature of their hypotheses and of the limited applicability of their doctrines, were seized upon by the journalists and politicians as the basis of a body of political and social precepts. That the common welfare would be best served by the unregulated play of individual self-interest became the rather generally accepted axiom of social policy. This, presumably, was the controlling "natural law" of economic life. Such incidental evils as were apparent could, under this scheme of thought, be reduced for the most part to the inevitable cruelty of the laws of nature. And in particular the patent distress of the wage-earning classes could, when descried by the more affluent classes, be regarded as the inevitable consequence of the natural fecundity of the human race. The dominant trends in philosophy and psychology, in political and economic speculation, and in the practical pursuits of trade and industry, converged to support the economic faith of nineteenth-century liberalism. Political economy was not something apart from the world of affairs. It was of the essence of the situation, in a sense an expression of the current common sense. Its professors were not without honor in their own country.

The range of dissent from the prevalent system of political economy was practically coterminous with that from Liberal statesmanship. It ran from Tory defenders of ancient privilege at one extreme to socialistic dreamers of "the new heaven and the new earth" at the other. In general the dissent emanated from persons who were not particularly impressed by the beneficence of the economic system as currently constituted. They were advocates of the use of political authority in various forms to eliminate what seemed to them deplorable and remediable defects of the social system. Social reform and economic dissent were generically related.

Later developments in the field of economic theory tended to destroy that generic relationship. It lies beyond our present purpose to inquire why Ricardian political economy lost the force of authority, or why economic speculation became, after about 1880, a somewhat academic diversion chiefly concerned with the subtle elaboration of consciously hypothetical systems of theory. With due allowance for the realistic influence of certain phases of Marshall's work, such certainly was the trend. Economists were engaged in working the "laws" or "principles" or "tendencies" of the normal case into systems of theory which postulated that the basic organizing force in economic life was competition among individuals animated by the hedonic impulse. A curious and anomalous situation thus arose. For, while economic theory continued to run in individualistic terms, the problems arising out of the growing complexity of social arrangements were leading to legislation of a more regulatory or collectivistic sort. If economists could contend that they were dealing with the more basic aspects of economic life, they were operating in a sphere increasingly remote from the workaday life of their time.

In this situation, economists were quite generally ignored by social reformers. Negatively, economic theory did not cast doubt upon the desirability of coping with such problems as poverty, though its implications might be of a distinctly conservative sort. Positively, it gave little aid or counsel to reformers. Economists, as individuals, might interest themselves in social reform, but they did so under the impulse of a humanitarianism largely unrelated to their speculations as professional economists. Reformers were able to charge that the problems with which economists engaged themselves were not the problems of real importance to modern society, and that, indeed, the very concepts and methods of economic science debarred it from furnishing any relevant aid in the solution of those problems.

The course of events dictated reform through collectivistic legislation. Economic theory lingered in the environs. Conservatives, of course, gathered strength from the ethical implications which some economists read into their analysis of an individualistic competitive economy. Moderate reformers were perhaps deterred thereby. The more radical groups largely ignored them. Proceeding by more realistic methods to play the light of publicity upon one after another of grave social ills, they forced the passage of remedial legislation in many directions. If much of this legislation was merely opportunistic legislative tinkering, the most active and coherent group in promoting it, the Fabian Society, was proceeding upon the basis of a rather clearly defined social theory and social policy. Moderate socialists by faith, the members looked to the eventual nationalization of the land and of industrial enterprises, while interesting themselves currently in the amelioration of poverty.

In the light of their more remote and more ambitious aim, the Fabians developed the theory, or perhaps one should say the ground plan, of a socialistic organization of economic life designed to fit the English scene. Constituting a skeleton plan for the reorganization of society, it rather failed to make a contact with the analysis of competitive production, values, and distributive shares found in orthodox economic theory. Mill's version of the Ricardian theory of rent was adopted as an argument for socialism. The principle of utility as expounded by Jevons was taken over. Beyond that the connection with economic theory was little more than a slight irritation that such theory lent their plan no support. Fabian theory never really came to grips with the problems of collective control of production, prices, and income—the automatic control of which under a competitive system occupied so large a share of the attention of the economists.

Economic theorists thus operated on a plan not quite the same as that of statesmen on one hand, nor of the radical social theorists on the other. From the point of view of social reformers, whether moderate or radical, this situation was unfortunate, since it frequently laid them open to the charge of advocating policies contrary to economic law. The charge could not but appear unwarranted to them, since they felt that the use of economic theory to discredit the attempts of the human race to remedy the ills which followed in the wake of modern civilization was rather a demonstration of the defects of that body of theory. The coolness between economic theory and social reform could, however, hardly be allayed until some one attempted to bridge the gap between their respective fields of interest and habits of thought.

This brief account of an interesting phase of British cultural history has seemed necessary to establish Mr. Hobson's relation to economic thought. He has been primarily interested in social reform. But he sensed the need of closing the hiatus between reform and economic theory, and attempted the task. In making the attempt he in one sense restored the earlier relationship between social reform and economic dissent. In another sense he was trying to establish a new body of theory which should bear to the practical conduct of affairs something of the relationship which Ricardian economics had borne at an earlier period. He wished to establish a theoretical foundation upon which to build precepts of public policy in a new age when *laissez-faire* had lost its message. His manner of accomplishing this task will be examined at some length a little later.

Meanwhile we may be assisted in grasping Hobson's point of view by looking briefly at a few personal facts concerning his life. Coming of a good upper-middle-class family, he received his university training in the classics at Oxford during the late 'seventies. That decade represented an interesting period in the history of political economy. It may be said to have marked the end of the ascendency of the Ricardian system. Upon its decline under the impact of influences too varied to mention here, there ensued a prolonged period of theoretical controversy and various restatements of economic doctrines. At Oxford these influences were felt in varying degree. It can be understood that, in a university where the humanities were elevated to the position of honor, and where, indeed, Aristotle was the high point to which human thought ascended and from which it fell away, the Ricardian political economy was alien seed. Carried, however, into such transcendental quarters by the genius and personal ascendency of John Stuart Mill, it maintained itself until this eventful decade.

An important factor in the decline of the old political economy at Oxford was the extraordinary wave of interest in reforming society which at this time swept through the university. John Ruskin had, of course, been belaboring the "huxter science" for twenty years. Though relatively inactive during this decade because of ill-health, his prestige and influence with a considerable part of the undergraduate body were enormous. It is not, perhaps, a mistake to attribute much of the moral earnestness of Oxford in the 'seventies to Ruskin's influence. This was also the decade of Arnold Toynbee's residence at Oxford, to mention no others. This amazing young man exercised a moral influence which has become traditional. While popularizing the religion of human helpfulness as one expression of his personality, he was at the same time expounding the ideas of the historical school in economics. The downfall of Ricardianism was simultaneous with, and in some degree related to, the sweeping through the university of a bursting sense of the social evils that had accompanied England's industrial expansion. The discrepancy between the expanding wealth of the country and the continuing misery of the masses, and the inadequacy of a policy of *laissez-faire* as an engine of social justice, were impressively borne in upon a generation of students.

It was to influences of this sort that Hobson was exposed during his undergraduate days and it is in this spirit of reformatory zeal that he has continued to labor. For seven years after his departure from Oxford in 1880, he was a master at Faversham and Exeter, teaching classics. For ten years thereafter he was engaged in giving university extension lectures for classes of working-class people, at first in English literature, but soon turning his attention to economic subjects. His earlier books were thus the outgrowth, not of quiet studies in the peaceful atmosphere of a university, but of attempts to explain to workingmen the structure of the industrial organization under which they earned their livelihood, and to indicate the solution of the problems bearing upon their material welfare. Sympathizing with the viewpoint of the workingmen, he had always in mind a primary problem, how to reshape the economic organization to promote their welfare. But back of this there lay in his mind a more fundamental belief for which he is directly indebted to Ruskin—the belief that English life was being debauched by its primary concern with commercial matters, and that any adequate philosophy of progress or program of reform demanded a larger place for noncommercial forms of activity. It is only in the light of these early influences and interests that one can arrive at an intelligent appreciation of Hobson's writings, and particularly of the unity which runs through their diversity of theme.

There was, of course, nothing unique about Hobson's devoting himself to the renovation of society and the education of the working classes. Many of the best men of his generation were sent by tender consciences to similar tasks. Among the Fabians and Radical Liberals they were legion, and Tory reformers were not few. It merely happens that Hobson was the one among them who addressed himself specifically to the problems of economic theory.

Hobson's early books were not primarily concerned with economic theory. Two of his first volumes were on the problems of poverty and unemployment, studies in industrial pathology. It was work of a sort to impress him with the heavy human wastage which attended the current organization of economic life. It raised problems toward the solution of which economic theory was ill designed to assist. The versatility of his talent was meantime shown by the publication of an excellent book on *The Evolution of Modern Capitalism*. A little book on John Ruskin in 1898 may be supposed to have brought to a head the rising dissent to prevailing types of economic theory which the nature of his early work had engendered. Even his earliest books gave evidence of an attempt to break through the concepts of the orthodox economists in unexpected and disconcerting ways. With the appearance in 1900 of his *Economics of Distribution* he was in a way committed to become the economic theorist of the group of middle-class reformers.

A certain tone has been given to his books by the character of his audience and the nature of his other preoccupations. As has been said, he was for a time a university extension lecturer. Since 1897 he has been a journalist connected with the London *Nation* and other liberal journals. Thus throughout his lifetime he has been writing for a wider and more popular

audience than is common to professorial economists.
Nor has his interest centered at all exclusively in economic theory. Much of his journalistic work has been
by way of comment upon current political questions,
particularly those in which the economic element was
large. His work upon the more abstract phases of social
theory has had to be sandwiched in between the daily
tasks of writing upon topics of current interest. The
range of his interest has been far flung and he has
seemed inevitably moved to burst into print upon every
question of the day.

The effect of this kind of occupation upon his theoretical writing has been twofold. In the first place, it
has placed him in possession of a range of information
concerning the moving forces in society quite outside
of and beyond that available to the closest economist.
It is about this raw material of life that he ponders,
moralizes, theorizes—about its processes, its shortcomings, its possibilities. In the second place, by
writing so rapidly, so extensively, and upon such a
variety of subjects, he has marred his work by stamp-
ing it with a certain superficiality and literary imperfection. His monstrous zeal and activity is evidenced by
the twenty-six volumes he has published in addition
to his writing for periodicals. It would be asking the
superhuman to demand that they should be notably
scholarly. His unquestionable intellectual ability has
been spread too thinly to impress scholars, but it has

not been scholars whom he has been mainly concerned about impressing.

In England, the defects of Hobson's presentation have led to a somewhat derogatory opinion of his work among professional economists. Men trained under the severe hand of Marshall find him distressing. Mr. A. W. Flux, for example, deplores his logic and finds that from generally sound premises he arrives at conclusions at variance with those of "sound thinkers." [1] And Mr. J. M. Keynes "comes to a new book by Mr. Hobson with mixed feelings, in hope of stimulating ideas and of some fruitful criticism of orthodoxy from an independent and individual standpoint, but expectant also of much sophistry, misunderstanding, and perverse thought." [2] If not too well received in the Olympian intellectual circles, Mr. Hobson has had a wide and appreciative audience among Liberal reformers, moderate socialists, trade unionists, and other groups interested in the remodeling of social organization. Nor is he without respectable intellectual associations. He has been given a respectful hearing in the universities in the United States, as representing at least an interesting approach to the problems of economic theory. It is not a little remarkable that, writing under such difficulties as he did, he should have achieved the influence that he has. If nothing more, it proves that the

---

[1] See his review of *The Economics of Distribution* in *The Economic Journal*, vol. x (1900).

[2] From a review of *Gold, Prices and Wages* in *The Economic Journal*, vol. xxiii (1913).

attempt to join economic theory with social reform movements filled a certain void in current thought.

If one were writing in the spirit of dialectical controversy, it would not be difficult to run Hobson's logic into numerous examples of the established fallacies. He is not less addicted to the use of deductive logic than other economists, and one is at times somewhat at a loss to discern the postulates from which he argues and the concepts in which his thought is couched. In reading his economic theory one bewails at times the absence of those clear-cut concepts and that impeccable logic which make Marshall a joy. A further difficulty arises from the fact that with the process of the years he picked up here a new idea and there another, and incorporated them into his thinking somewhat unconsciously and with rather inadequate correlation to his earlier thought. If some such preliminary warnings are necessary, it is still not to be denied that Hobson's system, in a very real sense, "hangs together." It will be our purpose much more to reveal it in its unity than to pick at its flaws.

Hobson has written that his reformulation of economic theory was prompted primarily by "a failure to find, either in the orthodox English treatment of Mill and Marshall or in the radical doctrines of Marx, Henry George, etc. (the formative thinkers in my early days), any intellectually satisfactory account of the inequality and economic oppression which I saw everywhere around me. Ruskin came later, clarifying and falsifying some of my opinions. Veblen a good deal later opened some new windows." [1] In the phrase "inequality and economic oppression" is to be found the key to Hobson's whole approach. He is, in the first place, seeking a formula which will explain the existence of "inequality" and "oppression," and, in the second place, a social policy that will eliminate them. The scientific search for the causes of social phenomena is never dissociated in his mind from the search for methods of ameliorating social ills. He is, in a current ironic phrase, "one of those persons who are always asking what we are going to do about it."

This view of the province of economic studies leads him to deny the separability of the social sciences, and particularly of economics and ethics. "Ethics do not 'intrude' into economic facts; the same facts are ethical and economic." [2] Every "is," it is contended, has its "ought," and economic facts are of significance only as they throw light upon how society may achieve for itself and its members, in the phrase of Aristotle, "the good life." This close relationship of economics and ethics is condensed into the phrases, "economic science" and "economic art" which run through Hobson's writing, not as antithetical, but as complementary ideas. Economic science is everywhere conceived as the handmaiden of an art, the aim of which is to reshape social relations and practices into a harmonious process em-

[1] From an unpublished letter.
[2] *The Social Problem*, p. 69.

bodying justice for all. Seen in this light, it is obvious that Hobson must hold a contemptuous view of what is called "pure economics." It is plain why he has come to be known, in the United States at least, as the principal exponent of the so-called "welfare economics."

No sharp line of distinction can, of course, be drawn between "pure" and "welfare" economics. Almost every economist, however "pure," has been interested in social welfare. Some, like Professor J. B. Clark, have considered the highest economic welfare to be the natural product of a system of competition. Others, like Professor Marshall, have considered their scientific examination of the operation of the industrial system to furnish a competent foundation of knowledge upon which to base such reforms as seem feasible. Still others, acutely aware of the hypothetical character of their science, have realized its limited applicability to social policy, and have dissociated their humanitarian feelings from their scientific pursuits. In practically all cases, however, they have naturally—such being the field of economic study as generally understood—confined themselves primarily to the analysis of the forces regulating values and incomes in a competitive order, whether in terms of the objective operations of the market or of the subjective states of mind underlying the market.

It is Hobson's view that, in the first place, their analysis has proceeded upon unwarranted assumptions concerning the competitive character of economic life; and that, in the second place, they misconceive their function in the scheme of things. Their aim should be avowedly ethical, to promote the attainment of harmony in social relations. And their analysis, he thinks, would operate to that end were it to proceed upon the realistic plan of inquiring into the reasons for the prevailing inequality of material welfare among various classes of people. Starting from the primary preconception, based upon his observation of the world, that the existing social and economic system does not automatically grind out well-being, he works backward in his analysis of the system to discover why not, then forward to discover how it might be able to do so.

Starting with such preconceptions, it is natural that Hobson's attention should be directed particularly toward the distribution of wealth, in the effort to discover upon what principles it is currently proceeding and in what ways it could be improved toward the end of increasing welfare. It is not too much to say that his entire system of economic theory revolves about that center. He finds it necessary to analyze the pricing process by which distributive shares are determined, to examine the social effects of present distribution, and finally to develop the content of the term "welfare." For a system of theory in which the actual is subordinated to the desirable is meaningless unless it presents at least the outlines of a plan of social organization toward the realization of which concrete social reforms may be directed. It is our present purpose to examine the lines of argument by which Hobson arrives at his characteristic body of economic doctrines. Interwoven with his constructive arguments will be found a steadily recurrent attack upon other types of economic theory, particularly upon such types of theory as are represented by Marshall and Clark, Pigou and Wicksteed.

II

Our attention will best be directed first to Hobson's analysis of the distribution of income, wherein he uncovers the causes of economic inequality and distress. [1] Any close examination of Hobson will reveal his great indebtedness to Marshall for his general concepts, terminology, and methods of analysis. It is, indeed, hardly too much to say that without a knowledge of Marshall, a reader of *The Economics of Distribution* and *The Industrial System* will find them obscure if not absolutely unintelligible. Ideas that Marshall has worked out with such painstaking analysis are taken for granted. There may be cited as examples the ideas of the equilibrium of demand and supply, the elasticity of demand and supply, the distinction between normal and market prices, and the extension of the concept of

[1] References on this phase of his work will be chiefly confined to *The Industrial System* (1909). Certain aspects of the theories there presented are more fully developed in *The Economics of Distribution* (1900) and *The Economics of Unemployment* (1922).

rent to other distributive shares. This is not to say that
the one system is at all a copy of the other, but merely
that the one has furnished a set of ideas which serve
as a point of departure for the other. Hobson pours
new wine into Marshall's bottles.

Our examination can be advanced most rapidly by
making plain exactly what it is that marks off Hobson's
theoretical problem in his analysis of existing prices
and distributive shares from that of Marshall and
most other theoretical writers. The usual analysis of
value and income shares proceeds upon the explicit
assumption that they are the outcome of a thoroughgoing system of competitive enterprise, in which
mobility of the factors of production and knowledge of
self-interest are present in rather large measure. Hobson's primary exception to the usual analysis is to the
assumption of "free" competition. His view is that
the interference with competition in the industrial system is too prevalent and too enduring to be disposed of
as "friction" for which allowance may be made. Beyond this, in his earlier works, he seems prepared to
proceed upon the assumptions laid down by "neo-classical" economists. He seems implicitly to rely upon a
hedonistic psychology, and, with occasional reservations
in favor of custom and convention, to assume a high
degree of rationality in the pursuit of economic ends.
What he is attempting, then, in *The Economics of Distribution* and in *The Industrial System* is to give a general theory of value and distribution which will make

adequate provision for all the special circumstances connected with stoppages in the competitive process.

The industrial system is excellently displayed as a complex structure of businesses, grouped into trades or industries between which there are innumerable connecting links, binding the whole system together so closely that no metaphor is adequate to describe it except that of a living organism. As goods flow forward from the raw material to the finished commodity stage, there is a reverse flow of money. At each stage this money must be distributed among the factors of production that have at that stage contributed to the productive process. Following the flow of money back to the earliest, or raw material, stage, it will be found that the money value of the finished product has been distributed, step by step, to individuals who have contributed some assistance in passing goods through the process of production. In grouping these individuals according to the factor of production which they control, Hobson follows the customary classification of land, labor, capital, and enterprise, or management. In the prevailing system, management stands at the center of the productive process, organizing the other factors into business units, paying them their shares of the value of the product, and holding for itself such residual amount as emerges. The money incomes thus distributed represent the respective claims of the owners of the various factors upon the current product.

In a static economy, the total money income of members of society would be the exact equal of the values of finished commodities and services produced and consumed during the year. In a progressive society, however, saving is necessary for investment in new forms of capital designed to increase the future output of commodities. "There exists at any time an economically right ratio of saving to spending," which will "assist to produce the maximum quantity of consumption goods," over a period of years. Less saving and capital increase than this will fail to provide for the possible growth of the industrial system. More will bring an increase of productive capacity greater than current income can keep pace with, thus producing a glut of goods and a slowing down of productive activity.

When the origin of individual incomes is approached, it is necessary to keep in mind that production and distribution are simultaneous and in a sense identical processes. Income arises from breaking up the prices of retail goods and new capital goods. Passing backward and into tributary channels in the productive process, it is broken up at each stage into rent, interest, wages, and profits. "The payments of money which constitute distribution are in effect orders upon the very goods which are being made or have just been made; the acts by which wealth is distributed are acts by which new productive energy is evoked and the general process of production is kept going." [1] One thus observes the integral character of production and distribution, linked

[1] *The Industrial System*, p. 57.

inseparably together in the processes of an organic system.

It will assist in comprehending the analysis of distribution which is to follow if the mechanics of Hobson's scheme are displayed briefly in advance. Two points of view are intertwined in a disconcertingly complicated fashion. On the one hand there is an analysis of the forces which actually fix distributive shares under the present economic organization. On the other hand, the various types of income are subdivided into elements which are rated on the basis of their effect upon the productive process, in terms of the fullest provision for the material welfare of the community. The first deals with income upon the basis of business principles, the second from the viewpoint of the social effects of current distribution. Hobson does not himself point out this diversity of approach, and one needs to be forewarned that he is in effect laying what is over against what ought to be.

Income is divided into the conventional categories, as arising from land, labor, capital, and enterprise. Then by a complicated use of analogy each of these various kinds of income is seen to include three possible elements, (1) a provision for the maintenance of the factor of production from which it arises, (2) a provision for the increase of the factor in response to the needs of an expanding industrial system, (3) income which does nothing to support the fabric or promote the growth of industry, thereby being marked as "unproductive surplus." The bargaining process is then examined to explain who gets the unproductive surplus. To explain the emergence and economic effects of this surplus is the goal of Hobson's immediate purpose. At a later point his theory of social welfare will be seen to revolve about the question of the proper disposal of the surplus. With this mechanism in mind it should be possible to steer a safe course through the intricacies of the following analysis.

Directing the attention to the problem of explaining the amount of distributive shares, Hobson observes the primary defect of conventional methods of economic analysis to be the "want of a clear system of measuring industrial energy." Labor is measured by the hour's or week's work; land by the acre; capital by its value in monetary terms. These separate forms of measurement, in his view, afford "no intelligible and consistent statement of the distribution of wealth." Searching for an intelligible principle upon which to base his theory of distribution, Hobson lights upon the idea that what *entrepreneurs* are interested in is not men or acres or machines as such, but "units of productive power." We are introduced, then, to "units of labor-power," "units of land-power," and "units of capital-power," neglecting for the moment the rewards of management. It is assumed that land, labor, and capital are rewarded not as acres, men, or money value, but in accordance with the number of units of power which they exert. It is a highly abstract conception. J. B. Clark, it will be remembered, adopted a somewhat similar method of analysis, arriving at the conclusion that each unit received as a reward the value of its specific product. Hobson, however, carries the analysis into more complex fields than Clark. Proceeding upon the analogy of the differential grading of land according to the use to which it is put, he grades labor and capital in similar fashion. For each grade of the three factors land, labor, and capital, there are conceived to be different units of productive power. Thus land may be divided into grazing land, wheat land, hop land, gardening land, and so on. Labor is divisible into unskilled labor and an indefinitely large number of grades of skilled labor. Capital is similarly graded according to the use to which it is put. Grazing land is of different qualities, so that any given area of it will be paid according to the units of "grazing-power" it contains. The same is true of wheat and other lands, and of each grade of labor and of capital. Two bricklayers, for example, will be paid different wages *because* one emits more units of bricklaying power than the other.

Before examining the implications of this unitary method in detail, it seems advisable to call attention to the other controlling idea of Hobson's analysis which he carries along simultaneously with the use of units of productive power. He conceives the first principle of industrial economy to be the repair of wastage and the provision for healthy growth. The first charge upon industrial income is the upkeep of the supply of the factors of production. In the case of labor this wear-and-tear fund consists of "subsistence wages"; for capital, the ordinary maintenance fund; for land, such expenses of upkeep as are necessary to maintain the supply of each sort of land in use.

Subsistence wages sufficient for maintaining the existing supply of labor power mean something more than the mere amount necessary for bare physical support. For wages must be sufficient to stimulate effort and to permit the upkeep of working efficiency and the support of a family. For the higher grades of labor higher standards of living are necessary for this purpose. "To evoke and maintain these finer sorts and uses of human energy will involve the existence of a higher standard of life and a higher rate of pay. For each unit of the finer sort of productive power a higher price is necessary than sufficed for a ruder power. It is partly a question of physical, partly of moral, motive." [1] Subsistence wages, thus viewed, are, however, merely capable of keeping the existing supply of labor and skill intact. An increasing number of laborers or an increasing degree of skill can only be produced through the stimulus of higher wages.

In a growing industrial system like ours something more than mere subsistence wages is a "necessary cost of industrial growth." There must be an added in-

[1] *The Industrial System*, p. 67.

centive in the shape of a "wage of progressive efficiency." There is, of course, no force operative which
automatically brings to every grade of labor wages
of progressive efficiency, or even of maintenance. In
depressed or declining trades, there are always some
classes of labor getting less. This condition is, however, only a relatively isolated phenomenon, and is
remedied in time by a falling off in the supply of the
depressed grades of labor.

What constitutes a maintenance wage can only be
understood in terms of the average earnings of all the
employed members of a family and of the conventional
requirements of the grade to which it belongs. The
opportunities for the labor of women or children will
affect men's wages, the total family wage being adjusted to customary standards of living. The provision
of the supply of labor for each grade and the character
of the customary standard of living for that grade are
the outcome of a very complex interaction of social
forces. "The possession and discovery of natural apti-
tudes, foresight, and outlay in the preparation for a
trade, personal connections and social opportunities,
mobility and trade organization, this complex of conditions, partly personal, partly adventitious, partly social, determines whether the sort of work a man does
commands a high or a low rate per unit of productive
energy."[1] Whatever the wages per unit of power in

[1] *The Industrial System*, p. 87.

a given grade, it must be sufficient to provide a maintenance wage for the marginal, or least efficient, worker,[1] employed in that grade, or shrinkage of supply will ensue. "In kinds of work where the difference of productivity between the best and worst workers in actual employment is large, their differential wage, marking the superiority of workers over the marginal worker, may be considerable." The analogy to differential rent is obvious. "The difference of weekly earnings between superior and inferior workers in a class of labour follows necessarily from the fact that so far as labour-power is treated as an article of commerce, to be bought and sold in a labour market, each unit of labour must be bought and sold at the same price. If, therefore, the marginal worker only gives out six units of labour per week, while the more efficient workers give out ten units, their weekly wage will contain a differential wage which measures this excess, most of which may be utilized in building a higher standard of comfort within the class."[2] One effect of the machine process, however, is to equalize productive power, with the result that, assuming mobility, "the wages of each class of labour tend to remain at a con-

---

[1] It should be noted that when Hobson refers to the "marginal worker" he refers to the least efficient worker actually in employment— i.e., the one embodying the fewest units of productive power. This is a different usage from that ordinarily employed by economists, where "marginal" refers to any one of a series of interchangeable or equally important units. It is analogous to the usual use of margins in the analysis of rent.

[2] *The Industrial System*, pp. 88-89.

ventional minimum for the marginal labour of each class." [1]

The effect of higher wages in any grade is conceived by Hobson to be "the lowering of the extensive or the intensive margin of employment." That is to say, it will bring into the grade workers from lower grades or those previously unemployed, on the one hand, and evoke greater intensity of labor on the part of workers already in the grade on the other hand. Here again the analogy between land and labor which pervades Hobson's analysis comes clearly to the surface. More remotely, general higher wages will increase the supply and skill of labor by their effect on population, by the industrialization of nonindustrial peoples (a feature of lowering the extensive margin), by improved standards of living, physical strength, education, and industrial training. Hobson regards the rise in wages during the nineteenth century as having resulted from the necessity for higher standards of life, strength, and skill which modern industry demands of workers. They were, in other words, the "necessary wages of progressive efficiency." It is apparent that his attention in connection with the wage problem is fixed upon the necessities of the workers, on the one hand, and on the needs of an expanding industrial system on the other. He nowhere gives adequate attention to the greater physical output per worker which is more generally

[1] *The Industrial System*, p. 89.

looked to by economists as the source of higher real wages.

It will be necessary a little later to examine the bargaining process by which wages, as well as other distributive shares, are actually fixed. At this point it is merely desirable to point out Hobson's general conception that the bargain-made wage cannot for long fall below the conventional needs of any grade, and that in a progressive system it must offer more than that to elicit the amount of strength and skill required for larger output, and for more difficult or refined processes of production. Under specially favorable conditions, such as strong union organization or rapidly growing demand, the bargain wage may include something over and above these two elements, an addition which serves in no way to elicit more or better labor-power.

Typically, however, the laborer is in a weak bargaining position, as the labor market is chronically overstocked. Thus labor seeking employment "is virtually obliged to sell its use for the marginal cost of production"—that is, for a maintenance wage. "If rigorous logic of bargaining prevailed throughout the field of industry, wages could nowhere rise, except in so far as increased intensity or higher quality of working energy involved in industrial changes required the provision of a larger human wear-and-tear fund." [1] But fortunately, "Custom, personal considerations, public opinion,

[1] *The Industrial System,* p. 91.

and legal enactments have always tempered competition." The force of this argument depends upon the assumption of an overstocked labor market or other weaknesses of bargaining position. The trend of Hobson's argument leads him away from any direct association of remuneration with product. Rising wages are, as noted at an earlier point, associated with the needs of expanding industry or improved bargaining power, to the neglect of the increasing productiveness of modern industrial methods.

The same type of analysis that has been made for labor is extended to the supply and remuneration of capital. Capital is defined as "all the non-human factors in a business, except the land" and is classified in the usual way as "fixed" and "circulating." The origin of capital is found in saving, and its continued existence involves a continuing postponement of consumption. Assuming a given state of capital accumulation, the necessary maintenance cost is the wear-and-tear, or replacement, fund. Hobson does not recognize the necessity of interest payment as a condition of the mere maintenance of the existing equipment. Interest arises as a necessary inducement to added savings for the progressive enlargement of the productive equipment. Where investment opportunities are free, and eliminating varying charges for risk, interest tends to a single, low rate. "Every unit of saving, like every unit of labour-power of a given sort, must be paid for at the same price. Some units of an output of labour involve no painful exertion, but since there is only one price in a market for the whole supply, they are remunerated just as highly as those units which cost most painful exertion. Similarly with saving." [1] A rising interest rate, in Hobson's view, stimulates saving and leads to the lowering of "the extensive and intensive margin of employment of capital." That is to say, it leads to speeding up or extending the uses of existing equipment, and to the scrapping of old plant and the substitution of more effective instruments of production. "This corresponds to the economy of high wages in improving the quality of the labour factor." [2] We find, then, in connection with capital, two "costs" analogous to those of labor, one a maintenance fund essential to the upkeep, the other interest essential to the expansion of industrial equipment. Over and above these payments it is possible for capital to secure an additional remuneration in some of its uses, due usually to some form of "contrived scarcity," and such payments are in the nature of an "unproductive surplus" in no way evoking an increase of productive effort.

When he comes to grading capital according to its uses, as he grades land by crops and labor by skill, Hobson's analysis appears to falter. So long as interest is looked at as a rate which must be paid to evoke a fund of capital, it appears, as has been noted above, that each unit must be equally rewarded. Such a view does not permit the classification of capital into grades with

[1] *The Industrial System*, p. 71.   [2] *Ibid.*, p. 74.

different rates per unit in each grade. Hobson, however, without giving notice of the change, slips quietly from the idea of interest as a market rate for savings to that of interest as the rental value of concrete forms of equipment. On this basis, capital can be graded according to the contrived restriction of supply which permits a greater or less return upon a given investment. This interpretation of his meaning is advanced with much hesitancy, because of the very vague treatment of the question which is to be found anywhere in his exposition. He holds the view, however, that interest payments may include an "unproductive surplus" analogous to that discovered in wages, and this would seem to be possible only under conditions of fortuitous or contrived scarcity. This interpretation is supported by his statement that "monopoly, combination, superior access to or control of markets, protection, and other public aids," permit very high returns to some enterprises or industries; and that such high "interest" does nothing to stimulate industry. This view seems to trench upon his treatment of profits, and it cannot be denied that his analysis falls into the very common confusion between the interest and rental aspects of the remuneration of capital, and between interest and profits.

The treatment of the payment of capital as a rent occasionally comes clearly to the surface. It is, in fact, a necessary condition to maintaining the analogy between capital, land, and labor. "It is the price per unit of capital-power in relation to the differential productivity of the various sorts of machine that will determine what is the worst sort in actual use. . . . If a machine of five-unit power is just kept in use, it is because the price per unit just furnishes a wear-and-tear payment and minimum interest." [1] The earlier phrase, "a unit of saving," could refer only to a given monetary amount available for investment. The present "unit of capital-power" appears to be applicable only to the capacity of a given piece of equipment to produce a certain value of product. The best that can be made of this analysis is, then, that capital is to be graded according to the capacity of those who control it to increase the rate of return upon it in various uses, while within such grades each item of equipment is considered to embody a certain number of units of power according to its capacity to produce value.

It will not be necessary, after what has been said, to consider Hobson's treatment of land at any length. "Land, so far as maintenance and improvements are concerned, is capital." [2] The expenses incurred for the upkeep of land are analogous to subsistence wages for labor and wear-and-tear funds for capital. Expenses related to the cultivation of new land, such as road-making, fencing, irrigation, and the like, are "costs of progress." The greater expenses involved in more intensive cultivation are also "costs of progress." Land may be divided into tolerably distinct grades, according

---

[1] *The Industrial System*, p. 101.   *Ibid.*, p. 76.

to the crop raised upon it. These uses of land, upon which Marshall lavishes such close and patient analysis, are taken for granted by Hobson. It is, however, implicit in the argument that the price of land use is dependent upon the value of its net product and that land will be put to the use in which the net product is largest. "These various prices of land use are the valuations set by social needs upon natural qualities of land which are scarce. They measure the utility of the several sorts of scarcity."[1] The sense of such a phrase as "the utility of the several sorts of scarcity" is not apparent. But the idea is plain and is not different from the usual economic analysis of rent. Instead, however, of measuring all rent as a differential from marginal, or no-rent, land, Hobson divides all land into grades, each with its own extensive and intensive margins. It all comes to the same thing in the end, however. For marginal wheat land carries a rental equal to what it would bring in its best alternative use, say as grazing land; while better wheat land, containing more units of "wheat-raising power," will carry a higher rent. A rise in rent for any grade of land, resulting from a rise in the price of its product, will lower the extensive and intensive margins of cultivation; that is, will bring into wheat-raising some land devoted to grazing at one side and to hops at the other, while increasing the intensity of cultivation of existing wheat land.

[1] *The Industrial System*, p. 139.

Hobson does not in the least differ from Marshall as to the relation of price to differential rents. He merely regards it as both obvious and irrelevant. He is driving at an entirely different objective, which is that all rents are scarcity rents. The whole supply of wheat enters into the fixing of the market price of wheat, whether it comes from marginal or from better wheat land. Wheat land all bears rent because there is a scarcity of land adapted to the raising of wheat. Some of it contains more units of wheat-raising power than other parts. Rent is merely the payment for these units, and the parts containing more units will get higher rent. "This scarcity price for the use of hop land is determined in precisely similar fashion to the scarcity or surplus payment for use of some particular kind of labour-power or capital." [1] It is obvious from this analysis that absolutely marginal, or no-rent land, for example the poorest grazing land in use, cannot be considered to contain any units of land-power whatever, since rent is, by definition, the payment for those units.

Rent, as thus conceived, is one with those elements of "unproductive surplus" which enter also into some wages and some interest. It arises, however, in the case of land because of a natural scarcity of the various grades of land, while with the other factors it is fortuitous or contrived. Like all such surplus, it is of no effect in stimulating production or land use. Its existence in this case cannot, however, be prevented, and

[1] *The Industrial System*, p. 95.

is not dependent on the existence of private property in land. Were it not appropriated by the landlord, it would pass on to the cultivator or to some more remote beneficiary, or, in case of public ownership, it would accrue to the state. Under private ownership it can be largely absorbed by taxation without deterring the appropriate use of land.

Though approached by this devious route, Hobson's analysis arrives at a point not very dissimilar to that of J. S. Mill, whose treatment of rent was seized upon by the socialists as the basis for part of their schemes for social reform. Plainly, the existence of the surplus known as rent was the analogy from which Hobson has worked to the existence of surplus in other forms of income. The unitary method was adopted to reduce all forms of income to a common basis and by that device to dispel the notion that, as economists have generally contended, there is anything distinctive about the income from land. "As soon as it is perceived that rent is the price of a unit of land-use in precisely the same sense that wages are the price per unit of labour-use, and that rent per acre depends upon the number of land units it contains, just as the weekly piece wage of a labourer depends on the number of units of labour-power he gives out in a week, the notion that there is a law of rent, differing radically from the law of wages or of interest on capital, will entirely disappear." [1]

It is now possible to draw together the strands of

[1] *The Industrial System*, p. 100.

this theory. For each of the three factors, land, labor, and capital, the minimum remuneration is the amount necessary to maintain the marginal (poorest) men, acres, or machines in each grade. The better ones, embodying more units of power, will secure higher differential pay. The marginal men, acres, or machines are of no more importance in fixing the amount of remuneration than any others; in fact, "in each case, the margin is seen to be determined by, and runs and falls according to the price per unit of, productive power."[1] An increase in the price per unit of any factor not only increases supply by lowering the extensive margin, but by introducing factors of the better sort, or by leading to more intensive use of the existing factors.

Hobson thinks, then, that he is arriving at the heart of the problem of distribution when he seeks to discover what the forces are that determine the price per unit. "The price per unit of each sort of industrial power is 'caused' or 'brought about' by a variety of forces of demand and supply, in which the marginal factors play no appreciable part."[2] It is, then, in the bargaining process by which demand and supply are equilibrated and a price fixed for each unit of power that the real solution of the distributive problem is to be found. We shall postpone the consideration of that problem while drawing together certain other strands of the theory presented to this point.

[1] *The Industrial System*, p. 102.   [2] *Ibid.*, p. 103.

Each of the forms of income known as rent, wages, and interest have now been divided into three parts, representing different sorts of charges upon the income from the industrial system. The first charge is the amount necessary to maintain the existing industrial fabric; the second charge, the amount of the surplus above maintenance necessary to evoke the growth of the supply of factors; the third charge, the remaining part of the surplus paid out in such a way as to evoke no increase in productive output or efficiency. This classification of income, in Hobson's view, entirely takes precedence over the more usual one, and is of the utmost importance to anyone who wishes to understand the basis for his subsequent theory of social reform. The full significance of the classification must wait upon a brief consideration of profits.

"Ability" or "management" has, in the industrial system, the function of organizing and directing production. The reward for the performance of this function is profit. This form of income differs from that of the other factors in that it is through the *entrepreneur* that the other forms of income are paid out, while his own income is the residual amount remaining in his own hands after making those payments. Socially viewed, the *entrepreneur's* service lies in the enlargement of output through the efficient organization of the other factors. So far as his efforts are directed to that end, his work is of a truly creative and essential character. To evoke these efforts the possibility of profit must be present, the anticipated amount varying according to the risk involved. "The chances of gain or loss are calculated and discounted according to the estimated apportionment in the several trades; ability is distributed among the various trades according to the genuine prospects of gain based on experience, though the distribution will be much less exact than in the case of other factors."[1] While a certain minimum profit is thus necessary to stimulate enterprise, it may under certain conditions be much greater. The maximum profit possible is the whole difference between the added product of the separate factors in an unorganized state and their greater total product when efficiently organized. Actual profits will lie between this and the minimum profits just mentioned. Within these limits they will be determined by the ability of the *entrepreneur* to hold them against the claims of the other factors, and this power will be strong in proportion to his ability to stifle competition or to occupy a strong bargaining position relative to some or all of the other factors. Such partial abeyance of competition is common in modern industry, in some cases transitory, in others long-continuing or permanent. To the extent that profits exceed the minimum amounts required to evoke the ability necessary to maintain and to increase the current fabric of industry, it is of the nature of an "unproductive surplus." Thus profits, while to a certain extent *sui generis*, are amenable, like other forms of

---

[1] *The Industrial System*, p. 130.

income, to division into three parts, as necessary to maintenance, necessary to growth, and superfluous, in relation to an adequate discharge of the social functions of business ability.

It is Hobson's contention that the existence of a surplus over and above the product necessary to maintain the industrial system is the source of economic discord in modern life. "If the result of the working of the industrial system were merely to produce a fund of food and other necessaries just sufficient to replace the wear-and-tear, and so to maintain intact the system, no problem of distribution would come up. . . . Improper distribution, or excessive payment to any factor of production is not possible, at any rate for long, in such a case."[1] Under such circumstances, "natural law of harmony of interests among the owners of the factors of production determines the distribution." This view appears to overlook the fact that surplus necessarily arises in the use of land, and at once raises discord over the social or private appropriation of rent. Even where surplus exists it could, in Hobson's view, conceivably be distributed so as to promote the maximum industrial development and efficiency, and thus to rank as "cost of industrial growth." Most income has been so "normally and naturally apportioned," under the conditions of harmony.

The growth of modern capitalism, has, however, greatly increased the surplus, with a consequent sharp-

[1] *The Industrial System*, p. 77.

ening of the struggle for it. "We may then . . . insist that every 'surplus' can theoretically be distributed so as to figure as a necessary cost of industrial growth, feeding the industrial organism. There is, indeed, in every progressive community a successful tendency towards such a natural or productive distribution of the surplus. But the success of this tendency is notoriously qualified; the surplus is not so distributed as to produce this maximum amount of economic progress. Portions of the 'surplus' which might have gone as stimuli of growth are taken as unnecessary or excessive payments, which, instead of stimulating, depress activity, and so the rate of growth is kept unnecessarily low. For, though it is possible and socially desirable that the whole of the surplus be distributed with the same natural equity that determines the distribution of the maintenance or wear-and-tear fund, it is not inevitable that this should happen. The abuse or uneconomical use of the surplus product is the source of every sort of trouble or malady of the industrial system, and the whole problem of industrial reform may be conceived in terms of a truly economical disposal of this surplus." [1]

We may turn now more directly toward the bargaining situation, out of which actual distribution arises. In dealing with the various factors of production, Hobson has used a method of analysis which appears to draw him very close to some sort of productivity theory of distribution. The implication of his analysis of dif-

[1] *The Industrial System*, p. 78.

ferential pay according to the number of units of pro-
ductive-power given out would seem to be that every
factor received its product as pay. But that idea is the
very opposite of his intention. He realizes this difficulty and hastens to remove it. "The real difficulty
which attends this reasoning is due to the fact that our
analytic method has tacitly assumed a separate productivity attributable to each part of each factor
employed in a business, whereas no such separate productivity exists." [1] It is not obvious how he can logically cling to this avowedly false assumption just long
enough to break down the conventional distinctions between rent, wages, and interest, and then hastily discard
it as unnecessary, even fatal, to his subsequent argument.
Hobson is far from lucid on this point.

However that may be, his view of the nature of the
industrial system must now be thrown into high light.
Production, in his view, is an act of organic coöperation.
The productivity of any one factor is inextricably bound
up with that of the others. Slow workers decrease the
productivity of capital, bad machines that of labor, poor
land that of labor and capital, and so on. The total
product is the outcome of coöperative activity and one
can in no conceivable way determine either what part
of the physical product or what part of its value has been
contributed by any part of any factor. Hobson avows,
thus, a position directly the opposite of that of Clark and
other proponents of the marginal productivity theory of

[1] *The Industrial System*, p. 106.

wages, on two main grounds: that no separable physical or value product is discoverable, and that, if it were, equality of competitive bargaining power is an unwarranted assumption in modern industry. But he is still faced with the unexplained fact that every unit is paid according to some imputed "utility" or estimate of importance. This importance, it is conceived, has no reference to any separable productivity, but is assigned to any unit as an integral part of the organic coöperative group. The actual price per unit of any sort of productive power will be fixed by a process of bargaining between *entrepreneurs* and the owners of the various factors. The only limit is the lower limit imposed by the necessity of a payment covering maintenance, and even this is flexible. The surplus disposes itself entirely according to the bargaining strength of the various factors—that is, their ability to "pull" a greater or lesser share of it.

Having arrived definitely at the bargaining stage, we discover the necessity of an underlying theory of value. Postponing for a little Hobson's treatment of commodity prices, it may be stated that his value theory is merely an adaptation of Marshall's notion of the equilibrium of demand and supply. He adopts uncritically the "law" that "the immediate cause of a rise of price is·always a decrease of supply or an increase of demand," and *vice versa*. As applied to the prices of productive units, the mechanism is a demand schedule entered by *entrepreneurs* for varying amounts of the various kinds of units, a supply schedule entered by owners of these units, the price emerging at the equilibrating point. For the services of *entrepreneurs*, the price must come in a rather more direct way as the point of equilibrium between society's demand for such services and the supply of such ability available. Land, labor, and capital are, in a sense, competitors for employment. The reservation supply price of each kind of unit is commonly merely the cost of maintenance. How much more than this any kind of unit will be able to secure (out of the surplus available for payment) is simply a question of its relative scarcity.

The scarcity of the various grades of land is fixed by nature, and the price of a unit of land-use of a given grade is an aspect of this scarcity. Viewed in this light, the rent of land is an element in the price of the products of the land in the same way that the cost of the other factors is. The supply of labor and capital is regulated by very complex sets of forces. The actual condition is, however, that labor and capital are both relatively plentiful. The abundance of labor puts it in a weak bargaining position, so that the price of it, and consequently its share of the surplus, remains relatively low. The same is in general true of capital so far as the general investor is concerned, but in some branches of industry some special advantage permits of very high returns on investment, a feature of distribution which Hobson vacillates between classing as interest and profits.

The striking fact about modern industry lies in the special advantages enjoyed by certain interests which permit them to control the supply of their special factor and consequently to draw to themselves a large share of "unproductive surplus." Such classes include monopolistic enterprises of all sorts—landlords, particularly owners of city property, makers of patented or protected articles, and the like. As against the laborer, all *entrepreneurs* enjoy a favorable bargaining position. The result is that a large share of the surplus product of the industrial system is absorbed by these favored interests, by reason of contrived or natural scarcity of the factors or products they control, at the same time that large classes of laborers are being deprived of the income that would serve to increase their numbers and efficiency. This misapplication of the surplus serves to slow down the development of the industrial system and to intensify discord, besides introducing certain specific evils to be touched upon later.

Hobson is at some pains to demonstrate that a strictly competitive theory of distribution furnishes no intelligible account of distribution. It can hardly be maintained that he is either lucid or convincing on this point. The "strict condition" of free competition is, he says, "an equal abundance of all the various sorts and qualities of land, labour, capital and managing ability, for, if anyone at any point is relatively short in supply, it can suspend free competition and extort a rack-rent or

enforced gain." [1] This is the most obvious nonsense.
An "equal abundance" of factors is simply a meaningless phrase, since there is no common denominator to
which to reduce a quantitative expression of the various
factors.   And all competitive theory takes into account
the scarcity of the various factors.   Hobson has a case
against the justice of current distribution, and is convincing in denying the applicability of competitive
theory to a system in which special advantage plays so
large a part.   But in pressing these points home he
occasionally goes to the untoward length of complete
unintelligibility.

Before concluding this part of our analysis, a brief
examination of the theory of prices needs to be made.
As it is our purpose only to bring out those points of
Hobson's theory which have exercised some influence
upon economic thought, we need not linger long.   The
mechanism of the value theory is borrowed entire from
Marshall.   There are normal prices and market prices;
prices are fixed at the equilibrium point between demand and supply; demand and supply respond to price
changes in accordance with their elasticity; normal prices
measure cost on the one hand and utility on the other.
There is a trick in it, however.   For the expenses out
of which prices are compounded include those forced
gains which, at one point or another in the productive
process, have been extorted by favorably situated agents,

---

[1] *The Industrial System*, p. 136.

such as monopolists, controllers of raw materials, labor unions, and the like. The dictum that "goods exchange according to their expenses of production, their prices being composed of these expenses,"[1] assumes that the gains of the retailer, or last seller, are included among the expenses of production, even though he be a monopolist; but attention is nowhere called to this aspect of the case.

The other main divergence from the "neo-classical" doctrine lies in an attack upon the use of margins in price analysis. Hobson contends that the cost of production of marginal units of supply is of no more effect upon price than that of any other unit. To impute separate costs to different parts of the supply is incorrect. The expenses of producing each unit must be considered equal and "it is only the whole output that has a true cost." In any industry, production is supposed to be almost wholly absorbed by firms of a "representative" size and efficiency, and it is the "mean" costs of such firms that "dominate the supply price."

The analysis of demand contains a similar attack upon the marginal utility type of analysis. It is assumed that there is a normal or "representative" group of consumers for each commodity, whose valuations are based not upon the added utility of final increments of commodities, but upon the place which these commodities play in their normal standards of consumption. The formula is thus worked out that selling price is

[1] *The Industrial System*, p. 146.

fixed at the point of equilibrium between normal supply price and normal demand price which are determined, respectively, by "mean" cost and "mean"
utility. In arriving at this conclusion, the terminology
wobbles noticeably at times. Supply price is confused
with normal price; normal price means at one time long-
time normal, at another merely the compound of all
necessary and surplus costs; and finally the distinction
between normal and market prices is entirely demolished by the remark that "the difference between
long-time, or normal, and short-time, or market, prices
has of course no logical basis." [1]

The objection to the marginal analysis of cost and
utility enters as a corollary to the organic character of
processes of production and of habits of consumption.
Why he should assail it with such warmth, as a subtle
defense of the existing organization of industry, is
never intelligibly explained. It constitutes, of course,
a mere bit of mechanism for explaining the adjustment
of prices and of the uses of various productive factors
under a hypothetical competitive situation. He may well
object to competitive analysis, either as unrealistic or as
often implying a defense of the present system. But
the attack on marginalism appears at best supereroga-
tory—particularly since he presents no adequate alternative explanation of price adjustments, and since he
adopts the formula that price results from the equi-

[1] *The Industrial System*, p. 154.

librium of demand and supply, a doctrine for which marginal analysis would seem fairly essential.

This analysis of prices presents a curious anomaly. Avowedly, the pricing of commodities and of the factors of production is supposed to be amenable to the same rules. At the same time, the analysis of distributive shares is necessarily anterior to that of commodity prices, since the prices are made to include the forced gains already reaped in the earlier stages of production. Prices appear to rise like a snowball, accumulating as goods proceed forward in the productive process. Another curious feature is that the analysis proceeds almost entirely on competitive assumptions. The whole mechanism of competitive price determination, taken over from Marshall, is overworked to make it include monopoly elements of many sorts. No attempt at a theory of monopoly prices is made, but the whole range of prices from competitive to monopolistic is rolled into a single formula. The theory is a sort of cross between that developed by Sidney and Beatrice Webb in *Industrial Democracy*, where everyone possessing anything of value impounds these values behind a barrier in the attempt to dam them up to the highest level possible, and the competitive analysis of Marshall. It is a sturdy, but one could hardly say successful, attempt to produce a formula of value more related to the actual forces affecting prices than is to be found in the usual competitive theory. If one may applaud the attempt, he can hardly deny that the result is a little preposterous.

It will be unnecessary to give at any length the ramifications of these theories of value and distribution as applied to the operation of the industrial system. Those types of business that, under modern capitalism, develop naturally into large units, such as transport, finance, and many branches of manufacturing, are seen to possess particular power to control their markets, and in consequence to draw to themselves a large share of the "unproductive surplus." This power is displayed in the modern trust movement, but is partially checked by the elasticity of demand and by the organization of labor. The real reason for the labor movement is interpreted as an attempt to increase the laborer's share of the surplus, which is a "standing challenge." And the fact that large sections of labor get less than adequate wages of progressive efficiency is regarded as an economic justification for this attempt. The customary English defense of Free Trade is put forward modified slightly with reference to the surplus. Protective duties are held to reduce the aggregate wealth of the levying country, and at the same time to reduce the share of this reduced aggregate paid as wages, thereby increasing the proportion of "unproductive surplus" to total income.

The primary function of money is conceived to be as a medium of exchange. Most transactions are effected with the use of credit money, which is based on property. Gold is necessary merely as a reserve against the possible collapse of the capitalized values of income-bearing property, against which credit has been extended. The volume of credit is principally dependent on the state of trade, and confidence, not gold, is its true support. Hobson has elsewhere extended his monetary theory,[1] but it is not relevant to the present purpose to display it. He is an opponent of the quantity theory, and his treatment is more notable for interesting suggestions as to monetary control than as a well-developed treatment of the whole problem. He finds it anomalous that the supply of the medium by which all transactions must be consummated should be controlled by profit-making private enterprises, practically underwritten by government, tempted to a misuse of their powers, and exercising a degree of private monopoly which tends to swell the proportion of the "unproductive surplus."

We have now examined in some detail one characteristic phase of Hobson's economic thinking. It centers about the emergence of the surplus, and is to be regarded as a theoretical statement of the causes of the inequality in the distribution of wealth. This is for Hobson merely the groundwork, and it will be necessary at a later point to examine the theory of social reform which is built upon it. At the present point we have reached a convenient place at which to pause and

[1] In *Gold, Prices and Wages* (1913).

cast an appraising eye over the scene. It is apparent
that what we have dealt with is highly abstract material, not less so than that of Clark, Marshall, or
Böhm-Bawerk. Illuminating his theory with constant
reference to the life about him, Hobson none the less
proceeds by the deductive method. The difference
between him and the "neo-classical" and "marginal"
economists whom he so roundly criticizes must lie, then,
in his premises and preconceptions. These economists
have been mainly concerned with analyzing the operation of a hypothetical competitive system in which men's
activities proceeded on the hedonic principle. And for
the most part they have entertained a bias toward competition as a social regulating force. Hobson, on the
other hand, with a wide first-hand observation of the
darker side of social life, entered the arena of theory
with a well-developed belief in the need of social reform and a fairly sound notion of the extent to which
competition was currently failing to function as theory
would have it. He was bound to take cognizance of
that feature of economic life and introduces it under
the phrase, "contrived scarcity." It is his tenacity in
clinging to this idea that holds his theory together at
all points, even when the thread of logic has worn
thin or snapped.

A further assumption that gives a characteristic turn
to his analysis is that what is paid for is not men, acres,
or machines as such, but units of productive power. On
this point he achieves a high and dry abstractness

worthy of J. B. Clark. It would delay us too long to
examine the logical difficulties in which the manipulation of these units involves him.[1] No one, of course,
has ever seen, felt, or been aware of the existence of
them except as intellectual concepts. Nor are they ever
anything but ghostly presences. They do not represent
physical product or the value of physical product. They
are manipulated in such a way that whenever the marginal worker, acre, or machine of any grade secures a
higher reward, the payment of a unit of productive-
power of the respective grade and factor is conceived
to have increased. Why was this metaphysical abstraction invoked? The answer is obvious, that Hobson was
intent upon some means by which he might break down
the customary distinctions between rent, wages, and
interest for the purpose of exposing the surplus element
in them all. Rent had long been pointed to by the
Socialists and all manner of reformers as a true surplus,
the private appropriation of which was socially indefensible. Hobson observed what appeared to be
analogous elements in other sorts of income, and
adopted this method to make his point. He is constantly tripping over these units in his effort to avoid
a productivity theory of distribution. He makes no
attempt to use them in analyzing profits except in the
no-man's land in which he cannot distinguish profits

[1] They have been well dealt with by J. L. Laughlin in the *Journal
of Political Economy*, vol. xii, p. 305, though with some misunderstanding of Hobson's position and in the light of a strong bias of his
own.

from interest, and definitely abandons them as soon as they have served to establish the rental analogy to other incomes. Hobson's idea of the surplus, though not original with him at all, shows some acumen and furnishes the basis for a desirable sort of criticism of current types of competitive theory. Nothing but regret is to be felt that he adopted so awkward an instrument involving such tenuous concepts and such a strain upon the imagination. Attempting to make economic theory conform more to the facts, he proceeds by a method the most abstract possible.

One further assumption must be noted. The whole analysis in this part of Hobson's work proceeds apparently on the basis of a hedonistic psychology. Men are conceived to pursue their selfish ends rationally and persistently, and the ideal consummation of the industrial system is to produce "maximum satisfaction." The main condemnation of the existing system lies in its inability so to dispose of the surplus as to promote this happy consummation. Being drawn into the dialectical controversies of the eighteen-nineties, Hobson unconsciously accepted the psychological postulates then prevalent. His philosophy is Utilitarianism. In other connections and particularly in his later work his conception of human nature is entirely different, as we shall see. The point is of interest as demonstrating that one is not permitted to find within his theoretical work a high degree of internal consistency. The really important part of our inquiry, indeed, is concerned with why so illogical and inconsistent a theorist must be considered important and significant in current economic thought.

Out of the theory of the "unproductive surplus" springs another of Hobson's characteristic doctrines, his explanation of the cause of economic cycles.[1] It is illuminating as to his general viewpoint that he treats the subject under the heading of "unemployment" and that he stresses the period of depression in which "welfare" is most damaged by the disorganization of industrial life. It is conceived that the surplus under modern industrial conditions has tended to become concentrated unduly in the hands of a limited, privileged class, the industrial and financial magnates who wax fat upon the gains derived from the "contrived scarcity" of the factors of production and the goods which they control. Among this class the conventional habits of consumption do not expand at all in proportion to the growth of income, and saving becomes practically an automatic process. Such automatic saving appears not only in large individual incomes, but in the accumulating surplus of large enterprises, reinvested in the extension of plant and equipment. So important a proportion of saving comes from this source that the supply of new capital does not respond readily to the lowering of the interest rate. The result of the large volume

---

[1] This is expounded briefly in *The Industrial System*, Chap. 18, and in more detail in *The Economics of Unemployment* (1922).

of saving is that investment in new enterprises is heavy. Temporarily, no ill effects are perceptible as the result of this process. More men are employed, consumer demand is good, credit is freely extended, and a general optimism goes hand in hand with active business expansion. As, however, the increased product begins to flow heavily into the market from factory and mill, there is not sufficient purchasing power in the hands of consumers to carry off the supply.

A smooth and steady operation of the industrial system demands a proper adjustment of purchasing power to purchasable goods. But here we have a case of productive power considerably in excess of the power of consumers to carry off the product. A glut of goods ensues, followed by the slowing down of the whole productive process, the laying off of workers, a decline in purchasing power, and widespread business depression. During times of depression this absurd or tragic situation exists: workers wishing to work but unable to find employment; wants demanding satisfaction without the purchasing power to back them; a glut of goods moving slowly from retailers' shelves because of diminished purchasing power due to unemployment; a very low rate of commodity production and almost no provision of new productive equipment. During this period savings go rather into buying up the enterprises which have been forced into insolvency by the depressed state of trade. The retardation of new saving for investment restores after a time the right adjustment between real capital and rate of consumption, and a spell of good trade with full employment for capital and labor ensues. And then the whole process repeats itself.

Hobson is not unaware of the financial and psychological aspects of cycles, but regards them as secondary or ancillary to the fundamental defect in the distribution of wealth which causes productive capacity periodically to run away from the power to consume. Since, then, cycles are due to "under-consumption," or, viewed from another angle, "over-saving," the obvious remedy is for society to save less, to put more purchasing power in the hands of the working classes in the shape of wages, and to extract more of the surplus from its owners by a policy of steeply graduated income and inheritance taxes for use by the state in promoting the common welfare. The desirable consequences of increasing wages are not confined to this particular problem, nor are they available as a defense for all policies designed to raise wages. But, in the present state of economic organization, the effort to secure a national minimum wage and the efforts of organized labor to increase wages must be considered as desirable steps toward the stabilization of industry and the elimination of unemployment.

Since the present inquiry is not particularly concerned with cycle theories, we shall not stop to criticize this one in any detail. The problem of cycles has received so much attention during the present century

that there exists rather a plethora of *a priori* explanations. There have been developed, too, rather extensive
statistical data, and informed opinion tends to look to
the further collection of concrete material, rather than
to simple theories, for light upon the subject. Hobson's
theory, however, considered in relation to the time when
it was propounded, the interest it continues to arouse,
and the extent to which a number of other inquiries
have resembled it, must be regarded as an evidence of
the author's perspicacity. Propounded in the 'nineties,
it was rank heresy. Economic theorists in that decade
were largely concerned, so far as they were not quar-
reling over "concepts," with establishing the laws of the
"normal" action of the competitive system.

So long as normality was the center of attention,
crises were studied more as isolated and unfortunate
episodes somehow disturbing the smooth current of
events. Their periodicity had, of course, been noted
long before, and some considerable study made of their
financial aspects. But the idea that there was some
innate characteristic that made business run through a
never-ending series of cyclical ups and downs was very
novel. It fitted badly into the idea of normality.
Rodbertus and Marx, and particularly Engels, had
rather approached it, and, of course, deprived it of
respectability among "sound thinkers." It can hardly
be said that Hobson had during that decade grasped
it very thoroughly. Yet in the fertilization of the idea
he must be accounted a pioneer. Placing his gaze upon

the period of depression and asking how industry got there and how it escaped, he called attention to the phase of the cycle that had been neglected, and by so doing helped to start scientific investigation of the round of prosperity and depression, of which the events known as crises or panics are but dramatic episodes. The theory of cycles is as yet too ill-developed to permit any final judgment of Hobson's explanation. Like most others, it will probably prove only partially, if at all, valid. But it must still rank as a distinctive and valuable contribution to economic theory, as advancing the study of one of the most elusive of economic problems. It is, indeed, this willingness of his to be heretical, to doubt the wisdom of the savants, and to suggest alternative views, that constitutes one of his most valuable contributions to economic thought. He has helped to keep the pot boiling and the wise ones on edge to confute his "fallacies."

III

We have considered to this point mainly Hobson's analysis of the actual operation of the industrial system, seeing at the same time some of his views concerning its vital defects. Of these, the most serious is a bad distribution of income, which generates conflict between classes of producers, intrenches the interests of a privileged class, grinds down the poor, and destroys the stability of industry. The analysis has run mainly in terms of the production of wealth and the conditions determining its distribution. We shall not have completed our survey of his contribution to economic thought until we have followed him into his "human valuation" of the processes of production and consumption, and given him the opportunity to relate economic theory to a wider sphere of social theory.[1]

Many economists before Hobson were interested in the subject of human welfare. In general, however, this interest has occupied no part of their scientific attention, but has been merely a humanitarian reaction to the darker side of the life of mankind. During most of the nineteenth century the preconception was prevalent that the economic, if not the whole, life of mankind is governed by fixed and immutable laws. The idea was derived from the physical sciences and was supported by a reputable line of philosophical approval. To the task of discovering these laws in so far as they controlled the economic life of mankind the economists were committed. During the earlier half of the century these laws as expounded by Ricardo and his followers were converted into practical precepts of action, designed to increase the production of goods and thereby to increase the sum total of human welfare, conceived in terms of material satisfaction. During the latter half of the century economic theory became increasingly

[1] These aspects of Hobson's work will be found best set forth in *The Social Problem* (1901) and *Work and Wealth: A Human Valuation* (1914). The latter is the far more mature and references will be largely confined to it.

and consciously hypothetical, and increasingly incapable of furnishing precepts for the guidance of political policy. The hypothetical laws of value and distribution were applicable to the guidance of public policy only by reason of carrying a faint connotation of approval of the competitive system. It was against the absorption of economists in the data of the market place, their vestigial defense of *laissez-faire*, and their abdication of leadership in pointing the path of economic advance that Hobson rose to protest.

In so doing he was, as he did not hesitate to point out, in very good company. For Adam Smith, the founder of the science, had been no mere dialectician, but a sturdy opponent of an outworn and corrupt system of government regulation. He was the proponent of a definite scheme of economic reform and his theoretical structure was designed to be the supporting foundation for the policy which he considered wise. His problem was simplified because his policy was to release men's economic activities from undue regulation and thus consisted principally in removing the débris of the mercantile system. Hobson, though working in the spirit of Adam Smith, is faced by a more difficult problem. For he starts from the preconception that, under modern industrialism, the "system of natural liberty" is obsolete and undesirable, an idea based on a wide knowledge of industrial and social ills. To construct a theoretical foundation for the regulation of industry, and to relate this theory to a general theory of human welfare is, of course, a superhuman task, but Hobson is valiant and attempts nothing less.

Moreover, he conceives it to be the appointed task of economists to construct the theory and collect the concrete data upon which to reconstruct the industrial system in accordance with some more ideal plan. He is contemptuous of economists who merely draw the foreordained logical conclusions from unrealistic hypotheses. His economist must be both investigator, seer, and physician, applying the scientific technique to the discovery and cure of social diseases. It is in view of this emphasis that he has come to be known as the outstanding representative of what is known in the jargon of the profession as "welfare economies." He does not much believe in "natural laws" which economists can merely discover. He believes in the power of mankind to shape its own ends and in the possibility of achieving a society in which men's interests will harmonize. The laws of human action by which this harmony can be realized must be sought by all the social sciences, and economists are assigned the task of finding so much of them as lies within the economic sphere of the production, distribution, and consumption of wealth.

In approaching this task Hobson clung to the modes of thought which Utilitarian philosophy had made familiar to his generation. The Utilitarian concepts satisfy his mind and come naturally to his pen. The "narrow and degrading interpretation given to the term" is unnecessary, and "the revolt of a few superior minds against the general conceptions and expressions embodied in a language is always futile and commonly mischievous." [1] This curious dictum would seem to be open to grave objections, but it gives a good impression of Hobson's thought, which clings to old methods and terminology, but reads new meanings into them. The "degrading" economic interpretation of Utilitarianism has, he conceives, identified "costs" with the monetary expenses of the production of goods, "utility" with the monetary valuations of their users, and "welfare" with large physical production. The problem is to divorce the terms "cost" and "utility" from their monetary connotations and to interpret them in terms of some standard of "human" welfare. Given a race of human beings with their faculties, their social institutions, and the available supply of natural resources, how may they secure from these powers "the most complete satisfaction"?

Hobson is at pains to display the shortcomings of the Utilitarian economists. He points out that political economy from Ricardo to Mill centered its attention on the production and accumulation of wealth. Consumption, or the use of goods, was neglected except in so far as it bore upon further production. The science was shaped, unconsciously but effectually, by the dominant class prejudices, interests, and passions which drove intellectual workers to build convenient systems for the

[1] *The Social Problem*, p. 4.

class of industrial owners. It took a statical and mechanical view of society and a narrow, sordid view of human life and character. Political economy from Mill to Marshall added generous thoughts and sentiments, but suffered no change of heart. It remained a commercial science concerned with marketable wealth. The attention given to consumption by Jevons and the Austrians was illusory, developing a mere mechanical toy for demonstrating the logic of hedonism. "The theory of production is still the only strongly and closely wrought portion of economic science,"[1] distribution and consumption being represented only by disjointed separate little theories. "A science which still takes money as its standard of value, and regards man as a means of making money, is, in the nature of the case, incapable of facing the deep and complex human problems which compose the Social Question."[2]

What is wanted to reform economic science is, Hobson thinks, a calculus of "human costs" and "human utility" against which to check "economic costs" and "economic utility." Upon this analysis must be built a policy designed to minimize human costs and maximize human utility, thus maximizing welfare. Welfare is not to be assessed in individualistic terms, but in relation to the organic needs of society. What it is desired to increase is "social utility" by a policy designed to harmonize the needs of individuals with those of the social organism, or "collective personality."

[1] *The Social Problem*, p. 37.   [2] *Ibid.*, p. 38.

Aware of the difficulties of applying the organic metaphor to the life of society, Hobson nevertheless considers it the only tenable view and regards the concept
of "organic welfare" as "generally accepted." He proposes to evaluate the processes and results of industry,
viewed as an attempt to satisfy the organic needs of
individual and society.

The first step in "the human scientific calculus of
industrial values "[1] is to break up the conventional economic categories of production and consumption into
the "human" costs and utilities involved in each. The
questions to be asked are, (1) what goods are produced? (2) what human costs and utilities are involved in producing them? (3) what human utilities
and costs are involved in consuming them? The result
should be to display two lists, one of utilities, the other
of costs. So far as these can be quantitatively expressed,
they can be balanced against each other and "a simple
sum in subtraction should then give us the result we
seek."[2]

In the development of this method of calculation,
productive activity is divided into seven classes—art, invention, professional service, organization, management, labor, and saving, for all of which an economic
cost is incurred. Creative artistic work is done for its
own sake and incurs no "net human costs." It would
be done for mere "keep." A human cost may be involved in the loss of self-respect of artists who de-

_____
[1] *Work and Wealth*, p. 227.   [2] *Ibid.*, p. 35.

bauch their art to reap a monetary reward for meeting the tastes of their clients. And in repetitive or imitative art, such as musical performances, some considerable human costs may be involved. But in general the human costs of artistic work are low and the human utilities to the artist high. Discovery and invention have much in common with art. They are pursued in response to an inward urge and are more play than work, yielding a net return of human utility. There is, however, a social human cost incurred by the lack of leisure and education to pursue artistic and scientific work on the part of many qualified for it, due to the existing unequal distribution of wealth and leisure.

Among the higher grades of the professional and administrative classes, the skilled mental work is largely interesting and pleasurable in itself and consequently yields a large net sum of utility over costs. In the lower grades, however, such as clerks, the human costs are heavy and the utility negligible, due to the routine and repetitive character of the work and the loss of initiative and independent judgment. The exercise of commercial and financial leadership carries a sense of power and an opportunity of creative effort which are distinctly pleasurable and greatly outweigh the costs of worry and uncertainty. A social cost is, however, involved in the moral callousness which is engendered by the pursuit of monetary profit, and in the misdirection of taste which it inspires.

We find, then, that, in those pursuits which are commonly best paid, the human costs are relatively light, and are in some cases outweighed by the utility involved in productive activity which is creative, varied, interesting, and pleasurable. Moreover, in relation to rent, which ranks as an economic cost, no human cost whatever is involved. The situation is far otherwise with laboring-class occupations. They are to a large extent, especially in machine-using industries, repetitive and uninteresting. Injurious fatigue from physical and nervous strain are incidental to them, leading to accidents, nervous disorders, lowered morale, debased character, and dissipation. Where these heavier costs are not present, the human costs of mere monotony and subordination are great, and are accompanied by those incidental to living and working in depressing or unhealthful surroundings. Large areas of the industrial field are, of course, not reduced to the discipline of the machine. Nor can all the effects of the mechanization of industry be counted as costs. Much routine has been taken over by machines, the exercise of judgment is necessary to their control, and they frequently lighten the physical strain of labor while facilitating the increase of consumable products. It remains, therefore, an open question whether machines increase or lighten the human costs of labor.

Heavy human costs are involved, too, in unemployment and uncertainty of regular work; in the moral degradation due to casual labor; in the labor of children and the aged; in the labor of women which damages

the health, disrupts the home, or injures the physical
functions; and in sex discrimination in regard to the
higher callings. Clerical work is costly by reason of
specialization, repetition, and inadequate scope for the
exercise of the higher faculties; domestic labor because
of the sense of servility and submission to the will of
others. At the same time, the conditions of modern
industry tend to divorce effort from any adequate
realization of the social ends which it serves. Nor
would the ends themselves appear rational, if realized.
For the products of industry are often of doubtful
social utility and the rewards are so little related to
effort.

Saving, so essential to the progress of the industrial
system, involves very different calculations of human
cost, according to the class of people who do it. The
saving of the rich and the accumulation of corporate
surplus funds are largely automatic and can hardly be
said to have any cost. The saving of the middle classes
is carried on with more rational calculation of present
and future benefits. So long as present needs are adequately cared for, saving against future needs may mean
a positive increase in utility, because it insures future
security. In any case, the human costs of saving for the
"comfortable" classes are light. As one proceeds downward into the lower income classes, the situation is found
to be very different. For most working-class families
the purchase of future security through saving is accompanied by a stinting of comforts or even necessaries, of

education for children, of house room, in general of the decencies or amenities of civilized life. From the point of view of individual or family conduct, such saving is sound if costly economy, but socially viewed it is wasteful and would be unnecessary under a sound social economy. "It is literally a coining of human life into instrumental capital." [1]

It will be observed that, in cataloguing the human costs involved in the processes of production, Hobson appeals to a number of different norms. Some costs relate to the undesirable social conditions entailed through the present organization of industry; some relate to the effects of physical strain; but predominantly they are psychic, relating to the irksomeness of labor, thwarted freedom of action, and the atrophy of abilities. It may well be kept in mind that, since Hobson is propounding a theory of welfare for an organic society, he is faced with the necessity of finding some formula for harmonizing the welfare of individuals with that of society.

Turning to a similar analysis of consumption, Hobson appears as the disciple of Ruskin. To the end of final use all economic activity is directed, yet economists have neglected it in favor of the attendant processes of production and exchange. The arts of consumption, being individualistic or conventional and lacking the profit motive, have not been highly developed as have the arts of production, and consequently have eluded eco-

[1] *Work and Wealth*, p. 105.

nomic investigation. The subject remains a dark un-
charted continent. So long as consumption is dictated
by man's organic needs or by the nature of his occupation it presents no problems. It is when the growth
of a surplus above such needs has developed that its
relation to welfare demands attention.

Utility refers to the satisfaction which is derived
from consumption. In economic analysis it is supposed
to be expressed objectively in the prices which people
are willing to pay for objects of consumption. In order
to cut behind the usage into the human effects of the
uses of goods, Hobson asks three questions: what goods
are produced? who get them and in what proportions?
and how far are the recipients qualified to get "vital"
value from them?

Under modern conditions of increasingly productive
industry, there has arisen a wide field of conventional
consumption, unrelated to the physical necessities of
organic life. Consumption of this sort is not to be dismissed summarily as extravagance or waste, since much
of it includes the more desirable amenities of life and
supports the sense of distinction, dignity, or interest
which adds to the worth of human life. It is, however, into this class of consumption that the expression
of the more absurd or damaging wants enters. And
here, too, Hobson finds the evil effects of the present
control of industry and distribution of wealth. For the
profit system is organized, not to satisfy socially desirable wants, but whatever wants can be satisfied at a

monetary profit. Against the wiles of producers, with their adulteration and their skillful use of psychological knowledge in the arts of advertising and salesmanship, the consumer is relatively helpless in his ignorant and unorganized present status.

Moreover, the inequitable distribution of wealth insures the further corruption of standards of consumption. Taste in the field of conventional consumption is formed principally by imitation. The upper class, consisting largely of recipients of the "unproductive surplus," hold a prestige of "immeasurable importance, . . . percolating through all lower social grades, and imposing, not merely elements of conventional consumption, but standards and ideas of life which affect the whole mode of living."[1] Unfortunately, the standards of consumption induced by "the definitely parasitical attitude and career" of the leisure class are directed by no sense of social responsibility. They are, indeed, to a large extent directed to the attainment of a sense of personal superiority through "conspicuous consumption," in Veblen's phrase. The corruption of standards of consumption, due to the lure of profit and to the imitation of the upper classes, results in the production and use of large amounts of what Ruskin termed "illth"—that is to say, wealth of a harmful or socially undesirable character. "Regarded from the standpoint of pecuniary expenditure, the misdirection of the surplus income into empty or depraved modes

[1] *Work and Wealth*, p. 141.

of recreation, culture, religion, and charity is the largest of all economic wastes." [1] And thus one sees the tragicomedy of modern life, the diversion of the large surplus which might serve to enlighten and ennoble mankind into nostrums, drink, sport, sham culture, and vain display, "in a descending scale of frivolousness and depravity, as they seize by imitation the awakening mind of ever larger strata of our populations." [2]

Hobson's analysis of consumption is thus in the nature of a diatribe against present standards. To his first question he is compelled to answer that the humanly useless or damaging goods produced represent a relatively large proportion of the total. To the second question, the answer is that they go in undue proportions to the recipients of the "unproductive surplus." And finally, the corruption of taste induced by wasteful expenditure on the part of the socially esteemed classes leads to a loss of vital usefulness in the goods consumed among all classes of the community. The corollaries to all this are, of course, (1) that the misapplication of productive energy deprives the community of really useful goods that it might possess and (2) that the misappropriation of income deprives the needier classes of the essentials of a satisfactory life. Regarded from the social viewpoint, then, economic utility or the consumption of goods contains an alarmingly large element of human cost.

Since it is the disposal of the surplus that, in Hob-

[1] *Work and Wealth*, p. 157.   [2] *Ibid.*, p. 158.

son's view, stamps "with the badge of irrationality and inequity the general process of apportionment of income" and impairs the consciousness of human solidarity, it is to its proper disposal that attention should be given. A "human law of distribution" would be designed to eliminate all those unnecessary human costs which arise out of present distribution and to increase human utilities by a rational care for the needs of individuals and society. "Distribution according to needs," which is Hobson's formula, is not interpreted as a Communistic equalitarian doctrine. It involves the destruction of excessive incomes and the establishment, as nearly as may be, of equality of opportunity, but recognizes the psychological necessity for differential rewards to stimulate good work. Nor can the formula be applied merely to individuals as such. It requires that the establishment of a harmonious functioning of organic society be kept in the foreground, and the claims or desires of individuals subordinated to the welfare of the social body.

The human claims of labor for a larger share of the surplus are supported by the analysis of the ills from which wage-earners suffer under the current operation of the industrial system, in the way of irregularity, uncertainty, overwork, sweating, and privation. The labor movement is not merely a demand for more pay and more leisure. It is also a demand that labor be no longer regarded as a commodity for purchase and sale, and that remuneration "be regulated on the basis of the human needs of a family living in a civilized country." [1] Labor is entitled to regular and adequate compensation out of the proceeds of industry, an end to be promoted by the establishment of a legal "living wage," and to proper provision out of the common funds for adequate education, old-age pensions, housing, insurance, health, and recreation.

The human costs of labor are in danger of being increased, too, by the increased standardization, specialization, and loss of initiative which are implicit in the new movement for scientific management. It is, of course, desirable to increase the effective use of improved industrial processes. Upon this basis may be built a higher standard of material welfare. But, so long as industry is based upon the profit motive and labor purchased as a commodity, there is no guaranty that the human costs of increased monotony, speed, and regimentation will not outweigh any material gains. Nor is there, indeed, any assurance that labor will ultimately gain, since the increase may be drained off into the surplus incomes of the rich. A human scientific view of industry must include much more than mere technical efficiency. It is therefore essential that industry be intelligently controlled in a way which will protect the workers as human beings, not as industrial automata, and will permit industry to perform its function of sustaining the organic life of society.

In view of the evils, antagonisms, and dangers in-

[1] *Work and Wealth*, p. 190.

herent in the current working of the industrial system, Hobson considers two lines of reform imperative. In the first place, there must be created in the popular understanding a realization of the social functions of industry and an ideal of the social purpose for which it is designed. Our higher aspirations are at present held in bondage to an exaggerated view of the value of industry and property. Viewing industry as a conflict, not a coöperative social enterprise, we sustain and nurture the anti-social elements in life, and these are intensified by the irrational character of the present distribution of wealth. Upon a felt desire to establish social harmony, upon a willingness to subordinate individual desires to the larger welfare, upon the existence of a large measure of public spirit in the performance of social functions, the good day must wait. "What is needed above all is a social soul to inhabit the social body in our industrial system. A conscious, coördinating principle. . . ."[1]

In the second place, social control of business must be established. For reconstructing industry closer to the heart's desire, Hobson has some concrete suggestions. The guiding principle is brief. "The substitution of direct social control for the private profit-seeking motive in the normal processes of our industries is essential to any sound scheme of social reconstruction."[2] It is, of course, a principle that might be

[1] *Work and Wealth*, p. 285.   [2] *Ibid.*, p. 293.

invoked for many different schemes of reform. Hobson gives it substantiality by suggesting an adequate policy of control. In his view there should be free and uncontrolled scope for all artistic activity. New or experimental industries should also be given a relatively free hand, subject to minimum wage laws and high taxation of profits. The professions should be for the most part socialized—that is to say, made branches of the government service. All industries which are largely reduced to routine operations, all those performing an essential public service, and all those tending to achieve a monopolistic position should be socialized. The result of this combined freedom and control, supported by proper wage and other social legislation, would be to divert to wages and to the public funds most of what is now "unproductive surplus" without stopping the wheels of experiment and progress. Higher wages would buy more leisure, better living conditions, higher efficiency, and opportunity for the pursuit of desirable noneconomic ends, in short, the conditions of "the good life." Taxation and receipts from socialized industries would permit the provision of better education, public amusements, adequate public-health service, adequate housing, parks, playgrounds, cheap transportation, and efficient public services of many sorts. The elimination of profiteering and of excessive incomes would place property upon "an intelligible social and moral basis," stop the corruption of standards of consumption, and stabilize the operation of industry.

Reorganized on such a basis and animated by a consciousness of social function, industry would distribute its rewards in conformity with the human law of distribution, wherein lies the solution of the major social problems of luxury and poverty, toil and idleness, the individual and society, authority and liberty. Intoxicated at times by his vision of a better world, Hobson wanders off into rhapsodies, much in the spirit of Isaiah, about the good time coming when there shall be an end of injustice, misery, and waste; when there shall have been achieved security and rationality in economic life, a remolding of all parts of human life, and a tapping of all the sources of human ability; when life shall be beautiful, rounded, free, and satisfying. "An economic reformation which, by applying the human law of distribution, absorbs the unproductive surplus, would thus furnish a social environment which was stronger and better in the nourishment and education it afforded to man. . . . So far as the economic activities can be taken into separate consideration, it is evident that this justly ordered environment would do much to raise the physical, and more to raise the moral efficiency of the individual as a wealth-producer and consumer. But its most important contribution to the value and growth of human welfare would lie in other fields of personality than the distinctly economic, in the liberation, realization, and improved condition of other intellectual and spiritual energies at present thwarted by or subordinated to industrialism."[1]

It is perhaps unnecessary to examine in detail the more metaphysical features of Hobson's organismic theory of society. It is of a kind with the speculations of those political philosophers who have invented diverse metaphysical theories of the state and is capable, as he admits, neither of proof nor of disproof. Society is conceived to have a personality of its own and a will of its own; its organic needs and purposes must take precedence over those of individuals; social harmony will result only from the realization by individuals of social ends and from submission to them. "The rights and interests of society are paramount, they override all claims of individuals to liberties that contravene them."[2] "This view of the nature of society . . . must, indeed, to the individual mind always remain as an hypothesis, incapable of full and exact verification."[3] Yet there is a moral obligation to believe in it. For, "so long as Society is spoken of and thought of as an abstraction, no social conduct can be sound or safe. For an abstraction is incapable of calling forth our reverence, regard, or love. And until we attribute to Society such a form and degree of 'personality' as can evoke in us those interests and emotions which personality alone can win, the social will will not be able

[1] *Work and Wealth*, pp. 299-300.
[2] *Ibid.*, p. 304.   [3] *Ibid.*, p. 308.

to perform great works." [1] The argument thus runs off into a distinctly theological terminology. Believe, and it shall be so! That which we know not, we know! "Society" is merely set up in place of God.

If society *is* an organism and if it has ends and a will of its own, it is not obvious what individual desires have to do with its functioning and development. But if the ends and will of society are but figments of the imagination, Hobson appears to be basing social progress upon a process of self-hypnosis. He falters between the literal and the metaphorical conception of the social organism. For the most part he is allied in thought to the theological party that denies foreordination, but believes in the divine purpose which can achieve itself only through the freely willed actions of men.

And so we come to grips with the mystery of mysteries, .the nature of the universe. It would be easy to scoff at Hobson's temerity in pushing an economic inquiry to the outer rim of philosophy. It violates, certainly, the professional habit of economists. Yet the problems are latent in the most conventional theory of the equilibrium of forces. They are escaped merely by an agreement in the initial postulates that certain things are so, thereby begging the whole question. It does not, therefore, disqualify Hobson as an economist if he feels at times the necessity of pushing his inquiries to the precipice of the unknown.

Being, however, of a practical mind, he withdraws,

[1] *Work and Wealth*, p. 309.

perhaps a trifle alarmed, from the contemplation of the metaphysical "great open spaces." He has avowedly attempted a "calculus" of human costs and utilities, "to assess the human worth which underlies the economic costs and utilities that enter into economic values." [1] But the mere attempt to measure human welfare demands a preëxisting standard of measurement. The division of the processes of production and consumption into human costs and utilities requires a principle of valuation. Hobson, driven to the necessity of producing this principle, finds it in the "enlightened common sense" of mankind. What enlightened men are agreed upon as social welfare *is* social welfare. Unfortunately, mankind is not greatly enlightened, and to raise up enlightenment and make it prevail is "the most pressing task of civilization in the self-governing nations of our time." [2]

Though such a common sense standard of human valuation is the best that is available, Hobson concedes that it will have little scientific accuracy. The significant facts of social life are, unfortunately for scientific precision, usually incapable of quantitative measurement. Only those phenomena can be scientifically valued or balanced against one another which are reducible to a common unit of measurement. In ordinary economic analysis a great many diverse kinds of things are reduced to monetary expression. It is upon the basis of this common denominator of economic value

---

[1] *Work and Wealth*, p. 320.   [2] *Ibid.*, p. 321.

that the ordinary processes of economic life proceed. These monetary valuations, however, merely tell us the proportions in which various goods and services exchange for one another, and nothing whatever about their relation to the welfare of either individuals or society. The basic reason for Hobson's protest against the dogma of conventional economic analysis is that it concerns itself only with monetary valuations and consequently gives no light or guidance upon the subject of welfare.

The things that really affect welfare are largely questions of kind and quality, good as against bad literature, symphonies as against prize-fights, sanitary as against germ-ridden houses, leisure as against overwork. The attempt, then, to maximize the human utilities of industry must, Hobson finally concludes, be in terms not so much of science as of art. It will be directed, not to mere increase of industrial output as measured in bulk or money, but to a control of the conditions of labor, a proper division of the product, and education in standards of desirable consumption. Such is the problem of the statesman and reformer, a task requiring a knowledge of conditions such as can be expressed quantitatively, but requiring much more the exercise of sound judgment in directing progress toward a sound ideal of social welfare. The direction of progress toward social welfare demands an adherence to three related guides, made valid by their appeal to "enlightened common sense," (1) the ultimate ideal,

(2) the operative ideal of a limited and practical nature, and (3) concrete measures directed to realizing the operative ideal. The first is, of course, Utopian, and, since we see at any one time "as in a glass darkly," would change as our enlightenment grew. For the second, "an operative ideal for an Englishman at the present time might be the vision of the State, as the collective will, securing by law a clearly conceived standard of sound efficient life for the ordinary working-class family." [1] The third would include the policy of socializing or regulating industry and of adopting such types of social legislation as have been heretofore mentioned. It is conceived that "no social-economic proposal, however distinctly quantitative it appears, can be humanly valued in any other way" than by reference to an ideal organic plan. "It is for this reason that a mere economist is always disabled from giving practical advice in any course of conduct." [2]

Driving his inquiry, ultimately into speculative fields, Hobson concludes upon the note that, however men may strive to cope with their problems, the course of progress must be regarded as the instinctive drive of the "general will" toward the ends of the social organism. The growing rationality of mankind, regarded as largely an aid in working out the lines of action prescribed by the instinctive protection of organic life, "may be regarded as a bringing of the individual man into vital communion of thought and feeling with the

[1] *Work and Wealth*, p. 347.   [2] *Ibid.*, p. 348

thoughts and feelings of the race." [1] The roots of the common sense by which the human valuation of industrial life must be made are thus to be found "in the silent, instinctive organic striving of mankind."

And there the story is ended—stranded upon a doubtful hypothesis of the purposeful evolution of the social organism. It is pertinent to ask whether this is a contribution to the literature of economic theory. Certainly not by the generally accepted understanding of the scope of economics. It appears more like a contribution to the inchoate science of sociology, of which economists commonly speak with contempt. But would it not be relevant to ask whether Adam Smith was not at least as deeply involved in philosophical difficulties? Is it less reasonable to postulate a social organism and welfare by control than natural law and welfare by the self-interested activities of innumerable contending individuals? And are there not implicit in the postulates of all systematic statements of economic theory philosophical problems just as troublesome as those which Hobson exposes boldly and explicitly? It will not do hastily to declare that this is not economics. It certainly is not economic "science" in the usual meaning of that term. If it must be classified, Hobson's terms of "economic art" may describe its subject-matter. It runs directly counter to the fundamental tenet of economic art implicit in most economic theory derived from Adam Smith—that is to say, noninterference. It

[1] *Work and Wealth*, p. 355.

is in effect a substitute formulation as against all theories that imply a blessing upon the state of things as they are, and all theories that "scientifically" detach themselves from considering the problems of human welfare.

How satisfactory a system it is, it is not our purpose to assess. The difficulties that are placed upon the imagination and understanding are many and serious. What starts out to be a "calculus" of human values turns out to be only a catalogue of the evils produced by the current operation of the industrial system. A calculus is nothing if not quantitative, yet the possibility of quantitative measurement of human welfare comes to be expressly denied. Before the logical necessities of the organismic concept the very idea of a calculus seems to break down, and enlightened common sense comes merely to represent the rational attempt to realize and promote the innate needs and ends of the organism. Though the ends sought are those of the organism, the evils recounted and the remedies sought are largely those affecting individuals as such. Such observations indicate the impression with which one is left that the whole framework of thought within which the problem of welfare is conceived has undergone a silent metamorphosis. And yet, one retains an equally strong impression that the analysis represents a useful and valuable addition to economic thought. An attempt at least has been made to cope with a set of problems, bearing upon economic activities, that cut in to the very heart of human life.

IV

We have now passed over the two phases of Hobson's work which represent his major contribution to economic theory. The first phase was an analysis of the current distribution of wealth out of which it came to appear that the major economic ills and discords of modern life arise out of a struggle for the surplus. That analysis proceeded in terms of the rational pursuit of individual self-interest, accepted in general the concepts and terminology common to recent systems of economic theory, and forced unorthodox conclusions into the framework of Marshall's theory. The particular turn of the conclusions was reached by keeping the light always turned upon those sources of income which represent exclusive property rights such as the ownership of land, or peculiar ability to reap an excessive reward through some contrived scarcity of productive power or salable commodities. The line of reform indicated is relatively conservative, admitting the necessity of the existing economic system, including in a limited way the profit motive, but requiring the state to intervene to enforce better distribution through various devices of social control.

The second phase is built upon the first. The evils arising out of the present operation of industry are more minutely examined, the remedies more specifically developed, and a whole theory of social reform built upon the assumption that social harmony is an attainable ideal. The analysis never departs far from the idea that the disposal of the surplus is the vital problem at issue, and that all the other desiderata of a healthy social life wait upon reform in that direction. We can thus perceive the consistency with which Hobson has, with good logic and bad, clung to his central tasks, (1) of disclosing the existence and effects of the surplus in the industrial system, and (2) of creating a method for the "human" valuation of wealth as the basis for social reform.

Between these two major phases of Hobson's analysis there exists a distinct discordance of thought. To a large degree it may be attributed to the lapse of time, during which he had been introduced to a number of novel ideas. As has been shown, his earlier analysis proceeds in conventional terms. Apart from indicating the incompetence of a competitive postulate to explain the distribution of income, it is thoroughly allied to other late nineteenth-century economic theory. Even the reformatory bias is distinctly, even crudely, hedonistic, proposing a method whereby to increase the physical productivity of the industrial system and to increase the mere physical complement of goods to the needier members of society. Out of such conceptions is the surplus theory distilled. Carried over into the theory of welfare, this theory finds itself strangely out of place in the midst of an organismic theory of society. Since welfare is conceived in terms of a proper distribution of the surplus, the organic theory of welfare's emasculated into little more than a theory of increasing individual welfare through the intervention of the state.

Hobson thus displays the influence of contradictory cross-currents prevalent in contemporary thought. He clings to the terminology and modes of thought of Utilitarianism. They do not, unfortunately, translate well from the language of the individualistic into that of the organic view of society. It is not, indeed, at all apparent how values can represent an equilibrium of forces except through the hedonistic calculus, or at any rate, through individual choices; nor how such a calculus, or such choices, can be fitted into the view of society as a true biological organism, living and growing. There is an uncertain wavering, natural to one who, trained up in the ways of "neo-classical" economics, has become conversant with and attracted to the organic theory of much sociological and political thought.

A further evidence of intellectual cross-currents is found in Hobson's use of psychology. The earlier work is based upon the assumption of the rationality of human action common to most economic theory. Later, in the discussion of standards of consumption, Veblen's theory of "conspicuous consumption" and Tarde's theory of imitation are appealed to. And still later human nature is portrayed as largely a matter of instinct, with specific reference to William McDougall's views upon the subject. Yet upon this latter base he proposes a scheme of reform dependent for its execution upon a rational calculus made by a democratic electorate gifted with "enlightened common sense." And this is in spite of the view that social progress is to be conceived as the instinctive striving of the social will to attain its ends. It is a curious mixture of ideas.

In his latest book, *Free Thought in the Social Sciences* (1926), he makes plain his belief that modern psychology has compelled a reshaping of all social theory. Modern psychology appears in his mind to be psychology of the sort of McDougall's *Social Psychology*, though that writer's later work is criticized in detail. He is impressed by the psychological approach to social theory as displayed by Veblen and Graham Wallas. In spite of his faith in it, it is not apparent that his acquaintance with psychological literature is large. One would surmise, however, that a growing knowledge of the bearing of psychology upon social theory is mainly responsible for the incongruence of Hobson's earlier with his later work. And this lack of congruity is heightened by a compromise between the individualistic and the organic social viewpoints.

That Hobson's mind should grow in stature and sweep should certainly not be a point for criticism. What appears is, however, that the new is overlaid upon the old with an inadequate process of fusion. The conclusions from an earlier stage of thought are carried over into a later stage a little uncritically. It is certainly an impossible feat to make the psychology of James Mill and of William McDougall lie down peaceably within the confines of a single system of thought. Only in the millennium shall the lion and the lamb lie down together.

Where his thought touches the field of political theory, Hobson wavers hesitantly between individualism and collectivism. The individualistic theory of the relation of the state to industry is attacked, and the attack upon "neo-classical" economic theory is made because it is supposed to support that objectionable position. The claims of society, as represented by the state, are regarded as paramount. Yet this leads to no thorough-going collectivism, but only to tinkering with the present organization of industry to remove its grosser evils. This, of course, may be very sound policy from the point of view of a practical reformer, but it appears to neglect some of the implications of the concepts used. The political theory is not carried far, only far enough to justify considerable inroads by the state upon the private control of industry. In England, it is the political theory of social reform that has been carried furthest, and by a somewhat sturdier race of reformers, including Sidney and Beatrice Webb, G. D. H. Cole, and H. J. Laski. Hobson is too conservative a reformer to be a good collectivist like the Webbs, and too devoted to the somewhat threadbare doctrine of parliamentary sovereignty to be a guild socialist or a pluralist. Yet he is too convinced a reformer to be an individualist. And so he is caught astride the fence, inclined to leap into the meadow where collectivists, social psychologists, and sociologists live on high thoughts and meager verdure, but loath to leave the fertile pastures of his early liberalism. Or it might better be said that he grazes in both fields without distinguishing the quality of the fare. No fence can contain the wandering of his mind.

Such is the situation of all practical reformers. Nor of them alone. Only workers in economic theory who labor behind barred doors can be unaware of novel and disturbing ideas developing in their sister sciences, or can be unconcerned with the progress of thought in psychology and politics, ethics and biology, history and law; or can fail to question the perfection of their own discipline. It has been Hobson's particular service to compel the attention of economists to subjects generally regarded as beyond their frontiers. He has demanded a new scrutiny of their assumptions, a new appraisal of their technique, and a new estimate of their use in the world. He has emphasized the unity of social life and its essentially artistic character, not thereby questioning the usefulness, but delimiting the scope of qualitative and quantitative analysis alike. He has attempted to demonstrate the barrenness of a social science which divorces itself from considerations of human welfare. He has insisted that the subject-matter of economics is human beings, with all their "trials and tribulations," and that their welfare is the paramount claim upon the attention of social scientists. The ideas are highly disputable. They are, nevertheless, Hobson's, defended in season and out. It may be admitted that, in developing a theoretical framework for his practical aims, he is at times guilty of faulty logic and a confusion of tongues, and that, in his criticism of other systems of theory, his misunderstanding or misinterpretation of them is serious. Yet there is still enough cogency and point, enough stimulating thought and illuminating suggestion, to entitle him to a place among the significant economic theorists of the present century. In his very confusions and inconsistencies he is as representative of the thought of his generation as in his more lucid intervals.

Hobson is in some degree the complement of Professor W. C. Mitchell. Mitchell believes that economists should engage in amassing quantitative data which can be used to promote social welfare. But he has not disclosed any definite view of welfare. Hobson attempts to give a theory of welfare in the light of which data can be collected and public policy directed. How satisfactory a theory it is each may judge for himself. It will please those who agree with the controlling preconceptions that social harmony is an attainable ideal and that laws of human action leading to harmony are discoverable. It will at least be regarded sympathetically by those who think the function of social science is to assist in the solution of current prob-

lems of practical importance. It will encourage, if
only by its temerity, all those unconventional souls
who are not impressed by the usefulness of economic
theory of the more orthodox sort. Behind the looseness of thought they will perceive a determined effort
to break through the crust of conventional modes of
thought in order to cope intellectually with some very
important practical aspects of economic life. Even
those critical persons who see in Hobson's theory a
tissue of absurdities can hardly read him without a
deepened sense of social forces and social problems.
And this will be particularly true if they go afield from
the work we have traversed into his less theoretical
writings. He is essentially the spokesman of a point
of view toward life. One may applaud his point of
view or not; one may or may not like his theory;
but one cannot escape their relevance to the present
problems of society.

It is a reasonable question whether, in the present
disordered state of knowledge and of human affairs at
large, any general theory of welfare can be framed.
And were it possible, it is not apparent that Hobson
possesses the synthesizing mind necessary to the task.
As a perhaps premature experimenter he at least brings
a mind full of relevant material. In a world not expectant of finality there is no doubt about the strength
of the influence of his ideas. He might well be made
economist "by special appointment" to the British Labor
Party. His surplus theory crops up in most current

discussions of social policy. And his view of the function of economists as that of forwarding the rational control of social processes for purposes of the general welfare is in a large degree sweeping the field.

In Hobson's apprehension the whole scheme of thought involved in the theories that we have presented was designed to be for the present day in some modest degree what *The Wealth of Nations* was for its day. It was to undercut the intellectual foundations of a socially wasteful economic policy, and to substitute the basis of a new plan designed to harmonize economic interests and maximize economic welfare. Without instituting any comparison, it may fairly be ranked among the more important contributions to economic thought during the present century.

Wesley C. Mitchell

Wesley C. Mitchell

I

THERE is a certain consensus of opinion among economists in the United States that the most capable of their number among the younger men is Professor Wesley C. Mitchell. Unlike most economists of earlier generations and the "elders" of the present generation, his reputation is not based upon any compendious or detailed treatise in the field of economic theory. His work has, in fact, been mainly concerned with a field so far from his subtleties of theory as the application of statistical technique to the investigation of economic phenomena. His peculiar competence in this field is the initial basis upon which the consideration in which he is held rests.

He has, however, joined to work of this character a sustained interest in the theoretical problems of economics. From time to time, in speeches and articles, he has developed his views on economic theory, and in his university classroom has perhaps been most effective and popular when dealing with the problems of theory. Concerning the importance or significance of his theoretical views there would be found no such

consensus as concerning his competence as an investigator. It is probable, however, that in his views can
be found a better expression than elsewhere of a newer
trend of economic thought which, in the United States,
is producing a marked hiatus between the ideology of
the older and younger generations of economists. He
may, consequently, be taken, not as the spokesman of
a generation of economic thinking, but as an illuminating example of certain currents of thought which, during the present century, have been recasting the intellectual concepts underlying economic theory.

It is only by a sort of license that one speaks of Professor Mitchell as belonging to the younger generation.
Having safely turned the mid-century mark and having
served his term as president of the American Economic
Association, he might well expect to be included among
those who are mature and wise. But one thinks of him
against the background of that distinguished and long-
lived group of American economists who have for a
generation adorned the scene of economic thought.
And one also thinks of him in terms of his spiritual con-
sanguinity. In these terms he is perhaps closer to the
youngest instructor than to the most venerable of his
associates upon the faculty of economics at Columbia
University.

Born in a small Illinois town, Mitchell passed
through the public schools of Decatur to the University
of Chicago. There is no record that he grew up with
any other complement of ideas than might be common

to any well-brought-up Middle Western boy. He doubtless approached the university armed with little more than small-town common-sense notions, a good mind, and an eager intelligence. He entered the university in 1892 and was there as a student continuously until 1899, with the exception of a single year when he pursued his post-graduate studies at the Universities of Halle and Vienna.

The decade of the 'nineties was marked by great interest in the theoretical aspects of economic study. The theoretical work centered largely on the refinement and elaboration of the marginal utility theory of value, and upon the discovery of a theory of distribution congruent therewith. It was during this decade that John Bates Clark was rising to the position of the foremost American economic theorist. The type of theory wrought out during the period, compounded out of the writings of Alfred Marshall, J. B. Clark, and the Austrians, has continued down to the present day to be the kind mainly taught in the schools.

Mitchell's theoretical position has been of quite a different sort, and it should prove enlightening to examine the curious, negative relationship of the development of his views to the drift of theory at that time. In spite of undergoing his apprenticeship during the 'nineties, circumstances combined to keep him from being swept into the main current. At the University of Chicago the outstanding figure in economics was Professor J. Laurence Laughlin, who, more persistently than any other American economist, clung to the classical tradition. Brought up on Mill, he remained true to Mill's type of analysis and was never seduced by the subtle blandishments of subjective economic theory. He was, indeed, its violent opponent and one of its keenest critics. So far as he made concessions to later thought, his sympathy lay much more with Marshall than with the Austrians. It was under Laughlin's tutelage that Mitchell was inducted into economic studies, and learned to look askance at prevalent doctrines.

Laughlin's primary interest was in currency questions and monetary problems, and it was under his influence that Mitchell undertook his first important task, a study of the greenbacks. This beginning was crucial and decisive, for out of the problems and technique of his doctoral thesis came the nature, scope, and direction of Mitchell's later work. It is not often that the dissertations of graduate students become classics, but such has been the fortune of the *History of the Greenbacks* which remains the standard work on one of the most important episodes in American monetary history.

The part played by Laughlin in Mitchell's development was to catch him young, assist in saving him from the methods of marginal utility analysis, implant in him high standards of scientific workmanship, and set him upon the statistical investigation of monetary problems. But he did not succeed in implanting an adherence to the doctrines of classical economics in his mind. The nature of the greenback investigation doubtless had something to do with this, as will be seen. But the primary reason may probably be traced to the presence of two men upon the staff of the University of Chicago, Thorstein Veblen and John Dewey.

Dewey was disseminating the novel doctrines of pragmatism from his chair in the department of philosophy, and Mitchell was one of his students. Dewey, of course, was doing nothing if not casting doubt upon systems of philosophy whose chief virtue was their internal logical consistency. He was exposing to view the social origins of the preconceptions upon which systems were built. He was attempting to rebuild philosophy upon a foundation of modern psychology and epistemology. And he was advancing a view of life and knowledge as an adventurous process in which mankind is attempting with developing intelligence to direct and control its increasingly complex environment.

Veblen was in a way the complement of Dewey, or his partner in crime. Dewey, of course, was a social reformer, and Veblen was a satirist. But both alike were under the influence of an evolutionary view of social development. The one in philosophy, the other in economics, was attempting to reshape the thinking in his own field into conformity with the findings of modern science. In their views upon the development of human thought and institutions their thought is to a considerable degree parallel and contiguous, and one infers that Veblen was himself indebted to Dewey. At the time when Mitchell was a graduate student

Veblen was in the process of constructing the devastating attack which he made upon formal systems of economic theory. He had been a student of Veblen's since his undergraduate days and was much impressed by the latter's philosophical attack and by his notion of the genetic approach to economic theory. It was, indeed, as an offset to the philosophical influence of Veblen and Dewey that Laughlin had suggested to Mitchell the very concrete and realistic subject of greenbacks for his doctor's thesis. The association was not terminated at the end of Mitchell's period of graduate study, for, after a year as a statistician at the United States Census Office in 1900, he returned to Chicago and was associated with Veblen upon the faculty of political economy at the university for a number of years.

It is plain that Dewey and Veblen, particularly the latter, had a decisive influence upon Mitchell's attitude toward systematic economic theory. From Veblen, too, he drew a framework of ideas into which to fit his thinking upon the problems which engaged his interest. In a limited sense, he may be regarded as a disciple of Veblen, and the extent of his debt our later exposition should make clear.

It would, however, be a serious misconception to regard Mitchell as merely some one to be explained in terms of Laughlin, Dewey, and Veblen. One must limit their influence to something of a germinal sort, providing him in his more impressionable days with, respectively, a direction for his work, a social and philosophical outlook, and a framework of economic concepts of an unorthodox sort. During his years of teaching at Chicago he was associated with other men who were struggling in an open-minded way with the problems of economic theory, particularly H. J. Davenport and R. F. Hoxie. He was associated, too, with a group of distinguished workers in the other social sciences, most of whom were working in a pioneering way to reshape their thinking in relation to the increasingly complex problems of modern society, with relatively little reverent adherences to traditional habits of thought. In just what way intellectual influences of this sort combined to shape Mitchell's thinking represents an aspect of the undiscoverable personal equation. It seems merely worth while to mention them in passing, in order to indicate the circumstances under which he worked, which were peculiarly favorable to the development of an independent and emancipated viewpoint.

The *History of the Greenbacks,* Mitchell's first work, was concerned only in a secondary way with theoretical questions. It was primarily a project in economic history. Yet it deserves some slight attention, as bearing upon the development of Mitchell's later views. The book covers only the period of the Civil War. The first part is taken up with a history of the Legal Tender Acts, and deals with the financial exigencies which led to them, and with the political situation out of which they arose. The second part, dealing with the economic consequences of the Legal Tender Acts, is an attempt to determine the influence of a fluctuating standard of value upon the economic welfare of various groups of the population, and upon the production and consumption of wealth. Economic theory of the normalizing sort has, of course, regarded money as a mere convenience and, for purposes of building up theories of value and distribution, assumed a stable monetary unit. Economists, reflecting upon the vagaries of monetary values, had from time to time arrived at various speculative conclusions concerning the effects of the "friction" involved in an unstable unit of money. Mitchell's was, however, perhaps the first extensive objective investigation into the subject.

His investigation was marked by two interesting variations from the speculative treatment of monetary theory. In the first place, he dealt with what, from the point of view of orthodox tradition, was an element of "friction" in the normal operation of economic forces. From the point of view of his own intellectual development, the important fact is that he was from the start interested in the "disturbing," and not in the "normal" aspects of economic adjustment. His mind was being compelled to run back from the objective facts of an unstable monetary unit, a fluctuating price level, and a shifting allocation of distributive shares to the less patent facts which lay behind them—politics, the credit of the government, popular sentiment and belief, and the unequal incidence of price-changes upon

the real income of various classes. He was exploring
economic processes, in which a complex system of
money payments stood between the production and en-
joyment of goods. Examining the influence of unstable
money upon economic welfare, his attention ran not to
any beautiful scheme of normal adjustment, but off
into the complicated scene of human institutions and
states of mind.

The other interesting characteristic of his study was
that it was based upon the use of a statistical technique.
The data with which he worked were sets of statistical
tables, showing the course of bullion prices, commodity
prices, wages, interest rates, rent, and profits under the
greenback standard. His primary conclusions then
dealt with matters of sequence, relative change, and the
like, and constituted an inductive display of the effect
of the greenbacks upon the purchasing power of the
recipients of various classes of income. In effect, his
task was the collection and interpretation of relevant
statistics. In attempting, however, to explain the meaning of his statistics and to establish causal relationships,
he was compelled to go outside his quantitative data.
His recourse here was to the economic arrangements
through which incomes reach their recipients, and to
the course of external events which, by affecting the
credit of the government and public confidence in the
greenbacks, led to price fluctuations and the further
disturbance of the relationship between income groups.

It is not necessary here to go into the nature of his

more general conclusions, except briefly. He found that profits increased at the expense of wages, interest, and rent. He concluded that prices fluctuated much more in relation to the state of public confidence in the outcome of the war than in relation to the quantity of the currency. He did not find that high profits stimulated an increase of physical production, nor that war-time "prosperity" was more than an illusion to the great mass of the population. These and other findings he attempted to give no general theoretical importance, presenting them as mere statements of fact for the brief period covered. The bearing of this investigation upon the development of his theoretical views was, however, of undoubted importance. For he was dealing with precisely those topics, value and distribution, upon which economic theory had most fully and confidently spoken. Treating them quantitatively in the light of a universally disturbing currency situation, he found that his conclusions fitted into no scheme of the normal equilibrium of economic forces. Such value as they had were merely by way of elucidating the course of economic welfare within a given period and under given circumstances.

It may be said in passing that the effects of the greenbacks continued to interest Mitchell, and he published in 1908 a companion volume to the *History*, entitled *Gold, Prices, and Wages under the Greenback Standard*, carrying the record down to the resumption of specie payments in 1879. This volume consisted almost entirely of statistical tables, with only text enough to explain the sources and methods, and to indicate the general character of the results. The intention was that the volume should furnish the statistical basis for a thoroughgoing investigation of the economic consequences of the greenbacks during the whole period of their inconvertibility. That task was never completed, due doubtless to the shifting of Mitchell's interest to a wider field of investigation. As anyone who has examined them will understand, the volumes on the greenbacks represent an amount and quality of work almost incredible for a man to have achieved by his thirty-fifth year in the midst of other duties. Thus, long before anyone knew or listened to his views on economic theory, indeed before he seems to have formulated them at all clearly, Mitchell had established a reputation as perhaps the most competent handler of economic statistics in the country.

Mitchell appears to have been jarred out of whatever predilections he may have held for classical or neo-classical economic theory by Veblen's essays near the turn of the century. He was impressed by the view that economics must approach its problems from the evolutionary point of view, and by the idea that the key to an adequate understanding of the working of the economic system must rest upon an understanding of the human habits of thought and institutions which direct economic activity. He was particularly impressed by the distinction which Veblen made between business, or pecuniary, and industrial, or technological, aspects of economic activity. This distinction, developed brilliantly in the *Theory of Business Enterprise* (which Mitchell considers "a great book"), became an essential instrument in his scheme of thought.

The distinction was one peculiarly designed to fit into Mitchell's handling of his own problems. As we have seen, he was engaged in an investigation of economic welfare from the point of view of the effects of an inconvertible currency system. He discovered, of course, that, while welfare depends upon an abundance and equitable distribution of concrete goods, the most remarkable variations in the well-being of classes of the population arose merely from the financial disturbances related to a fluctuating monetary unit. He found, too, that the fluctuations in physical production were in no way parallel or comparable to the extraordinary variations in money prices and pecuniary rewards.

In other ways his investigations were designed to throw his analysis of economic activity into other terms than those of an equilibrium of economic forces. For example, the monetary system which could play such extraordinary tricks upon people's income and their physical well-being was purely a human institution, devised and instituted by a legislature in extreme ignorance of its ultimate consequences. It appeared that the application of human intelligence to the solution of economic problems and to the planning of economic life was a more fertile and fruitful field of study than the subtle elaboration of what logical results would flow from the play of the self-regarding impulses under a competitive organization of economic life. Briefly, economic theory seemed to make too simple and abstract a picture of the institutions through which economic activity found expression. It was through the channel of monetary history that Mitchell became acutely aware of the decisive importance of humanly devised and humanly changeable institutions. And it was these that increasingly caught his interest.

Again, his studies centered attention upon the controlling importance of prospective money profits in directing and controlling industrial processes. It became apparent how loosely profits were related to the supplying of useful goods, how largely they depended upon mere differential trading advantages, and how directly they were affected by exigencies and circumstances of every conceivable sort. There thus sprang up in his mind a vivid interest in the relationship between the business man's pursuit of profits and the community's concern for the well-being of all its members. Concrete data seemed not to fit in, for example, with J. B. Clark's view of the automatic solution of this problem.

Moreover, the period of time with which Mitchell was concerned in his earlier studies was one of most rapid and spectacular change in American economic life. In business methods, technical methods, population, agriculture, labor relationships, indeed over the whole field of economic organization, there was a rapidity of development which could hardly impress an objective observer as less than a revolution. It was, in fact, the industrial revolution getting thoroughly under way upon the American scene. Other observers, of course, continued to speculate in static terms, while recognizing the immense significance of this "dynamic" movement. It was these phenomena that J. B. Clark had in mind as the fruitful field of the economist's labor. But somehow the older methods of theoretical analysis seemed never quite to come to grips with the facts. No one could classify or codify this sweep of events into economic laws. A puzzling and prominent aspect of the period was that the growth was not regular, but proceeded by fits and starts. Backward and forward swung the pendulum of high profits and low profits, intensity and dullness of industrial activity, plenty and want for laborers.

All these things and a variety of allied questions came of necessity under Mitchell's attention in the course of collecting and interpreting his greenback data. The whole nature, scope, and method of his earlier work came, therefore, to serve as a sort of apprenticeship for his most important contribution to the economic thought of our times, his study of business cycles.[1]

---

[1] Mitchell's book, *Business Cycles*, was published in 1913. It was written during the period of his residence at the University of California, 1909-1912, where he had gone from Chicago, and during the following year when he was unattached to any institution.

II

Crises and panics had long attracted the attention of economists, but during the nineteenth century they were generally entered in theoretical treatises as an afterthought to monetary or banking theory. By the early years of the twentieth century, analysis had, to a limited extent, moved from the earlier recognition of the periodicity of crises to a recognition of the somewhat regularly recurring round of alternating periods of prosperity and depression, or of greater and lesser intensity of business activity. The mounting interest in the subject is attested by the considerable number of theories propounded in explanation of cycles during the first decade of the century. These theories, by well-known and competent economists, were for the most part highly plausible, but suffered from the one major defect that they all offered different explanations. The subject was therefore wrapped in not a little mystery which the diversity of explanations only deepened. At the same time, it was of the most immediate and practical importance, in that the instability of business activity served to accentuate all the imperfections which marred the efficiency of the economic system in serving the needs of the community. It constituted therefore a standing and stimulating challenge to the intellectual faculties of scientific investigators.

It is not unlikely that Mitchell's imagination was

most directly touched by Veblen's treatment of the subject in the *Theory of Business Enterprise*, and grew as he became acquainted with the theories of Hobson, Beveridge, Aftalion, Sombart, and others as they appeared. One defect he found in them all, that they betrayed a great paucity of facts. From a certain antecedent standpoint of general theory and from certain limited if relevant facts, each succeeded in raising a logical structure of explanation, the plausibility of which was only marred by the fact that no one was any more plausible than some of the others. Mitchell's approach was novel and, in a degree, revolutionary. And since his approach to this problem is in a considerable degree the key to his whole contribution to economic theory, we may examine it with some care.

His primary conviction was that little could be done with logic, or with mere casual knowledge of a limited range of facts. These had been tried with no better outcome than the mutual defeat of competing theories. What was required, he conceived, was "the collection and analysis of elaborate records of business experience in quantitative form." It seemed to him necessary to consider not some, but all of the facts that might measurably affect the regularity of business activity. The facts, too, must be of a sort not merely capable of discovery, but of measurement. And the only facts which seemed to admit of scientific treatment were statistical facts. "Since in his effort to make accurate measurements the economic investigator cannot devise experiments, he must do the best he can with the cruder gauges afforded by statistics." [1]

He was, moreover, convinced that the data should not be gathered with reference to any theory already in mind, but that, on the contrary, after the collection of all the available relevant facts had been completed, they should be carefully analyzed and made to yield such conclusions as they themselves contained. Here then we find Mitchell engaged upon a study for which his greenback studies had eminently fitted him, both as regarded the use of statistical tools and as regarded a certain detached and objective viewpoint. The scientific task was enormously larger since his problem ramified into the most remote corners of the intricate processes of the economic system and carried the burden of suggesting remedies for business instability, as well as of discovering its causes. Concerning the theoretical bearing of his task it is not probable that Mitchell gave much thought or had any clear conception at the outset, and the point may be postponed. Probably he saw merely an interesting and important investigation awaiting some one, and saw in it possibilities of quantitative statistical analysis of the sort of which he was master.

However objective one might wish to make such a study, it was nevertheless essential to have some framework of ideas into which to fit the data. In short, there must be some test of relevancy. In setting up this test, Mitchell displays an implicit theoretical position. For

---

[1] *Business Cycles*, p. 20.

he prefaces his investigation by a brief statement of his view of the operation of the economic system. And in this statement, negatively, or by neglect, he may be said to discard adherence to any orthodox view of economic processes; while, positively, his descriptive analysis rests upon the distinction, taken explicitly from Veblen, of the distinction between business and industry. From an isolated sentence in the *History of the Greenbacks* [1] one supposes that he was then beginning to think in those terms. The distinction is more clearly stated in *Gold, Prices, and Wages under the Greenback Standard* in an incidental way. [2] But in the writing of *Business Cycles* Mitchell made it the fundamental conception upon which his whole examination rested.

His approach to the study of business cycles depended, he conceived, upon an adequate understanding of the rôle of money in the economic organization. In the second greenback volume he had written, "Writers upon money usually state that it performs three functions, serving as a common denominator of value, a medium of exchange, and a standard of deferred payments. To enumerate the functions of money in this fashion, however, is very far from suggesting the importance of the rôle which money plays in economic life. To understand this rôle attention must be fixed upon the complex mechanism of prices, rather than upon money itself." [3] "Money prices, in brief, are the formal basis on which the economic relations of indi-

[1] Page 395.   [2] *Op. cit.*, p. 280.   [3] *Ibid.*, pp. 279-280.

viduals in modern society are organized and the formal mechanism by which economic processes are carried on." [1] "The system of prices has a quasi-independence of the will of individuals or even of the whole community. . . . Men who make use of the system of prices in their economic activity are constrained to obey its logic and to adapt themselves as best they may to its technical exigencies." [2]

This view is enlarged upon and clarified in *Business Cycles.* On its economic side, modern life is organized within the confines of the "money economy," an institution of which the essential feature is "not the use of money as a medium of exchange, but the fact that economic activity takes the form of making and spending money incomes." [3] To the community as a whole, material well-being is determined by the abundance of useful goods. But to the individual, or family, it depends, not upon efficiency in making useful goods, but upon the command of an adequate money income.

Under the money economy, the production of useful goods waits upon the prospect of profit. "The elaborate coöperative process by which a nation's myriad workers provide for the meeting of each other's needs is thus brought into precarious dependence upon factors which have but a remote connection with the material conditions of well-being—factors which determine the prospects of making money." [4] The industrial and

---

[1] *Gold, Prices, and Wages under the Greenback Standard,* p. 281.
[2] *Ibid.,* p. 281.
[3] *Business Cycles,* p. 21.   [4] *Ibid.,* p. 22.

commercial processes of producing and distributing
goods comprise a highly complicated concatenation of
processes, linking the whole industrial system in a mechanical interdependence. The functioning of these
mechanical processes, however, awaits the exercise of
the discretion of business men whose interest in the
processes is almost solely confined to the money profit
to be obtained from them. In other words, goods produced are a by-product of the process of earning profits.

The business enterprises, whose interests are primarily pecuniary, are themselves bound together in a
system of financial interdependence, somewhat analogous to the mechanical interdependence of industrial
processes; and the most marked aspect of this interdependence is the endless chain of interlocking indebtedness between business enterprises. It is the logic and
exigencies of this scheme of financial relationships that
everywhere dictate the course of action of enterprises
engaged in the pursuit of profits; from which "it follows that a theory of modern prosperity must deal
primarily with business conditions—with the pecuniary
aspects of economic activity."[1] Fluctuations of business activity must therefore be regarded as a problem
in the fluctuating prospects of profits. Until that point
has been reached, the problem has not even been stated.

From the business man's point of view, the fundamental condition of business prosperity is the price
margin between purchase prices and sale prices, in con-

[1] *Business Cycles*, p. 25.

junction with the volume of transactions. The quest
of profits thus takes place through the mechanism of
the system of prices. Three types of goods—commodities, services, and rights such as securities and bank
credits—are objects of purchase and sales. Between
the prices for the various kinds of goods there exists a
complicated set of relationships which bind them into a
system. "The prices ruling at any given time for the
infinite variety of commodities, services, and rights
which are being bought and sold constitute a system.
That is, these prices are so related to each other as to
make a regular and connected whole." [1] The retail
prices of commodities are related loosely to one another,
and more directly to wholesalers' and manufacturers'
prices. The prices of producers' goods are related in a
variety of ways to those of consumers' goods. As goods
proceed through the series of transactions which carry
them to their various ultimate uses, the price margins
at one point and another are marked by great diversity;
but these diversities are sufficiently regular to furnish
to business men a tolerable basis for making profits out
of supplying the community with the goods it habitually uses.

Without going into Mitchell's careful analysis of
price relationships in any detail, we must grasp his
conception that the price system constitutes a closed
system, "an endless chain." "The prices of producers'
goods do not form the ends of the series of price rela-

[1] *Business Cycles*, p. 27.

tionships, but the beginnings of new series of relationships which run backward with countless ramifications and never reach definite stopping points." [1] "The price system has no definable limits in time. No analysis can get back to the ultimate term in the endless series of bargains which helped to make the prices of the present. . . . Nor has the system of prices any logical beginning or end." [2] It is "a system infinitely flexible in detail yet stable in the essential balance of its interrelations, a system like a living organism in its ability to recover from the serious disorders into which it periodically falls." This system is the "social mechanism for carrying on the process of providing goods," and its distinctive rôle is to "render possible the rational direction of economic activity by accounting."

The high development of corporate organization and the complicated division of functions within it cause Mitchell to regard as obsolete and negligible the usual simplified view of the direction of economic activity, according to which the "capitalist-employer" is supposed to supply the capital, assume the risks, superintend the operation, and take the profits of his business. He is attempting to set forth a realistic view of the direction of economic activity.

A primary defect of economic organization under the money economy is the lack of effective coördination between the operations of independent enterprises. "In detail, then, economic activity is planned and directed

[1] *Business Cycles*, p. 28.   [2] *Ibid.*, p. 31.

with skill; but in the large there is neither general plan nor central direction." [1] Production is "controlled by no large human purpose." It follows the line of prospective profits, not the line of human good. The money economy insures no humanly desirable distribution of goods. It merely assures abundance to those sufficiently canny to intercept a generous money income. Moreover, the smooth functioning of the system is marred by large elements of uncertainty which increase as progressive technique and widening markets baffle the intelligent planning of enterprisers. It is, then, in the nature of the money economy, the structure of the price system, and the defective coördination of the separate business enterprises that one must look, under modern conditions of complex economic life, for the explanation of the recurring disorders of the economic system.

It should be understood that the range of ideas which we have been discussing does not constitute any of Mitchell's conclusions from his detailed analysis of business cycles. It is the framework of preliminary ideas within which he proposes to fit his findings. The controlling preconception is the subordination of industrial and commercial processes to the money-making process. "The ebb and flow of economic activity is brought into dependence upon the profits of business enterprises. Upon this basic fact the whole investigation rests. Profits, in their turn, depend upon the mar-

[1] *Business Cycles*, p. 35.

gins between buying and selling prices, and upon the
volume of transactions." "First, then, we must seek
for data to measure variations in prices and variations
in the volume of trade. . . . The prices of importance
in gauging profits are not merely the prices of commodities, but also the prices of labor, of loans, and of
business enterprises themselves." [1]

The test of the relevancy of data therefore becomes
their bearing "upon the crucial problem of business
profits, either by dealing with the factors which determine profits, like prices and volume of trade; or by
dealing with necessary conditions for the successful
quest of profits, like the currency, banking, and investment; or by offering direct gauges of business success
and failure, like the statistics of profits themselves and
bankruptcies." [2]

It may be contended that this descriptive framework
has no particular bearing upon one or another type
of economic theory, but Mitchell would not concur in
that opinion. Marginal-utility theory is mainly concerned with an analysis of subjective values, of which
prices are the objective monetary expression. Mitchell
is not concerned directly with the subjective side of
the valuation process, but emphasizes the organic character of the price structure. It may be held that he
does not discredit Austrian theory, and that he is concerned with quite a different problem which does not
cut across the value problem. The same comment could

[1] *Business Cycles*, p. 92.   [2] *Ibid.*, p. 92.

be made concerning the relation of his descriptive analysis to the neo-classical value theory, as represented by Marshall's theory of the normal equilibrium of supply and demand. It is true, of course, that his problem is a different one from theirs. But the introductory chapters of *Business Cycles* cannot be intelligently read without perceiving that they rest upon a groundwork of ideas incompatible with any of the variant statements of orthodox economic theory.

The difference centers around Mitchell's conception of the rôle of money, and the distinction between pecuniary and industrial factors in economic activity. Most modern types of theory with a classical genealogy trace the motives of economic activity back to certain fundamental human traits which may be roughly divided into two classes—those which incite to activity in order to secure the satisfactions of consumption, and those which discourage activity because of the irksomeness of effort. Upon these underlying "real forces" is built up the conception of the system of normal prices representing an objective expression of an underlying human calculation of alternatives. Money enters into the case merely as a convenience, to facilitate the smooth working of the economic system, but not giving it any of its fundamental features.

Mitchell, on the other hand, sees money, or the pursuit of a money income, as the primary motive in business activity. This pursuit may be of a highly rational sort, but it is rational only in the sense that the money economy enjoins a certain kind of activity on pain of the failure to acquire the desired income. The money economy is itself a dominating feature of our institutional life which shapes the nature and direction of economic activity. It provides the logic of business, and the fact that business enterprise is guided by that logic throws no light upon and bears but a loose relationship to the material well-being of the community. One may, indeed, follow the logic of pecuniary gain to the patent damage of the community's well-being.

It must, then, be plain that Mitchell's scheme of thought is antipathetic to the methods and conclusions of marginal-utility analysis, to all theories of distribution based upon it, and to all notions of an equilibrium of "real" economic forces which are expressed in a system of prices. He regards economic motivation as largely the outcome of the institutions by which human nature is disciplined. His concern is to discover the nature of these institutions, and then by the study of objective data to explain the consequences of their operation.

As we are interested here only in the more general aspects of Mitchell's theoretical position, it will be unnecessary to follow the detailed argument of his study of business cycles. It may be said briefly that it follows the plan which he had so thoroughly learned to use in his previous greenback studies, of gathering, ordering, and interpreting statistical data. His statistics cover the period from 1890 to 1911, and are drawn from the United States, Great Britain, France and Germany. He follows the course of price fluctuations of consumers' goods at retail and wholesale, of producers' goods, of manufactured goods and raw materials, of organic and inorganic goods. He follows the course of wages, of interest, and of security prices in detail and under various methods of classification. He examines the physical volume of trade; the volume of currency; the condition of banks; the course of saving, investment, new enterprises, and speculation; and the records of profits and bankruptcies. Out of this imposing mass of statistical evidence is drawn a comprehensive statement of the sequence of events during the course of a cycle, accompanied by a series of suggestions of ways and means for stabilizing business.

Quite apart from theoretical considerations, the factual data in *Business Cycles* added enormously to the existing knowledge concerning business fluctuations. And the study, by demonstrating the advantages of realistic treatment, was the decisive factor in turning the investigation of cycles from speculative to quantitative analysis. By tracing the ramifying effects of cyclical fluctuations into endless relationships to other aspects of the economic system, Mitchell gave the lead for many new investigations; so much so, in fact, that within a decade after the appearance of the book the study of almost all current economic problems had been in some considerable degree revolutionized.

Out of his collected data Mitchell attempted to distil a theory of cyclical fluctuations. His theory was, however, of a sort quite distinct from preceding ones. For, while they had, on the basis of certain limited data, proceeded by logical processes to trace fluctuations to one or two outstanding "causes," Mitchell's theory consisted of a statement of certain sequences or relationships which his statistics showed to recur more or less regularly during the progressive movement of business activity from depression to "prosperity" and from "prosperity" to depression. In studying one cyclical period after another, he had, of course, to give due attention to the fact that each cycle was affected, in the process of "cumulative change," by unique, non-recurring forces such as war-demands. In interpreting his statistics he was convinced, however, that these unique forces, though they made each cycle differ characteristically from every other, could be sufficiently abstracted to permit a statement of the regularly recurring sequences and relationships between prices, incomes, physical production, profits, and the other phenomena included in his investigation.

In advancing a theory consisting of a statement of these sequences and relationships, Mitchell appealed to no final or ultimate "causes" of cycles. It appeared to him that the round from prosperity to crisis to depression to recovery, the continual alternation of expansion and contraction of business activity, is cumulatively "caused" by the exigencies of business enterprise as it operates through the money economy under modern industrial conditions.

In a certain definite sense, then, one may say that Mitchell's theory is of a "static" sort. That is to say, he uses the ideas of "process" and "cumulative causation," not to describe the evolution of the institutions through which economic activity takes place, as Veblen had done, but to describe the fluctuations which business undergoes within the confines of a given institutional situation. So far as his investigation is concerned, institutions are a relatively constant, not a highly variable, factor.

Just what the institutional situation is, in terms of which he works, he is at no pains to make clear. He does not, for example, attempt to say how far modern business is competitive, and how far monopolistic, nor whether these alternative modes of business organization affect his results. One will, in fact, search in vain in Mitchell's work for an explanation of what he means by an "economic institution," though he stresses so strongly the importance of institutions. He emphasizes only one, the money economy, but that, of course, is an aspect of economic life which has existed almost immemorially and in the face of the most disparate institutional situations.

If one may cavil at the indistinctness of the institutional picture, it must be admitted, on the other hand, that the conducting of the investigation in the light of a given institutional situation gave to *Business Cycles* its great theoretical importance. The principal argument of orthodox economists against Veblen's evolutionary approach has been that, while it might throw light upon the development of economic institutions, it could add nothing to our knowledge of the process of the economic system as at present constituted. They have, in the more self-conscious atmosphere of the twentieth century, regarded their analysis as concerned with a cross-section of time, and have elaborated their systems of normality with the qualification that the principles which they expound are applicable only to the present situation—whatever may have been the economic organization of times past.

By confining himself to the present and immediate past, Mitchell undercut this defense of the orthodox discipline. The whole bearing of his study, in fact, tended to discredit the notions of normality and of an equilibrium of forces. He writes that, "One who turns from reading economic theory to reading business history is forcibly impressed by the artificiality of all assumptions of a 'static' or even a 'normal' condition in economic affairs. For, despite all efforts to give technical meanings to these ambiguous terms, they suggest the idea of an unchanging order, or of an order which economic principles are always tending to reëstablish after every aberration. But a review of business annals never discloses a 'static' or a 'normal' state in either of these senses. On the contrary, in the real world of business, affairs are always undergoing a cumulative change, always passing through some phase of a business cycle into some other phase. . . . In fact, if not in theory, a state of change in business conditions is the only 'normal' state." [1]

This disbelief in normality was doubtless held by Mitchell previous to the initiation of the study. But the result of the investigation was to confirm the disbelief. For nowhere could there be discerned any line of normality from which prices diverged or to which they were drawn back. On the contrary, there seemed to be an inevitable cumulation of events which carried business activity through successive phases, to the constant and never-ending disturbance of the material welfare of various classes of people. In the end, therefore, Mitchell was confirmed in the conviction that the only way in which to formulate a realistic statement of economic activity was in terms of a process, of a cumulative sequence of events. In those terms nothing is "normal" and nothing "abnormal." All events and eventualities are equally a part of the process. The economist is obligated, so far as may be, to throw light upon the process, and the only way in which to do this is by way of careful examination of all the objective facts bearing upon whatever problem he may have in hand.

Veblen had, of course, propounded the theory of process as the fundamental notion of economic speculation. Working in those terms, Mitchell succeeded in

[1] *Business Cycles*, p. 86.

making the greatest single contribution to knowledge concerning one of the most mysterious phases of current economic life. It may not be too much to say that he only succeeded in doing so by reason of the freedom of his mind from the constricting hold of any formal system of theory. Yet one cannot say that his work demonstrated the uselessness of the more speculative attacks upon this problem. For most of the clues which he followed were furnished by men whose speculations were formally tied to some system as he himself pointed out. And his results demonstrated less any lack of perspicacity on their part than the incompleteness of their theories. They were for the most part not wrong; they merely attributed causation to factors which, on more intimate view, appeared only as a few among many factors in the cumulation of causes. Mitchell would perhaps say that speculative thinkers are useful people to supply leads to stimulate the thinking of scientific investigators. But he would hold that cogitation is no substitute for laborious investigation if we are to arrive at any adequate comprehension of the complicated processes through which the economic system functions.

That, of course, was an idea which had been suggested by such theorists as Clark when he marked out "economic dynamics" as the fertile field for future economic investigation, and Marshall, when he suggested that quantitative analysis must be the field of future importance. Mitchell is decidedly the apostle of quantitative analysis. But he would say that such analysis could only be handicapped by working in subservience to a preconceived system like Clark's, and that the problems encountered would not fall into the categories of Marshall's qualitative analysis. The only scientific generalizations are those which arise out of the data available. Speculative generalizations are only a second-best in the absence of other knowledge, and logical systems deduced from simplified postulates cannot by any stretch of the imagination be held to give an adequate or accurate account of the operation of the economic system.

Enough has perhaps been said to permit the relation of Mitchell's findings to orthodox economic theory to be crystallized into a single point. Veblen's method of demolishing systematic theory is to cast doubt upon its *postulates*. Mitchell appeals to his mass of facts and distills them into a convincing picture of economic processes which lends no support to the *conclusions* of systematic theory. He thus appears, not as a parrot of Veblen, but rather as his complement, proceeding, from a different angle and with a wholly different technique, to complete the discrediting of the scheme of thought in which economic theorists have framed their systems.

Quantitative analysis, in the hands of its very competent user in the field of economics, has thus come to take the form, not of verifying or modifying the conclusions which have been arrived at by qualitative analysis, but of marshaling facts without reference to "principles" and drawing such conclusions or generalizations as the facts themselves afford. It is possible to see, then, why *Business Cycles*, which was not primarily a project in economic theory, has achieved a position of such outstanding importance in the field of theory. The gradual dissemination of the point of view and the conclusions contained in it has not only had the effect of weakening the hold of orthodox economic views upon the younger generation of economists, but has at the same time introduced them to a type of analysis which contains the promise of fruitful results. One may perhaps say that Mitchell's outstanding contribution to the economic thought of his time has consisted in promoting the metamorphosis from the attempt to normalize economic life to the attempt to comprehend the complicated processes of economic life through a realistic quantitative investigation of the facts.

We have perhaps given sufficient consideration to the aspects of Mitchell's theoretical position illustrated by his study of business cycles. It is curious to recall how little attention the theoretical implications of the book elicited upon its appearance. Widely praised by economists as a factual study of cycles, it received only belated and partial consideration as a treatise on economic theory. Its formidable size did not invite full and careful reading, and one must suppose that economic theorists did not generally read, nor fully comprehend, the significance of the second chapter and the other brief scattered passages within which the theoretical framework is stated.[1]

There has been no intention of intimating that his work on the subject was authoritative or final. He himself concluded his study with a modest disclaimer of finality, and with suggestions for future investigation. It is strictly consonant with his view of the economist's task to admit that finality is an unattainable ideal. Impressed with the enormous complexity of the institutional arrangements under which we live, he thinks it the task of many men and many years to uncover and display an accurate understanding of them. His own work thus ranks as but one item in a vast cooperative scientific effort to trace economic processes into their endless ramifications.

Moreover, the ceaseless changes which develop tend to doom any study of current facts to early obsolescence, and to involve investigators in the eternal process of keeping pace with the facts. For, in Mitchell's view, which is a moral view, the facts most worth investigating are those most immediately bearing upon the well-

---

[1] Professor Pigou, for example, in a commendatory review in *The Economic Journal*, vol. xxiv (1914), states that this "massive work— by far the most elaborate treatise on the subject that has yet appeared in the English language—must command the attention of all students of industrial fluctuations." He makes no mention of its relation to general economic theory and, though quoting at length on the general viewpoint, appears not to recognize that it represents a scheme of thought quite antipathetic to his own doctrinal system. Merely to call it a study of "industrial fluctuations" is, of course, to misconceive its nature and to overlook the significance of the title, in which the word "business" is used in a technical sense as contrasted to "industrial," with malice aforethought.

being of the social body. Such facts are, of course, present facts. The search for them is dictated by problems of social maladjustment, and the end in view in social amelioration.

His study of business cycles established Mitchell as the foremost student of that problem, but it was perhaps the fortuitous circumstance of the disconcerting behavior of prices during the war and after that swept him into wider prominence. Under the saddening impact of recent experience, the problem in which he pioneered has come for the time being to be ranked as perhaps the most important and fundamental of our economic problems, with the consequence that Mitchell has come to be regarded as one of the foremost American economists. The fortuitous character of his rise is not, however, likely to detract from the influence of his example, because, for one thing, the problem with which he has been primarily concerned has been recognized as intimately related to almost every other economic problem, and, for another, the objective investigation of economic problems has pushed perhaps permanently into the foreground of the attention of economists. At the same time, a growing recognition on the part of the responsible leaders of political and economic groups of the complexity of our economic arrangements has led them to expect economists to play the part of experts.

There is thus transpiring a removal of the circumstances which earlier inhibited American economists from any appreciable influence upon the course of events, and turned their attention largely into speculative channels. Mitchell was, in a sense, the forerunner of this current phase, and is the recognized leader of the group of economists whose interest lies in a realistic approach to economic problems. Of course, other economists before Mitchell had made excellent monographic studies, particularly in the fields of currency, transportation, monopoly, and taxation. Perhaps the difference which marked most of them off from Mitchell and others who work in his spirit was that their investigations started from the preconceptions of a definite system of logical theory. Mitchell's primary preconception, on the other hand, is that the economic process cannot be constrained within the bounds of a system of logic. His goal is objective reality, not logical consistency.[1]

[1] Before taking up other general aspects of Mitchell's theoretical position, a word may be said concerning his more recent interests and occupations. He has since 1913 been a professor at Columbia University, except for a short period as lecturer at the New School for Social Research. During the war he was chief of the Price Section of the War Industries Board. In this capacity he edited the official publication, *History of Prices During the War*, and wrote, in collaboration with others, *International Price Comparisons*. Since the war he has, in addition to his university duties, been Director of Research of the National Bureau of Economic Research, the object of which is "to ascertain and to present to the public important economic facts and the interpretation thereof in a scientific and impartial manner, free from bias and propaganda." Its works has been mainly statistical analysis of cycles and national income. During recent years he has been co-author of *Income in the United States—Its Amount and Distribution* (1921) and editor of *Business Cycles and Unemployment* (1923), the report of the President's conference on Unemployment. He has also recently prepared the first volume of a revised edition of *Business*

III

If Veblen is the Messiah, Mitchell is at least the high-priest of what has come to be called in the United States "institutional economics," the devotees of which are coming to include a considerable proportion of the more capable younger economists. It cannot be said that there is any particular unanimity among them as to the proper scope and method of this new and well-advertised brand of economics. They hold in common a highly skeptical attitude toward the "principles" of all variants of classical economic theory. Their common aim is to throw light upon the institutional arrangements through which the economic process functions. They entertain a somewhat attenuated hope that out of their labors may ultimately arise some sort of synthesis that will constitute a generally acceptable body of economic theory. Loosely bound together, they recognize one another by these signs.

They are in the meantime delving each in his own corner of the economic system under the impulse of various motives. Their work at present consists for the most part of monographic studies. They maintain a high ideal of scientific objectivity, but are in general guided in their choice of subjects for investigation by the desire to be of assistance in an intelligent scheme of social reform. Wherever the operation of our eco-

Cycles. His later work has thus proceeded along lines for which his earlier experience had eminently fitted him.

nomic institutions appears to raise some human problem
they will be found, whether in questions of international finance, railroad administration, business combination, labor relations, legal institutions in their economic bearing, the distribution of income, corporation
finance, or what not. Their scent for problems is like
that of bears for honey.

For such a group there can obviously be no official
spokesman. As the most eminent of their number,
Mitchell speaks with somewhat more authority than
others. He has, too, given more thought to the general theoretical problems of this type of economics than
any of his fellows, and in a disconnected series of
papers and articles during the last fifteen years has
given expression to ideas which may be pieced together
into a sort of philosophy of the institutional approach
to economics. We shall briefly examine these ideas in
so far as they run in other terms than those imbedded
in the framework of *Business Cycles*. It must not be
supposed that they represent any consensus on the part
of institutional economists. But it must at the same
time be understood that they roughly reflect the intellectual background to the work of a great many
economists.

It has already been pointed out that Mitchell accepted Veblen's view that economic studies must be
congruent with the evolutionary viewpoint. This is
the basis for fitting facts into a conception of "process"
instead of "equilibrium," and for eschewing the con-

cept of "normality" in economic life. It has further been noted that, while Veblen utilizes his idea of the genetic approach by interpreting history in the large in its economic bearing, as the introduction to rather sweeping generalizations on contemporary economic organization, Mitchell gives the idea content by a minute analysis and interpretation of facts and figures bearing upon a particular limited problem. The genetic approach is obviously one that lends itself to a great variety of method. Taken as a somewhat vague orientation of ideas, it may be said to rank as perhaps the primary preconception of institutional economics, and as an essential part of Mitchell's armory of general ideas. It serves both as the basis of his dissent from older types of theory and as the foundation for the framework of his constructive work.

No problem of economic theory seems more significant to Mitchell than the economist's view of human nature. It is one of the fundamental items of his viewpoint that no theory can be considered scientifically tenable which rests upon a view of human nature at odds with the best authenticated views of psychologists upon the subject. Since modern psychology gives no support to the hedonistic view of human nature, with its emphasis upon action as the result of rational choice between the alternatives of pleasure and pain, all systems of theory that explicitly or implicitly rely upon such a view become in his mind at once untenable. His interest in this aspect of economic theory has led him to follow at least as closely as any other economist the recent literature of psychological investigation, and to take his bearings anew from time to time with the advances in psychological knowledge. To most economists with an interest in psychology the rapidly changing views and diversity of opinion in that field have been frequently disconcerting, not to say irritating. For, attempting to build upon a sound psychological foundation, they find that they have built upon shifting sands. The reaction, among those who demand a feeling of certainty in their economic principles, has been in the direction of a relative or even absolute denial of the dependence of economic theory upon psychology.

Mitchell, however, is plagued by no such impatience. For he thinks that no fields of knowledge dealing with human behavior, as economics does, can attain to thoroughly scientific generalizations until we know "why we act like human beings." He has a sufficiently modest apprehension of the achievements of modern science to admit that there is very much that we do not know. And he is willing to reserve judgment upon doubtful points in the absence of authentic knowledge. He is the better able to do this, in that he is not wedded to any scheme of logical theory which demands at least an implicit set of psychological assumptions.

Like most students of the social sciences who took the trouble to examine it, he was much impressed by William McDougall's *Social Psychology*, which appeared in 1909. Dealing with the functioning, rather than the structure, of the mind, it appeared to bear directly upon the problems of human behavior, with which the social sciences are concerned. This approach to psychology strengthened his disbelief in the psychological postulates of current types of systematic economic theory.[1] And he has, for purposes of his own thinking, for the most part accepted McDougall's central thesis that the instincts are the prime movers in human activity. In this view, the *ends* of life are instinctive, and the instincts which dictate them are stable and enduring. The factor of intelligence, or rationality, enters into the case as an instrumental *means* by which men seek to realize the instinctively appointed ends. For the most part the means employed represent merely types of action which have become habitual. They operate through the agency of established institutions which are themselves no more than crystallized habits of thought and action.

Where, as in business enterprise, the element of rational calculation is obviously an important factor in economic activity, rationality is not related to the underlying ends of life. No more is apparent than that certain types of action are rational in relation to the institutions through which they function. Business enterprise functions through the "money economy" and

---

[1] See *e.g.*, the discussion of Pantaleoni, Fisher, Clark, and Marshall in an article, "The Rationality of Economic Activity," in the *Journal of Political Economy*, vol. xviii (1910). "A man who reads books like McDougall's and accepts their conclusions may well become skeptical of the value of economic theory like that provided by Jevons, Fisher, and Clark."

can be rationally practiced on the basis of a system of accounting. But this means only that men exercise intelligence in the pursuit of a money income and tells us nothing about the relationship between money incomes and the "psychic incomes" or satisfactions which are derived from spending the money incomes. The arts of consumption are, indeed, so almost completely customary in character that they are not at present reducible to analysis in terms of rationality. The point of the argument is plain—that economic rationality is itself a social phenomenon calling for explanation; that it can be explained only by resort to a scientific explanation of human nature; that it grows out of a certain type of institutions, or means to ends; and that rational action comprises only a limited part of economic activity.

One approaches thus the reason for the peculiar tenderness of economists of Mitchell's type for modern psychology. It forms an inseparable link in the argument for the genetic approach. When it has appeared that the more fundamental, if obscure, ends of action are imbedded in stable instincts, it follows that the great majority of human actions are but the habitual means through which these obscure ends are sought. Habitual action is the creature of time and place, endlessly changing. An adequate understanding of most of our behavior is thus to be sought by tracing the mutations of the institutions which have led up to the present situation. Some notion of the future may be derived from a thoroughly realistic understanding of the present. Mitchell's position here is not far removed from that of Veblen. It crystallizes about the conviction that the important field of economic investigation is the institutional structure of society. Original human nature is, in a sense, removed from the economist's problem. Interest comes to center on that part of behavior which cumulatively changes under the molding influence of institutions.[1]

Mitchell is particularly receptive to the opinion of Professor Thorndike that human nature is highly plastic, in the sense that action is the result of a highly complex interaction of instinctive propensities, and that what passes for human nature is largely types of action called forth by a given institutional situation. He applauds the substantially similar view of Graham Wallas that the "human nature" of one generation is determined chiefly by its nurture at the hands of the preceding generation.[2] The corollary of these views is, of course, that under different institutions men might be-

---

[1] "If our present beliefs are confirmed, that the human nature which men inherit remains substantially the same over millenniums, and that the changes in human life are due mainly to the evolution of culture, economists will concentrate their studies to an increasing degree upon economic institutions, . . . the factor which certainly admits of change and perhaps admits of control." From the presidential address, "Quantitative Analysis in Economic Theory," delivered before the American Economic Association, December, 1924. Published in the *American Economic Review*, vol. xv (1925).

[2] See an article, "Human Behavior and Economics," in the *Quarterly Journal of Economics*, vol. xxix (1914).

have quite differently without in any sense violating the dictates of original human nature.

The peculiar appeal of such views to Mitchell is that they form the basis of optimism concerning the possibilities of social reform. They catch him on his moral side, which is strongly developed. They wipe out the conservative defense that this or that reform is "against human nature." They ally themselves naturally to the psychologists' view that intelligence, or thinking, is an instrument reserved for use on special occasions when men are faced by problems not amenable to an habitual solution. It thus appears that, as society is faced with major problems, it may effect an effusion of intelligence which will guide its course toward ends which it has set for itself. The prerequisite for intelligent guidance to socially determined ends is an adequate understanding of our present institutional structure. Thus the social scientists who are engaged in supplying this knowledge are playing an essential part in the progressive solution of social problems.

It follows from Mitchell's attitude toward psychology that the relation of economics to that science is something more than a mere debt. Not only does psychology give economists a framework of ideas within which to conduct their investigations. Conversely, economists are uncovering a mass of facts concerning how men behave and to that extent are making a contribution to social psychology. "It was because hedonism offered a theory of how men act that it exercised so potent an influence upon economics. It is because they (the social psychologists) are developing a sounder type of functional psychology that we may hope both to profit by and to share in the work of contemporary psychologists. But in embracing this opportunity economics will assume a new character. It will cease to be a system of pecuniary logic, a mechanical study of statical equilibria under nonexistent conditions, and become a science of human behavior." [1]

The logic of this viewpoint has led Mitchell, in recent years, to incline toward the "behaviorist school" of psychologists. From the standpoint of that school, knowledge of human nature is confined to the observation of its objective manifestations. In the light of that preconception economics becomes less a debtor than a contributor to psychology. It supplies the necessary data concerning one type of behavior. To what extent Mitchell accepts this view he has never taken occasion to say publicly. In any case it would little affect his general viewpoint, and it is safer doubtless to interpret him in the light of his published declarations.

Mitchell's viewpoint has by this time been sufficiently examined from various angles to demonstrate the convergence of all his arguments upon his central conviction—that the economist's appointed task is to examine the nature and functioning of social institutions. That

[1] *Quarterly Journal of Economics*, vol. xxix, p. 47.

conviction is the logical outcome of the genetic approach, or one may say preconception, by which one thinks of a given cultural situation, not as final, but as a passing phase of an endless process. It is supported by the views of many psychologists. And in Mitchell's case it is supported by a strong predilection to assist in the rational guidance of a great and complicated and in some degree mysterious society which, under the bondage of custom, has stumbled somewhat blindly into a forest of human problems.

It is the problems that fascinate him, challenging his intellect and his sympathies, making his scientific work both mentally exciting and morally satisfying. "Whether economics is to us a subject of thrilling interests or a dismal pseudo-science depends upon ourselves. If we come to it with literal minds, seeing only what has been definitely accomplished, we find the discussion dull and the conclusions dubious. But if we come thinking of man's long struggle to master his own fate, then the effort to solve economic problems seems a vital episode in human history, a hopeful portent for the future. Seen in this perspective, economic speculation represents a stage in the growth of mind at which man's effort to understand and control nature becomes an effort to understand and control himself and his society. . . . The future of economics, the question whether men will ever succeed in establishing a serviceable science of human behavior, becomes one of the crucial issues on which hangs the doubtful fate of humankind." [1]

Mitchell's loose formula for economics, that it is a science of human behavior engaged in examining the structure and functioning of the institutions through which economic activity takes place, is plainly comprehensive enough to include studies of widely differing range and character. It includes orthodox economists in so far as they realistically portray the processes of current life; it has a particular niche of honor for Sombart, Sidney and Beatrice Webb, and Veblen, who learned from Marx "the scientific possibilities of his way of working," and are "studying the evolution of economic institutions in a scientific, as opposed to a historical or propagandist, spirit." [2] There is a place for the monographic study of the problems of transportation, labor, banking, trusts, and so on. The realization that theoretical economic inquiries cluster about the working of institutions "establishes upon a common plane the work of those who seek to know how economic organization has developed in the past, of those who seek to know how it functions in the present, and of those who seek to know what changes it promises to undergo in the future." [3] "When, however, economic theory is made an account of the cumulative change

---

[1] From an article, "The Prospects of Economics," in *The Trend of Economics* (1924), p. 3.

[2] *Ibid.*, p. 18.

[3] From an article, "The Rôle of Money in Economic Theory," in the *American Economic Review*, vol. vi, supplement, p. 160 (1916).

of economic behavior, then all studies of special institutions become organic parts of a single whole. . . . Economic theory will cease to be a thing apart from applied economics, because economic theory will itself deal with genuine issues." [1]

The reason for undertaking these various sorts of investigation is very plain to Mitchell's mind. It is no detached "idle curiosity," nor any coldly objective desire to know. "In economics as in other sciences we desire knowledge mainly as an instrument of control. Control means the alluring possibility of shaping the evolution of economic life to fit the developing purpose of our race." [2] Without dropping his insistence upon the scientific method of accurate observation, he allies himself to Dewey's conception that human thought and action are inevitably intermixed, to the end of achieving the goals which are more or less clearly set up. In Mitchell's thought these goals seem something more than the immediate goals of individuals or groups. He tacitly personalizes society; and appears to assume that society as such has a will of its own and goals of its own. Social evolution takes on a somewhat dramatic form, as a sort of cosmic struggle, in which the social will is striving, in the midst of the discordant purposes of its members, to achieve its ends, by and with the advice of its more intelligent counselors, the social scientists. It is not to be supposed that Mitchell ever permits himself to be drawn so far

[1] *The Trend of Economics*, pp. 24-25.   [2] *Ibid.*, p. 25.

as this into the imponderable marshes of social philosophy. We wish merely to indicate that, were he more a philosopher and less a statistician, this is where his footsteps would seem to lead.

Enough has been said to indicate the broader outlines of Mitchell's conception of economic theory. It leads him to the very borderland of philosophical speculation. But across that boundary he never steps. For, though Mitchell is somewhat philosophically minded, one is aware always of the restraining influence of a lifetime's work of realistic investigation, of marshaling statistics and interpreting their meaning. He does not have what one would call an original mind, but rather a workman-like mind. His dissent from orthodox economics is not original. It is taken from Veblen. His subordination of economic investigation to ends of social welfare runs in terms that may be traced to Dewey and Hobson and others within whom the moral urge is dominant. For the general terms in which his thinking runs he is in the position of a debtor to a considerable range of thinkers. The cathartic effect of Veblen's early influence cleared his system of tradition, and left him with a hearty appetite and sound powers of absorption for innovating and progressive thinking in the social sciences. Omnivorous in his reading, catholic in his sympathies, and eclectic in his thinking, he has done much to popularize new approaches to social problems and to make them intellectually acceptable and professionally respectable.

But it is not as a loud-speaker for any set of second-hand ideas that he has achieved his significance in the field of economics. It is in the alliance between his intellectual approach to economic problems and his technical handling of them that he is eminent and important. His method is that of a quantitative analysis. He is the prophet of facts and figures. He believes that in dealing with the mass of phenomena of social organization our one authoritative and impartial source of information is statistics. Much of his energy has been devoted to improving the sources of statistical information available to economists. The rest of it has been largely devoted to collecting such information, interpreting the economic significance of the data which he handles, indicating the relation of the facts disclosed to the common welfare, and devising methods for the social control of the aspects of economic organization where his investigations have indicated that it is possible and desirable.

His enthusiasm for quantitative information is so great that on one or two occasions he has almost permitted himself to say that intelligent social reform is only a matter of possessing the necessary factual data on which to build.[1] Never committing himself quite that far, he nevertheless insists that statistical investigation is the most scientific instrument of economic analysis, and that it constitutes an essential, if not

[1] See, e.g., an article, "Statistics and Government," in the *Quarterly Publication of the American Statistical Association*, for March, 1919.

the most important, tool of rational social development. As might be expected of so ardent a champion of facts, . he is not a little impatient of mere agitation and propaganda as instruments of reform. They appear to him unintelligent.

This conviction that knowledge of facts, particularly statistical facts, is essential to the proper coördination of our complicated economic organization has been pretty thoroughly disseminated and accepted, not only among economists, but among business men, officials, reformers, trade-union leaders, one might say among responsible or intelligent people in general. The manifold problems of social adjustment—wage disputes, minimum-wage laws, railway rates, marketing arrangements, business fluctuations, unemployment, allocation of taxes, and what not—all occasion resort to the tangible evidence of quantitative data. It is not Mitchell, of course, who has done this. The phenomenon grew out of a complicated social situation. But, so far as one man can be singled out for credit, he has played a preëminent part. He has pioneered in the application of statistical method to economic problems and in all seasons urged the importance of this instrument. He has demonstrated the advantages and uses of statistical analysis, and has been its spokesman and its philosopher.

When so much has been said, one may perhaps wonder whether the nature of Mitchell's work has not decidedly colored his conclusions. For a quarter of a century and more his work has been mainly concerned with price studies, a field within which statistical technique is the primary instrument. His studies have centered around the pursuit of profits, wherein he finds the key to business fluctuations. It is at least an open question whether his own successful use of statistics has not been generalized into an exaggerated statement of their place in the scheme of things.

Moreover, his concern with distinctly "business" processes and "business" habits of thought may explain the primary causal influence which he attributes to the "money economy" as the rationalizing influence in economic activity. One might understand the following passage as a criticism of orthodox economic theory, but it appears as a strangely narrow view for one who assumes the province of economic theory to be the descriptive analysis of economic institutions: "Because it thus rationalizes economic life itself, the use of money lays the foundation for a rational theory of that life. Money may not be the root of *all* evil, but it is the root of economic science." [1] Such bias as Mitchell displays in an exaggerated view of the place of quantitative analysis in economic investigation and of the institutional importance of the money economy in shaping economic activity may reasonably be explained in terms of a lifetime's preoccupations.

It would not, as we have indicated, be true to say

[1] *American Economic Review*, vol. vi, supplement, p. 157 (1916), "The Rôle of Money in Economic Theory."

that Mitchell sees quantitative analysis as the sole method for advancing economic studies. He merely considers it the most scientific, and stresses the instrument with whose use he is most familiar. He recognizes the existence of important facts that do not lend themselves to quantitative treatment and admits the essential service of qualitative analysis in institutional economics. He says, for example, "Quantitative work cannot dispense with distinctions of quality. In the thinking of competent workers, the two types of analysis will coöperate with and complement each other as peacefully in economics as they do in chemistry." [1] Such passages are, however, of a parenthetical sort, and represent a field of thought upon which he has not been moved to bestow much consideration.

The sort of union between qualitative and quantitative analysis which Mitchell foresees is not of the sort that was in Alfred Marshall's mind. Marshall thought that the *kind* of forces that operate in the market place had been pretty well canvassed. Limiting the scope of economic science primarily to the problem of value, he limited the qualitative analysis, which he thought so nearly complete, to the aspects of economic activity bearing upon that problem. He recognized, however, the broad implications of value theory and permitted his analysis to roam widely over the surface of human affairs and to penetrate into their hidden

---

[1] *American Economic Review*, vol. xv, p. 12 (1925), "Quantitative Analysis in Economic Theory."

depths. His view was that statistical analysis would give objective evidence of the relative intensity or importance of the play of forces comprised within his general scheme of thought. Concerning the general outlines of value theory, his view displays something of the naïve self-esteem exhibited in Mill's famous dictum a generation before.

Mitchell thinks quite otherwise. He considers Marshall's view of economic behavior, as controlled by two opposing sets of motives, an obsolete conception. He does not, therefore, look for any statistical measurement of the force of motives, nor think it desirable that quantitative analysis should be subordinated to any preconceived analysis of the forces at work. He wishes quantitative analysis to address itself strictly to the objective phenomena at hand, supported by whatever analysis of unmeasurable forces is relevant to the particular problem.

Qualitative analysis, relieved from supporting any particular system of theory, takes on a double nature. It is, in the first place, a subsidiary instrument for handling the incommensurable factors which arise in any particular quantitative investigation. Its second and more important use lies in setting the ends of human endeavor. Holding that economic science is the handmaiden of the race in attempting to increase its economic welfare, Mitchell is compelled to recognize that welfare is not a concept that lends itself to measurement. At bottom, concepts of welfare are based upon our sympathies, prejudices, interests, or preconceptions. Mitchell, for example, could doubtless trace the genealogy of the humanitarianism of which he is so warm a partisan. These simple truths he recognizes only to neglect them. One feels it not a little paradoxical that one who views the life-process of the race as an attempt to achieve its dimly perceived and changing purposes should glorify the statistical instrument almost to the point of discounting the ends to which it is a tool, and certainly to the point of neglecting the manifold if intangible forces which enter into the institutional situation.

Mitchell is not a little critical of economic theorists like Jevons, Clark, and Fisher, whose love of logical precision eventuates in the mere "mechanics of utility." It would appear that his own love for facts and figures opens him to a somewhat similar criticism, that his economics inclines to be the "apotheosis of statistics." Statistics, no matter how complete, will not explain the social philosophy underlying a demand for minimum-wage legislation, or trust regulation, or lower railway rates for farm products, or government operation of the coal industry. All this Mitchell would doubtless admit. He might well say that under the necessities of a division of intellectual labor he was willing to let others speculate upon the immediate and remote ends of social policy while he busied himself with collecting the data with which responsible men might assess the ends or upon which they might build a better order.

Such strictures as one may bring against Mitchell, in terms of his own scheme of thought, are principally matters of emphasis. Being so much the spokesman of his own craft, he appears at times to be something less than an adequate spokesman for the institutional approach to economics. He shrinks from the philosophical, the intangible, the incommensurable. And if such reticence is pardonable in the economist whose gaze is centered upon the marts of trade, it ill becomes one who thinks of economics as the study of human behavior and human institutions, in which those elusive characteristics are so pronounced.

Enough has perhaps been said of Mitchell's work, and of his views concerning the scope and method of economics. To inquire whether those views constitute a body of "economic theory" would carry us into a controversy too warm to be comfortable, and not relevant to our purpose. Certainly he has no "system" of economic theory in the sense that Marshall or Clark or Fetter has a system, logically tied together. He has, on the other hand, a foundation of theories upon which his approach is based. He builds upon the biological theory of evolution; the sociological theory of a developing organic society; an epistemological theory of a pragmatic sort; a psychological theory embodying stability of instincts and the subsidiary nature of intelligence; and a theory of the institutional origin of most overt human behavior. He would say that these theories are based upon modern scientific research, and furnish as sound an ideological basis as is obtainable for scientific research into the processes of human society.

He might further contend that systematic economic theory, when run to its source, has a way of merging into psychology, epistemology, metaphysics, and analogy to the physical sciences, wherein its footing is less stable than that of his own scheme of thought. From this he might argue that his view that the central task of economics is an objective study of institutions—their history, processes, direction, and effects upon human welfare—may be validly called a form of economic theory. He might further add that within the confines of a given investigation there would often be need for the use of highly theoretical work of the logical sort by way of filling in the interstices where factual data were not available. He could even admit the uses of systematic theory within the bounds of his approval, as an enlightening display of the logic of certain forces.

Of some such material is compounded Mitchell's claim that he and other "institutionalists" are economic theorists. The claim is perplexing and distressing to those who draw their scheme of thought from orthodox sources. Obviously Mitchell's formula for economic theory is highly eclectic, loose, and inclusive. It has a resting-place for all and sundry, if only they are engaged in elucidating human behavior on its economic side. Hospitality, it is true, proceeds on a plan of graded warmth, from a certain coolness toward logical processes at one extreme, to an effusive cordiality toward statistical analysis at the other. But all are welcome.

Over and around the whole position is wrapped the warm mantle of a high moral purpose. That the function of economics, in conjunction with the other social sciences, is to aid in social melioration, is the enveloping preconception. That, of course, is a matter quite apart from science. There is no scientific reason to suppose that the evolutionary process of cumulative causation is amenable to intelligent social control. It may be a matter of blind force, of electrons or chemical processes. And then again it may not be. There is no guide here but faith. And it is in this homely human trait that Mitchell's approach to economics ultimately rests.

Meantime, the view of economics of which Mitchell is the outstanding figure represents the most marked trend of the present time in the United States. Economic theory with a longer classical pedigree is still formally dominant in the schools. Objective economic investigation is to a considerable degree tied to business enterprise, with the immediate incentive of a favorable effect on the credit balance in the profit-and-loss ledger. But an increasing share of the sound scientific work is being devoted to monographic studies of the economic system in detail, to the immediate end of disclosing the manner of its working, to the ultimate end of assisting in intelligent social guidance. Realism is Allah, and Mitchell is his prophet. Paradise may be around the corner.

It is not a little curious that the most eminent of our economic workmen in the field of minute analysis of statistical data should be so heavily indebted to an impressionistic cosmic philosopher like Veblen, who heroically distorts facts and shows no evidence of commerce with figures. Mitchell's work is of the sort that would have pleased Marshall. One thinks of a certain resemblance between them in the union of moral and scientific interest in their problems, and in the scientific precision of their methods.

But Mitchell's work proceeds within a general framework of ideas not consonant with the general ideas of that excellent economist. It serves, therefore, to make more crucial the debated question of what constitutes the essential theoretical equipment of a competent modern economist.

NOTE.—Since this essay was written there has been published the first volume of a re-written edition of *Business Cycles*. A hasty examination of it leads to the belief that the changes incorporated in it would necessitate no essential revision of the foregoing analysis.

The Present Impasse

The Present Impasse

NOTHING can be more evident to anyone surveying the field of contemporary economic thought than that those economists who concern themselves with general theory hold widely divergent ideas of the purpose, scope, and method of economics. When one remembers that the objective data upon which economists must base their beliefs are the same for all, an explanation of these divergencies must naturally run in terms of the difficulties which beset the economic theorist in the complexity of his data, or of the inadequate media of thought which men have devised for scientifically explaining their own activities, or of the astigmatic contrariety of the human mind, or perhaps of all three. Mark Twain observed that no matter how learned and authoritative an opinion may be expressed upon one side of any question, equally irreproachable authority may be adduced upon the other. One might rest in the shadow of that cynical observation. The curious mind, however, desires no such disillusioned respite.

When one has comprehended the diversity of thought of the five men who have been exposed to view he is in a position to see the difficulties which beset

the bold person who essays to develop a general theory
of economic life. The difficulties converge upon the
economic theorist from various directions. He becomes
entangled in psychology, to his almost inevitable dis-
comfiture. He is faced by a choice of methods—the
systematic formulation of principles with the aid of
deductive logic, or the accumulation and interpretation
of data, whether historical, quantitative, or descriptive,
of a character not readily available for the construction of broad generalizations. He must delimit the
scope of his inquiry. He is under the necessity of rely-
ing upon some general theory of the nature of the
social process. And of such theories there is today a
glut. He has need of a set of criteria concerning the
nature, aims, and methods of scientific inquiry, and must
decide which, if any, of the diverse disciplines in the
field of natural science furnishes the best basis upon
the analogy to which a scientific instrumentality for
dealing with social facts may be modeled. No task of
his is more fundamental or more difficult than the creation of a terminology in which social facts can be scientifically described. He is faced with the fact that the
explanation of the individual's relation to social groups
has not proceeded much beyond the stage of metaphysics. Between the limits of an extreme individualistic and an extreme organismic theory of society lies a
field for infinite diversity of view.

Apart from such imponderable difficulties, troubles
of a different sort arise to plague the economist in the

very profusion and complexity of the objective data with which he has to deal. The infinity of economic groups, pecuniary transactions, productive activities, organizations, marketing methods, customs, legal restrictions, and human incentives out of which the conception of an economic order is compounded, permit a wide diversity of view concerning the nature and relative importance of the forces at work. Moreover, they are with difficulty reduced to orderly classification and treatment. Pondering this situation, the economist has a range of choice running from the uncritical acceptance of traditionally established concepts and categories all the way to a complete denial of the possibility of achieving sufficient order in this mass of facts to permit generalized scientific explanations.

When one perceives the problems which beset an economist setting forth to the development of a body of general theory which will explain economic facts in a scientific way, the reason emerges why the economist himself is so important a factor in the situation. Working in the midst of a field of uncrystallized ideas and recalcitrant facts, his treatment of them will be conditioned by his intellectual bents, by the ideas he has accepted in the malleable period of his youth, by the range of his reading and of the phenomena he has observed, by all manner of influences which have shaped what may be called his "point of view."

So long as economists looked not askance at the scientific and philosophical dogma imbedded in their discipline, they succeeded in achieving a certain common point of view concerning the scope and method of their science. They were carried forward on the flow of a tradition. Some such consensus appears to have been reached toward the end of the nineteenth century. Or it may perhaps be said to have prevailed throughout the century, though disturbed by such streams of thought as the historical school and Marxian economics.

Agreement, however, toward the end of the period was limited to the general proposition that economic science, in its general aspects, was concerned with the search for a logically articulated statement of the laws which govern the fixing of economic values and control the distribution of income. In approaches to that problem, personal viewpoints and doctrinal refinements abounded. Wider and narrower definitions of scope, subjective and objective aspects of economic life, varied applications and analytical uses of doctrine, divergent concepts and terminologies, had each its professors and advocates. In spite of the sedative influence of Marshall's work, the closing years of the last century and the early years of the present century were marked by continuous and vigorous controversy between economists whose general positions were not too far apart. This period resulted in a very great refinement of concepts, and the infinitely careful elaboration of principles, the meat of which was derived from Clark, Marshall, or the Austrians, or all three.

Unable to agree, apparently wearied by controversy,

and perhaps impressed by the futility of further refinements of abstract theory in the face of the complex
facts of modern life, economists for the most part made
an end of controversy some fifteen or twenty years
ago, and turned their attention more largely to a realistic study of the life about them. Text-books continue
to be written or revised, perpetuating or combining or
mutilating their doctrines. Few economists, however,
are any longer disturbed by the diversity of text-book
principles, and, in the face of larger issues, it has come
to be thought a minor matter whence a student derives
his knowledge of economic principles, if only it be
from a spokesman of the old tradition. Economists,
so they be "orthodox," find themselves today enjoying
a restrained amity similar to that which envelops the
evangelical churches.

In the meantime, an attitude of irreverence toward
the ancient traditions was arising about the turn of the
century. Economic historians like Ashley were not impressed by the facile development of static laws. Sidney and Beatrice Webb took to exposing the historical
roots of contemporary economic organization and to
protesting against the kind of economic theory which
would imply the presence of some beneficent principle
in the competitive order—a work not original in its
socialistic bias, but impressive as a presentation of
neglected facts and forces. Hobson, also buttressed
with historical facts and a knowledge of social ills, undertook the comprehensive revision of economic theory

in the attempt to mold it to the uses of social reform. Again, this dissenting attitude took the form, as with Veblen, of translating analysis of economic phenomena out of the ideology of the physical sciences into developmental or evolutionary terms.

In certain aspects, the new attitude took forms which caused it to be described as a recrudescence of the influence of the historical school. Something more than that, however, appears to have been contained in it. What appears to have happened was an infiltration of ideas from other fields of knowledge. A serious inquiry was instituted to discover whether economics might not have to revise its discipline in the light of contemporary knowledge or thought in the natural sciences or in the other social sciences. The movement was related, and in some degree directly indebted, to the effort of William James and others to revise philosophy in the light of modern science. The idea of evolutionary social change was appealed to, as bearing upon the validity of statically conceived economic laws. Functional and social psychology, anthropology, history, politics, and law began to yield their tribute. Crystallizing gradually as a movement, this new approach came to center its attention upon the careful study of contemporary economic institutions and relationships, viewed as the temporary and evanescent aspects of a process of social evolution. Veblen was, of course, the outstanding and for a time almost solitary spokesman of this viewpoint. But time has recruited his legions.

It is a viewpoint that calls for no orthodoxy, with the consequence that those who work somewhat in the spirit of the new movement are at no particular pains to define the scope of economics or to engage in controversy. Whatever falls within the sweep of modern industrial or pecuniary relationships is their raw material, and their problems are chosen from those aspects of such relationships as appear to them important or interesting. For the most part the Veblenian disdain of "purpose" has been discarded, and they conceive themselves to be furnishing the data upon which may be instituted an intelligent policy of social control in the interests of the welfare of the race. Thus vaguely bound together, the dissenting economists can hardly be regarded as forming a "school." Their unity lies mainly on the negative side, in a common critical attitude toward economic analysis of the traditional sort. On the constructive side they are a race of free-lances, with rather a common failing for historical research and interpretation, quantitative analysis, realistic description, and only such abstract theory as is necessary to the analytical treatment of specific problems. In their interpretation economics loses much of its character as a science with a well-established body of controlling laws. It is the scientific spirit of the investigator, not the accumulated body of truth, that achieves the position of importance.

It also has been said that the economists who work in the new spirit are occupied merely with what was in an earlier phrase called "applied economics." That opinion seems to involve a misapprehension. For the newer movement represents an effort to discover what tale the facts themselves tell, while the older, in so far as it was not divorced from theoretical considerations, was an effort to describe or explain or modify or justify existing institutions and practices in the light of established economic truth. Economists have, of course, always been interested in the peculiar manifestations of economic activity in their respective generations. But the newer trend seems definitely away from the older division into "pure" and "applied" economics which holds over from the days when economic truth was deduced from the Utilitarian philosophy.

One is in danger of becoming enslaved by tags, in any attempt to classify contemporary economists. To speak, as is often done, of "neo-classical" and "institutional" economists may perhaps do more to obscure than to clarify the current scene. For, in the midst of the many difficulties which beset an economist in the definition of his task, there have emerged such numerous combinations of ideas and such distinctive and personal points of view as to defy any authentic scheme of classification. In consequence, it must be admitted that the five economists who have been passed in review are to be taken less as examples or leaders of "schools" than as illustrations of a strange state of affairs. Were

other names to be added, the gallery would become
more diverse as it grew more ample and one would be
often at a loss upon which wall to hang the portraits.
But some rough line of demarcation seems to be called
for between those who cling, in however attenuated a
fashion, to the older tradition of scope and method and
those who conceive the scope of their enterprise in
different terms.

Diversity of theoretical approach to economics appears in recent years to have been much more marked
in the United States than in Great Britain. This is not
to say that there are no marked trends, but merely
perhaps that what is thought of as the Veblenian influence has created no such striking counter-types of
theory. Marshall's *Principles* or some adaptations and
extensions of it have been the main sources of theoretical knowledge for a generation. Professor Pigou
notably perpetuates this scheme of thought. Since his
work and that of others of the Cambridge "school"
have, however, been more by way of extending its application rather than merely polishing it to greater bril-
liancy, and since they use it, as Marshall wished, as a
tool for further analysis rather than cherish it as sacred
dogma, they appear to have justified its continued usefulness, in the absence of better tools for the theoretical
analysis of such problems as at present call for attention—problems of trade, poverty, currency, and the
like. There are in evidence in England reversions to
J. S. Mill such as Professor J. S. Nicholson's, and even

sundry vestiges of Manchesterism, and Austrian theory has been carried to a very high level of development by Mr. Wicksteed. Probably the train of ideas set in motion by Professor Cannan marks the most noticeable trend affecting many younger British economists, not in the direction of forswearing systematic theory, but of supplementing it by a more careful study of the facts out of which it grows and by a reorientation of ideas, particularly in regard to the distribution of income. Hobson, however, remains the only economist who has developed any comprehensive body of dissident thought, and the abstract character of much of it separates it from the contemporary American impatience with schematic abstractions.

On the other hand, the British literature of general social dissent has been copious. Writers of the type of the Webbs and Mr. Tawney are somewhat allied to Veblen in their view of the transience of institutional arrangements, in their delving for explanations of existing economic modes of action, and in their analysis of institutional trends. Such an attitude is naturally essential to socialistic reformers. In spirit, however, they are much more closely allied to Hobson's dogma that economic facts are inevitably charged with ethical meaning, and that the economist's labors may not abstract that meaning, nor be dissociated from it. An equally propagandist use of economic organons of thought has been widely practiced in defense of existing forms of economic organization, but not usually by any but amateur economists.

On the whole, effective thinking has been largely turned away from more general theoretical considerations and has been concentrated upon the ways and means for the provision of future well-being for the nation. In a country so beset as England by economic problems, so torn by group conflicts, so uncertain as to the future basis of economic and political control, it is not surprising that the broader analysis of economic processes should be somewhat in a position of decline. Indeed, the social basis for such analysis is most unstable. Should the present distressing conjuncture, however, lead into a period of comparative composure, it is to be supposed that some attempt will be made to give concrete meaning to Marshall's opinion that his *Principles* was by way of becoming "waste paper." [1]

In the United States the theoretical scene is more complicated and difference of opinion runs more on strictly intellectual lines. Theorists who work within the limits of the orthodox tradition seem each to have a personal and characteristic slant, and such wide variations of emphasis and treatment are to be found as separate Professors Taussig, Davenport, Fetter, and Fisher, to mention no others. Professor Taussig displays a liberal eclecticism similar, both in spirit and in results, to Marshall's. Professor Fetter, trailing originally in the train of Clark and the Austrians, has

[1] See *Memorials of Alfred Marshall*, p. 490.

attempted a revision of the psychological postulates of economic theory to relieve it from the taint of hedonism, and he conceives the important trend in economics to be the emphasis upon the human factors which lie behind the price system. Professor Davenport, narrowing economics to an objective study of prices, has within the bounds set conducted a highly illuminating investigation of the logic of business enterprises under the pressure of pecuniary motivation, relieving economics of all ethical associations and placing in high relief the acquisitive character of economic activity. Professor Irving Fisher, with the aid of a mathematical training, has carried further than any other American the investigation of the mechanics of the principle of utility. He is the nearest American approach to the continental mathematical school. He exhibits, as do other mathematically minded economists, that infinite precision of analysis which a mathematical training appears to engender. But precise deduction demands precise postulates, and it is around the postulates which support a deductive-mathematical analysis of prices that much of current theoretical disagreement in economics centers.

The absence of any really original work in the field of systematic theory during the past decade or two seems to indicate that some sort of obstacle has been encountered. Various views may be taken. The established body of theory may be thought fairly satisfactory and in need of little revision. Or the prevailing theories may be thought somewhat futile, as representing conclusions too simple to explain satisfactorily even the restricted groups of phenomena with which they **are concerned**. Or the construction of generalized and technical theories of value and distribution may appear a less fruitful use of time than the investigation of other aspects of the economic system. Or one may be skeptical of the possibility of reducing the complicated and changing facts of modern economic life to a logically articulated system of general principles. All those points of view are to be found represented among contemporary American economists. Whatever the causes, there is no doubt that American economists have been turning their attention more largely into other fields than their concern for systematic theory. And when one turns to survey their occupations in these fields there are few criteria by which to group or classify them.

There appears little reason to doubt that most economists entertain the idea that they should perform some function in the world beyond the development of theories. They are pretty universally, and one would say rightly, bitten with the notion that they should be providing data which will assist in the intelligent formulation of public policy in regard to banking, tariffs, immigration, railways, and similar important matters, or in the adjustment of the interests of economic groups. Almost all are, to that extent, exponents of the idea that economics should promote welfare. The increasing complexity of modern economic organization may be supposed to have provided absorbing and re-

stricted fields of investigation which have lured economists from their wider speculations. So far has this
specialization developed that many economists are
almost unspotted with any taint of theoretical knowledge beyond some few general ideas that they have
retained from university days, or are without interest
in it except in so far as their specific work demands
some theoretical background. Plainly, a man may collect statistical data upon Mexican immigration or the
wages of miners without regard to his opinions upon
the marginal-productivity theory of wages.

The fact remains, however, that the background of
general theoretical ideas with which an economist enters
upon his career is liable to be influential in affecting
the decision as to what subjects he will undertake to
investigate, and crucial and decisive as to the form in
which he shall cast his problem and the terms in which
he shall elucidate it. For example, the statistical study
of business cycles, which has lately come to the front
of the attention of many competent economists, while it
of course attracts economists with every theoretical bias,
seems particularly to fascinate men who have discarded
theories of the "normal" action of economic forces, and
who are interested primarily in the analysis of factual
data. This observation appears to fit the American
more than the English situation, due, one would suppose, to a more general adherence of English economists
to systematic bodies of doctrine. The more wedded an
economist is to normalizing theories the more ready

he appears to be to set up hypotheses in explanation of cycles, and the more his explanation seems to run to the operation of accidental or "abnormal" factors in the situation. Conversely, one's views upon the causation of cycles appear to react upon his general theory, for admitting the "normality" of cycles casts doubt, not upon the logical correctness, but upon the explanatory usefulness of theories of normal value or normal wages. It is probably no exaggeration to say that recent investigations into the causes of cycles have done as much to destroy adherence to older types of theory as any other single cause. And it has led to the casting of their problems by many economists into terms of a changing process rather than into terms of a static situation.

The economists who pursue their investigations undirected by older theories cannot be contrasted sharply with the exponents of orthodox theory. For they do not write logically systematic treatises. They cannot, since their original assumptions preclude them from so doing. Nor do their fields of objective investigation mark them off sharply, since they share these fields with economists of more traditional general views. But to some distinguishable degree they produce results of a sort not obtainable in the light of traditional assumptions. A point of view, of course, is one thing and its application to economic analysis is another. "The institutional approach to economic theory" is becoming a standardized phrase in the United States, but it gains content only by acquaintance with the projects of a variety of economists who interpret it in diverse ways. And, such is the evil way of formal categories, one may classify under it the work of men who do not apply it to themselves.

The late Professor Carleton Parker may, if one is permitted a certain looseness of his categories, be regarded as an important influence in the development of the new viewpoint, in spite of the objective smallness of his contribution. He broke new ground in the attempt to bring a realistic psychology to bear upon the explanation of economic processes, and stimulated the recently considerable activity along that line. Professor J. M. Clark, also requiring a stretching of our classification, pursues his investigations into what he, like his father, terms the field of "dynamics." But his analysis of overhead costs carries him to conclusions which do not permit themselves to be subsumed under, or subordinated to, any scheme of static or normal theory, since cyclical variations, excess productive capacity, human short-sightedness, and similar disturbing phenomena enter too decisively and too permanently into his economic scene.

Perhaps Professor W. H. Hamilton is as extreme and as articulate an exponent of the institutional approach as can be found. In his study both of wages and of the coal industry one may find an analysis of those diverse features of the social process related to changing legal precepts, technical developments, social groupings, business conditions, and acquisitive practices, not amenable in his view to reduction to the customary concepts of economic analysis. The income and cycle studies of the National Bureau of Economic Research represent a type of statistical analysis at least dissociated from systematic theory, though its ultimate bearing upon the validity of such theory is hardly at present determinable. Mr. H. G. Moulton has found monetary facts too complicated to conform to the simple monetary theories that usually pass as corollaries to general economic theory, and has felt it necessary to explain them, with a minimum of abstraction, with reference to the whole financial structure of present-day society. The field of legal-economic ideas seems in recent years to have exercised a particular fascination for some minds, and this interest has pushed Professor J. R. Commons, in *Legal Foundations of Capitalism*, far in the direction of a counter-type of economic theory of a sort that he calls "volitional" in contradistinction to the "mechanistic" quality of both orthodox and Veblenian theory.

One may, however, make an end of such citations. They serve no purpose beyond indicating certain channels down which the institutional interest is flowing. They prove nothing concerning the validity or usefulness of one type of analysis as against another. On the side of concrete performance, institutional economics appears still in a position to show a becoming modesty. Its great merit appears to have lain in stimulating interest in historical and descriptive work, and in unloosing a youthful experimental spirit upon economic analysis. Since a certain contempt for old ways and old thoughts marks its adherents, it has still to show that, in the everyday analysis of economic affairs, it has a firmer grasp of facts or a sounder organon of thought than economists of more orthodox leanings. It appears, indeed, that in the analysis of details and of concrete data, the intellectual divisions of economists are often not too pronounced. It is when the area of discussion broadens to consider the wider, the less observable or measurable, the more speculative aspects of economic life, that divergence of thought sharpens into active disagreement. But one cannot say that the divergence is negligible or unimportant, since a general point of view may in the long run exercise a remarkable objective influence, as the history of economic thought, or merely of thought, amply testifies.

Since there exists such unanimity of opinion that economists may best be occupied during the present generation in providing a more thorough knowledge of the nature and social effects of the economic environment, one is forced to the opinion that the unsettled state in which economic theory finds itself arises, not merely out of the complexity of the facts with which it deals— though this no doubt adds to the confusion—but more particularly out of the confused currents of thought which prevail in the modern world at large. There is no mere family quarrel in economics—one sees there an illustration of the intellectual world at odds with itself. Economic theory was developed with its roots driven into Utilitarian philosophy. It developed as the mechanics of self-interest in a competitively organized world. It has gradually changed its form by concessive adjustments to other ideas than those that furnished its early sustenance. It has largely cast off the agency, if not the guiding principle, of Utilitarian ethics. Allowance has had to be made for abeyances in the competitive process, and recognition given to the complex of forms which are in their totality called the competitive system. The hedonistic view of human nature has given way to varying modifications or complete denial. Darwinian ideas of perpetual change have shrunk universal laws to mere principles applicable to a given time and place. Concepts applicable to a relatively simple economic organization have had to be revised to fit a situation of infinite complexity. Such adjustments as these many economists have found it possible to make while remaining true to the central problem, the value problem, the central method, the method of logical deduction, and the central scientific preconception, the mechanical analogy, of the science. It is this loyalty that permits them to be grouped as "orthodox." It is their varying manner of making the adjustments that accounts for the diversity of their systematic doctrine.

The major division of economic thought has arisen, however, in the twentieth century, not from these internal diversities within the bounds of an honored tradition, but from a denial of the adequacy of the adjustments and a denial of the validity of the remaining norms. It is not to be denied that the study of prices and markets constitutes a profitable use of the economist's time. For it is through the guidance given by the price system that, under our present arrangements, economic activity takes on the semblance of orderliness. The protest is rather against a too exclusive attention to the problems there encountered, against the terms and concepts in which economic analysis has proceeded, and against the limitation of scientific performance in the field of economics to analysis of the price-making process.

The sources of these denials are of the most varied sort. Partly they arise out of observation of current economic phenomena. It is a competitive postulate alone which gives systematic orderliness to economic theory. Competition has become to many economists, however, something to be investigated, not assumed. Current business practice takes on an aspect less and less recognizably related to the ideal competition of the economic treatise. The competitive system, as the principal regulator and coördinator of economic activity, can now be plausibly denied, with a good show of evidence drawn from the practices of voluntary business and labor combinations, from collectivistic legislation and the regulatory activities of governments. The study of the price-making process thus tends to become more an objective study of the practices which condition it, and less an elaboration of the mechanics of competitive activity. Moreover, faith in the social efficacy of competition is worn thin, and the spiritual descendants of those who once advocated *laissez-faire* are now concerned, not with extending the bounds of individual freedom, but with achieving some desirable modicum of public control. Nor does control any longer mean to them, as it did to J. B. Clark and the authors of anti-trust legislation, the enforcement of competition.

In like manner, over the whole economic field, the complexities of business practice are turning assumptions into problems for investigation. Simple monetary theories are giving way to detailed examination of the agencies and effects of credit. Simple wage theories are neglected before a wider examination of the conditions of the efficient application of labor in industry. Simple theories of international trade stand aside while the nature, extent, and effects of national regulations are examined. Simplicity and logical coherence in economic theory are, in important circles, no longer deemed sufficient. They are being submitted to the inexorable test of their relevance to objective reality.

This concern for realistic data, while it has been a factor in limiting the acceptability of economic doctrines, has perhaps had less effect in actively reshaping economic theory than a new ideology which has found its way into economics from such varied sources as philosophy, psychology, and natural science. It is an ideology which is affecting all the social sciences alike, drawing them together, and obscuring their characteristic frontiers. History is becoming more a "genetic" account of the development of human societies. Anthropology is less a system of classifying races through skull measurements and more a study of the functional content of primitive cultures. The law is becoming less a body of principles and more a heterogeneous expression of bygone sanctions of conduct, as modified in the light of a new and changing social situation. Political science is turning from philosophical theories of the state to the comparative study of political institutions. And so in economics, the search for sweeping generalizations is being subordinated to finding by what chain of circumstances our present institutions came into being, how they at present work in detail, whither they are carrying us, and by what means and to what ends we can direct their future development.

Run ultimately to its source, if one may hope for ultimates, this enveloping movement away from the concepts and intellectual systems of the nineteenth century seems to be primarily traceable to the evolutionary principle. The usefulness of this principle as a standpoint from which to conduct a scientific investigation of social phenomena is at last being widely, if tentatively, tested. Its applicability to social development has been fortified by historical studies, and its acceptance hastened by its timely appearance just in the midst of a period of very rapid social change. Gingerly handled by earlier economists, it was used for purposes of a rather half-hearted modification of economic theory, by picturing the competitive system as the agency through which "survival power" was tested. It was Veblen, as we have seen, who first pressed home the wider implications, involving a denial of the fixity of any human institution, including the competitive system. Since then, statically conceived systems of economic doctrine have been somewhat on the defensive.

The evolutionary idea carried with it an implication of the organic character of human society, bringing social theory around full-circle to a mediæval idea, but in a radically different setting. It seems of minor significance for economic theory whether organic analogies applied to society be taken as literal or metaphorical, the negative fact being that they have undermined the individualistic terms and concepts in which economic theory has been couched. The economic process in recent years has thus come more commonly to be treated in terms of organic functions rather than of contending individuals.

The evolutionary principle as applied to economic theory has been buttressed by the influence of modern psychology. The so-called "psychological school" of economists achieved its name by stressing the subjective factor in the valuation process. But those economists who have recently emphasized the bearing of psychology upon economics have usually had a different idea in mind. They are frequently men who consider the analysis of value as a minor technical aspect of economics, not its whole scientific scope, and they expect to get from psychology, not a theory of value, but a working explanation of why human beings in organized society act as they do. The prevailing answers, imported from psychology, have run partly to the influence of an instinctive "original human nature," partly to that of the rational faculties, but predominantly to environmental factors, of which the chief are institutionalized habits of action. Consequently a psychologically valid explanation of economic behavior is presumed to demand an account of the prescriptive force of established forms of action upon human behavior. It is the changing character of these forms that calls for the application of the evolutionary principle. And it is the fact of such change that leads to a widely held view of the purpose of economics, as furnishing economic data upon which the rational faculties of man may base the intelligent guidance of a changing situation.

Of such stuff has been built up that counter-type of economic thought which belittles both the usefulness and scientific validity of the generalizations arrived at by an essentially mathematical process of logical analysis in static and individualistic terms. The point of view is not one which originated within the field of economics, and it has been best expressed by writers not themselves professional economists.[1] Though subject to variations due to the fluid condition of contemporary psychology and to the varying judgments of the applicability of biological analogies to social development, it forms the ideological setting within which a great many economists, especially younger ones, frame their work. The viewpoint is foreign to the thinking of many economists whose methods of economic analysis have been shaped by other influences and who conceive this range of ideas irrelevant to the economist's peculiar tasks. It is, no doubt, this difference in the sources from which contemporary economists secure their general ideas that accounts for the unbridged gap which separates them.

To display in so sharp a contrast the antithetical points of view which condition the theoretical thought of contemporary economists is, no doubt, to distort the picture. Most economists, probably, do not define their position so sharply. The contrast, nevertheless, appears necessary to an explanation of why a situation approaching an impasse has arisen in the field of economic thought. It has seemed the part of wisdom to avoid too definite a use of such current phrases as "neoclassical economics," "institutional economics," and "welfare economics," since they appear to have an overlapping connotation. When, however, one has seen that some economists assume a psychological and in-

---

[1] As, for instance, by John Dewey in *The Reconstruction of Philosophy*, C. H. Cooley in *Social Process*, and Graham Wallas in *The Great Society*.

stitutional situation as a point of departure for their reasoning while others wish to examine the postulates, that some conceive the task of economic science to be the reduction of economic phenomena to an orderly presentation of controlling laws while others wish rather to explore the intricate pattern of modern life, that some work more in terms of physical and others of biological analogies, the more fundamental cleavage of thought appears to emerge.

This cleavage, as developed by the more ardent champions of the opposed points of view, appears to take the form of antithetical dogmatisms. It has about it the general cast of a theological controversy. By definition, economic science is to be couched in individualistic or organismic terms, by definition it is to deal with value or with economic behavior in a larger setting, by definition it is to be static, dynamic, or evolutionary. One suspects that the advocacy of the evolutionary, or genetic, or institutional approach to economic theory as the sole defensible approach conceals a dogmatism and a naïve faith as fundamental as the eighteenth-century system of natural liberty, and quite as pronounced as that entertained by any intelligent contemporary advocate of orthodox economic analysis. If it is true that the broader generalizations of orthodox theory are difficult of acceptance in our complicated world, it is not less true that institutional economics has no tool to substitute for deductive analysis in coping with many problems of economic cause and effect. Professor Pigou's work would seem to prove that orthodox tools still perform a useful service as surely as Professor Mitchell's work is a demonstration of the uses of quantitative analysis applied in the light of institutional preconceptions.

It may well be, as Marshall contended, that the important thing for an economist is that he be armed with tools adequate to the tasks of analysis which he undertakes, and that economic laws are of secondary importance. Even so, the general ideas within which he frames his specific tasks are an essential complement of his kit. Perhaps, in a world so buffeted by diverse currents of thought, no unanimity of general theory is to be hoped for. One might wish, however, that economists would spare more time from their narrower preoccupations to contemplate the construction of a framework of thought which could command more general agreement, and remove at least the central scientific area of their discipline from the shriveling blast of every intellectual wind that blows.

One might develop to much greater length the diversities of opinion that exist in tangled confusion in the minds of contemporary economists, running from the scope of the subject and the scientific method to be used down to the minutiæ and subtleties of specific theories. Such a task, however, goes beyond the purpose of the present essay. The confusion of the picture cannot but indicate the fact that economic science is caught in that wider confusion of thought which is typical of the present generation. The growing complexity of economic data only adds to a confusion which has its roots in changes in the technique and canons of thought in such diverse fields as natural science, philosophy, and psychology, and the varied application of ideas obtained therefrom to the analysis of social facts. The simple faith of the nineteenth century that the life of society in its totality might be scientifically explained has departed from our midst. The developed scientific technique for the analysis of economic activity has fallen under a cloud.

The situation need not, however, be diagnosed as a turn for the worse. Under the impulse of enormous curiosity, impelled by the pressing character of economic problems, economists in increasing numbers and with improving technique are amassing data which permit the light to play upon the detailed processes of our social organization. The social sciences are being thrown into closer coöperation and dependence. Society in detail is under the microscope in unprecedented fashion. That society in the large is too extensive to fit under any instrument yet created need not be too distressing. So long as the scientific spirit continues to animate those who search for the obscure causes of economic effects and the obscure effects of economic causes, one may with some equanimity accept the fact that they fall short of unanimity in their opinions. Whether economics in the future shall consist of a body of *doctrines*, or a body of *facts* scientifically ascertained,

or a *technique*, or more or less of one and the other,
is on the lap of the gods. There appears to be a place
in the general scheme of things for technical studies
of the price system, for studies of changing economic
processes and institutions, and for philosophical appraisal of the meaning of economic life. By what
methods these tasks may best be performed is to be
tested in the crucible of time. And just when any results shall have passed over into the sacred precincts
of scientific truth will wait upon professional consensus
in some future period when men's minds are more
generally agreed.

One may not journey through the diverse fields of
economic thought in our own times without soon dis-
cerning that, afflicted with the myopic quality of the
human understanding, men may not agree upon which
are wastes and which are meadows. One recalls, with
sympathy, the thought which came to Henry Adams
as he pondered over the development of mundane
affairs from the twelfth century to the twentieth, that
unity gives way to diversity, simplicity to complexity.
Axioms defer to questions, and certainty to groping.
Caught in the swift stream, economists, like others, are
swept past the familiar landmarks. In the presence of
a new and bafflingly complex phase of economic development, of novel philosophies, and of fluid scientific
concepts, they are grappling as they may with their
problems. Lest they slay one another, instead of their
enemies, they may well give some attention to defining

their scientific task and to forging instruments of thought adequate to its performance. It is in the realm of ideas, more than of facts, that the issues are drawn. In this realm it appears of some importance that economics, if it is to retain the semblance of a science, should lay itself less open to the remark of a character of Disraeli's that "Few ideas are correct ones, and what are correct no one can ascertain."

INDEX

	DATE DUE	
NOV 3 1976		
NOV 2 3 1976		
DEC 5 1978		
APR 8 1980		
OCT 1 4 1986		
OCT 2 2 1990		
FEB 0 6 1998		
RESERVE		
OFF RESERVE		